THE WORLD'S MASTER POTTERS

THE
WORLD'S MASTER
POTTERS

Their Techniques and Art

Materials, Processes, Design, Decoration, Styles:
The Development of Ceramic Art from Ancient
to Modern Times

Charles Platten Woodhouse

PITMAN PUBLISHING

Pitman Publishing Corporation
Library of Congress Catalog Card No 74-83400

© Charles Platten Woodhouse 1974

ISBN 0-273-07081-9

Printed in Great Britain

CONTENTS

PLATES

FOREWORD

Interest in the character and development of ancient and modern ceramics, together with growing appreciation of the potter's art as a creative medium, are reasons for this introductory survey of the techniques and art of some of the world's master potters. For ease of reference, the contents are arranged in East-to-West sequence, approximately following the historical development of ceramic art. As far as space limitations allow, the techniques and productions of celebrated master potters at various periods from the remote past to the present day are reviewed, also the work of groups of anonymous potters in civilisations and countries where a high peak of artistic development was attained. Industrial ceramics and, with a few exceptions, mass-produced wares lie outside the scope of this book.

Pottery is an extremely ancient craft, or art, dating back perhaps some 15,000 years. Identities of master potters in ancient times are almost totally unknown. For example, only a few names of celebrated Chinese potters have come down to us, yet for hundreds of years the most superlatively beautiful porcelain ever seen was produced in China by master potters who attained unsurpassed skill. The manner of development of Chinese pottery techniques and styles was practically unique and for convenience is usually classified under successive dynasties. In Japan, on the other hand, where ceramic art developed and flowered comparatively late, outstanding potters emerged concerning whose activities documentary evidence has survived.

In respect of China and other ancient civilisations and cultures ceramic techniques are considered in general, those employed by potters in respective periods, as identification of wares by individual potters is usually impossible.

Brevity concerning a potter or his work has occasionally been unavoidable. Nevertheless, it is hoped that readers will find adequate coverage given to potters and their productions, periods, and varying methods and styles in cultures and civilisations.

As an introduction to the subject, the techniques and art of the world's master potters, developed through thousands of years, this book may serve to whet the appetite of the interested layman, scholar, student and collector for extended study which, needless to add, will be found infinitely absorbing and rewarding. To this end a bibliography is included, comprising a selection of informative, authoritative publications relating to ceramics at various periods in different parts of the world. Most works listed in the bibliography contain useful bibliographies.

I

ASIA

CHINA

The early development of ceramic techniques in China is associated with the remarkable race who in prehistoric times dwelt in the region of the Yellow River (Hoang-Ho) in the north-east of the country. Chinese historians recorded that the first pottery was made during the reign of Emperor Huang Ti in about 2698 BC.

As already noted in the foreword, very few potters are known by name in the long history of Chinese ceramics. In certain instances it is possible, by comparison of wares with affinity in style and technique, to recognise the productions of one factory and even decoration probably executed by one artist, but at best such identification can only be based upon surmise. Experimentation and invention were undoubtedly encouraged in the day-to-day work in a pottery. When a new process was satisfactorily developed and introduced, or new forms and modes of decoration evolved, ultimate success usually depended upon gaining favour at the imperial court, the finest wares almost invariably being supplied to the emperor and nobility. This was particularly so under later dynasties.

At the end of the Stone Age, a period when China was frequently invaded from the West, it is reasonable to assume that the invaders brought with them primitive clay vessels which were subsequently copied by Chinese potters. Stonewares were certainly produced in China at a very remote period, but their origins and the techniques used in making them are not known. It is conjectured by some authorities that the first Chinese pottery was produced under the Chou dynasty (1122–249 BC). Although Near Eastern potters achieved remarkable results in production of glazed wares in a range of colours obtained by refining natural minerals, and the Chinese learned the techniques, it was not until the establishment of the Han dynasty in 206 BC that the most dramatic Chinese developments in high-fired glazing techniques occurred which gave Chinese potters the lead.

Prior to the commencement of the Han dynasty (206 BC–AD 220) ceramic wares produced in China were mainly coarse and primitive in character. The potter's wheel was known and used in China at a very early period, probably introduced from Egypt by way of Asia Minor and Central Asia, where it had been in use since almost 3000 BC. Chinese wares made in pre-Han times, though coarse in texture and unglazed for the most part, were vigorously modelled. Ancient Chinese pottery tomb-wares, gradually becoming more refined by careful selection of clays and higher firing, were inspired by the bronze vessels used in religious ceremonials. Simple forms and subdued colouring are typical. Improvement in quality from crudity in shape and workmanship was brought about over a period of several centuries. A successful conclusion to the prolonged search for a more durable body

13

was achieved just prior to the beginning of the Han period when a strong non-porous body was invented. It was only the first of innumerable inventions and the beginning of technical prowess attained by Chinese potters through the centuries, not the least being an unequalled mastery of techniques in the production of high-fired pottery and porcelain.

It may be useful at this point to define the nature of pottery and porcelain. Pottery – earthenwares and stonewares – is basically composed of clay – often blended clays – baked until hard, the degree of hardness achieved depending upon the intensity of heat to which wares are exposed and the time spent in the kiln. Comparatively low temperatures – around 800 °C – are employed for baking soft earthenwares, rising to around 1,450 °C in the final firing of certain porcelains. When a degree of heat is reached sufficient to render the baked clay non-porous it becomes stoneware. Clays vary greatly in manner of reaction to heat. It is upon the extent of his knowledge of the potentiality of clays, especially when blended, that the potter's success depends. The body, which is the biscuit or clay object fired once, may be left unglazed and decorated or covered with glaze which serves as decoration as well as a protective covering for the body. The creation of fine glazes is perhaps the master potter's most exacting test of technical skill.

Porcelain, known to the Chinese as *tz'u*, as is also porcellanous stoneware, probably accidentally evolved when feldspathic material made fusible was incorporated in a stoneware body. Decayed feldspar, known to the Chinese as *kaolin* – meaning 'high place' after its place of discovery – is more familiarly known in the West as 'china-clay'. In China, a less decayed, more fusible feldspathic material, known as '*petuntze*', was originally supplied to potters in pulverised state. *Petuntze* or china stone serves as a white cement binding together the particles of less fusible *kaolin*. From the Chinese viewpoint a true porcelain body need not be translucent or white. Production of fine translucent porcelain vitally depended upon correct firing procedure at a carefully calculated and controlled high temperature, a difficult technique the Chinese potters mastered in the highest degree.

So-called true porcelain, a *kaolin* hard-paste body is, as the term implies, basically opposite to artificial soft-paste or simulated porcelain. Hard-paste porcelain is exceedingly smooth and glassy, obtained by firing at very high temperatures. Soft-paste porcelain, translucent and lead-glazed, is composed of ground glass mixed with various ingredients, including white clay, fired at low temperatures resulting in a somewhat oily or greasy appearance. In production of a soft-paste body Chinese potters used an ingredient they called *hua shih* or 'slippery stone', now thought to be pegmatite.

Prolonged exposure of ingredients to weather was always an essential part of Chinese preparation for pottery-making. When sufficiently weathered, rock was pulverised by machine, reducing the material to fine powder, and mixed with water to form a paste. By means of flotation, mixing with water and drying off, which eliminated coarse particles, a fine paste of the desired consistency was obtained.

Indigenous stonewares of the early Han period reveal complete mastery of tech-

1 EWER. Glazed pale buff pottery. T'ang dynasty, Chinese. *H* 11$\frac{3}{4}$*in*

niques and notable technical development. Throughout the Han period, and for long after, many Chinese potters erected large chamber-kilns on open hillsides or artificially created mounds. Beehive-shaped chambers were built, often in a series of three connected by a low passage. Protective brick walls, known as 'saggers', which screened wares from harmful gases and served to conduct flames upwards away from the wares, did not appear in Chinese kilns until later times, probably not before the twelfth century. The use of a downdraught, causing deflection of flames and gases, prevented heat from escaping up the chimney. By conserving heat the potter achieved the necessary high temperatures in the high-firing process. Naturally, the kiln itself was constructed of refractory materials capable of withstanding great heat within. Sandy fire clay was used in kiln construction. Kiln walls were never thick, insulation being achieved by coating the outside of the structure with wet coarse clay left to harden.

Glazes developed by Chinese potters in the early period served a twofold purpose, as decoration and, when applied to earthenwares, as a seal for porous surfaces. Non-porous stonewares and porcelain were glazed for the sake of decorative effect. Chinese potters used two different types of glazes, one of glassy character produced by fusing silica of quartz or sand by means of a flux, usually of lead oxide, the resulting lead glaze being applied in one or more coats over the surface of the ware. The Chinese also evolved a type of glaze which varied in form but was basically composed of feldspar or some other fusible rock. Salt glaze, as later used in Europe and introduced into the English potteries in Staffordshire with enormous success, was probably not unknown to the early Chinese potters but does not appear to have been used by them.

From the earliest times Chinese potters concentrated their inventive genius upon the development of fine glazes. In all probability, the attractive feldspathic glaze which enhanced early Chinese stonewares, and was subsequently applied to porcelain, was not an accidental discovery but evolved through experiment. The feldspathic glaze was obtained by mixing a composition of burned limestone and potash with *petuntze* and water. The glaze was applied to wares in various ways, including painting, blowing through gauze covering the end of a bamboo tube in much the same way as English potters centuries later obtained 'mottled' lustre effects, or by immersing wares in liquid glaze. The fusibility of the glaze was increased by mixing in larger proportions of ash and lime.

Unlike European potters, who first fired the clay object to biscuit state before applying glaze, the Chinese submitted clay wares already coated with glaze to the oven and fired in a single operation. High-temperature firing in the so-called *grand feu* techniques, first applying feldspathic glaze to hard-paste wares, was carried out with unqualified success by Chinese master potters. The *grand feu* palette was limited to coloured oxides which would withstand the intense heat required to unite feldspathic glaze to the hard surface of the wares. Coloured oxides were principally obtained from cobalt, iron and copper.

In their endeavour to create beautiful glazes the Chinese constantly experimented

2 (*left*) TEMMOKU
SHALLOW CONICAL DISH.
D 5⅞in; (*right*) KUAN-YAO
VASE *H 5½in*. Both
Southern Sung dynasty,
Chinese

with all kinds of soil and rock they hoped would yield rich colourings. Continued success in experiments gradually brought a more extensive range of glazes, and novel colour variations were introduced. Such effects as 'crackle' glaze and other types were probably accidental discoveries made during experiment.

Some of the earliest Chinese pottery is a type of redware found on excavated sites near Yang-shao and a similar type of ware found in Kansu province, both wares in certain respects resembling examples unearthed in parts of the Near East and the Indus valley. From this fact it may reasonably be concluded that the Chinese wares were derived from wares brought into the country by invaders. The primitive unglazed wares of Yang-shao and Kansu consist of a superior hard reddish-brown earthenware. Modelling was evidently carried out by hand, although the wheel was probably used to impart a gloss to the outside surface of wares. Decoration consists principally of black, red and white spirals, trellis and serrated bands, foliated and abstract patterns painted on white slip. Early wares of the type were probably used for mortuary purposes, their date being variously set from as early as 2500 BC as in the case of the somewhat finer Kansu specimens, to the Shang-Yin period which ended in about 1122 BC.

It is unlikely that glazed pottery was produced in China on an appreciable scale before the Han dynasty (206 BC–AD 220). Notwithstanding that Chinese potters almost certainly imitated Near Eastern pottery brought in by invaders near the end of the Stone Age it cannot be doubted that during the centuries just prior to the commencement of the Han period a completely indigenous type of pottery evolved in China, developed in pure concept of form with embodiment of techniques and styles that owed nothing to foreign inspiration. Chinese ceramic art in the centuries

17

preceding the Han period centred upon increasing mastery of vital techniques and reveals an enterprising spirit which enabled potters to achieve remarkable technical prowess in a relatively short time. This is apparent from the manner in which, following the invention of glaze, a rapid development of glazing techniques occurred during the early Han period, resulting in the introduction of fine lead-glazed ware. Especially impressive are some remarkable splendid large glazed stoneware jars hardly surpassed in their monumental beauty by similar productions of later Chinese potters.

Partially glazed examples of pre-Han pottery exist that are possibly the result of fusible ash accidentally settling on an object in process of firing. The melting ash formed into glaze which spread over part of the ware while baking in the kiln. Such occurrences, caused by draught through the kiln, were prevented in later times by the construction of saggers to protect the wares during firing. Pre-Han potters, observing the effect of intense heat on fusible materials such as wood ash and clay, or feldspathic rock, were not slow to make use of the discovery, with the result that sometime before 206 BC, the year of the Han ascent to the imperial throne, the first glazed stoneware was produced in China.

Under the Han emperors Chinese ceramics assumed the character and direction that were to prevail for the ensuing ten centuries. Tradition endured through successive generations with only slight modification of techniques and styles: yet despite convention, the master potters of ancient China were never so conservative in ideas and outlook that they refrained from making technical improvements and inventing new wares.

It is feasible that two distinct classes of ceramic wares were produced under the Han. Large potteries were established for what amounted to mass-production of utilitarian wares for common use, while potters of exceptional skill, recognised as masters, worked in their potteries almost exclusively for the court and nobility, creating fine ornamental wares some of which were destined to be placed in the splendid tombs erected in the period.

During the Han period Chinese pottery became more refined in body, form and decoration. Glazes continued to be of the greatest importance. Alkaline and lead-silicate glazes, otherwise glazes produced by fusing silica, usually of sand, aided by an alkali flux such as oxide of lead, were much favoured. The glazes were coloured with metallic oxides and, being soft, could be fired at fairly low temperatures. The use of lead glazes on stonewares became characteristic under the Han dynasty. Wood ash predominated in the composition of lead glaze, imparting the familiar dullish brown, or grey-green colouring, somewhat blotchy and sometimes iridescent. The hue of lead glaze was wholly natural, with no artificial colouring agents incorporated. It does not appear that even the resourceful and inventive potters of the early Han period knew how to colour lead glazes by artificial means. Even so, a distinctive durable slate-grey or red earthenware appeared in the Han period coated with mottled green lead glaze thought to have been derived from copper. Examples taken from Han tombs are often iridescent, caused by centuries of burial.

Green-glazed pottery was extremely popular during the Han period. The wares were usually modelled after the bronze vessels of the time used in the household, in temple ritual, and buried with the dead. Objects were freely and boldly modelled, usually devoid of formal rigidity, with clear-cut lines and well-balanced proportions even when of monumental dimensions. Ornamentation was in excellent taste, restrained yet vital and energetic, mainly comprising lion masks, ring handles, animals in low relief and broad bands.

Various sources are cited for the origin of lead-glazing techniques as practised in China in Han times. Some authorities believe that the process was invented in Egypt and introduced into China by a Persian, a theory supported by the English potter Bernard Leach. *Lui-li*, the ancient Chinese term for what is nowadays believed to have been glass frit imported into the country, may have first been used in China at a period when native potters were beginning to experiment in the development of glazes. Whether or not Han green-glazed ware was made solely for mortuary use has never been conclusively established.

It is firmly believed by the Chinese that the first porcelain made its appearance during the Han period. The earliest vitreous wares, often referred to as 'proto-porcelain', preceded the development of a type of white vitreous ware more deservingly described as porcelain. Significantly, a single Chinese word, *tz'u*, is used to designate both vitrified pottery, otherwise stoneware, and white translucent porcelain. Even if in fact its invention did not occur until after the eclipse of the Han dynasty, the earliest porcelain lacked most of the attributes of translucency and whiteness which aroused such admiration in Europe when porcelain was seen there for the first time. The ultimate sheer perfection of Chinese porcelain was an objective not attained until long after Han times.

Under the Han dynasty Chinese potters moved rapidly forward in improvement of techniques and greater understanding of materials. Imperial patronage of celebrated master potters capable of producing refined types of wares encouraged effort and experiment in the creation of new types. While the clay body was improved in quality, however, as a result of over-refinement a marked degeneracy in form and design occurred towards the end of the period. On the whole, late Han pottery was made with firm grasp of techniques and admirable stylisation, as is apparent in finer types of wares removed from tombs. But such wares, though providing sample evidence of the technical accomplishment of the potters who created them, cannot be regarded as being representative. In all probability they were superior wares supplied exclusively to the court or produced as mortuary wares.

Vitrified stonewares with feldspathic materials included in their ingredients were produced in the turbulent period between the end of the Han period in AD 220 and the beginning of the T'ang period in AD 618. The so-called period of the 'Six Dynasties', with a struggle for imperial power being fought in China, allowed little

3 OCTAGONAL BOTTLE.
Kuan-yao. Southern
Sung dynasty, Chinese.
H 8½in

opportunity for cultural and artistic progress, although several important potteries continued active. While it is seldom possible to recognise any particular wares as being the productions of one or other of these factories, the names of various famous kilns are known. In the neighbourhood of Yüeh Chou, subsequently renowned for beautiful celadon ware, the kiln of Tung Ou is thought to have been in operation as early as the middle of the third century AD. At Ch'ang-an a pottery recorded as flourishing in the sixth century AD became the first of several factories erected in the important imperial porcelain manufacturing centre of Ching-tê-chên.

With the expansion of the T'ang empire during the seventh century westwards into Central Asia and southwards into Indo-China, the Chinese potter absorbed new ideas and acquired new techniques through contact with foreign craftsmen. Yüeh celadon wares, high-fired and of great technical merit, their beauty celebrated throughout China, exemplify the remarkable advance of Chinese pottery-making techniques under the T'ang. The early development of Yüeh celadons belongs to the period preceding the establishment of the T'ang dynasty (618–906). With a continuous improvement in materials and techniques, whilst following a gradual change in style, production of Yüeh celadon ware endured at least until the end of the tenth century. Yüeh ware is not translucent, but in its characteristic hardness of body and glaze it approaches porcelain in quality. Obviously the Chinese delighted in Yüeh celadon by reason of its resemblance to jade, a rare substance to which magical powers were attributed and which was almost worshipped in China. Some authorities contend that Yüeh celadon is the earliest ware of its kind produced in China. The hard body is usually carved in high relief, following an incising technique which Chinese potters employed with remarkable dexterity on celadons and which was also used with success in the decoration of other wares. The chief attraction of Yüeh celadon is its distinctive grey-green glaze which occasionally shows a brownish tint. Glaze was applied over the grey body. So superior in quality, and in consequence universally admired, became Yüeh celadon wares that it is believed that by the eleventh century the princes of Yüeh and Wu reserved the entire output for their exclusive use.

Under the T'ang dynasty the artistic and cultural development of China entered upon a golden age of fulfilment. From surviving reports of travellers and ancient records preserved outside China it is evident that all foreign visitors to the country were impressed with its magnificence and the flourishing conditions which embraced all classes of the populace. As with artistic achievement in other spheres, T'ang potters expressed the vital, vigorous creative spirit of the age in their production of finely modelled, brilliantly decorated ceramic ware. Fired with the enthusiasm which gave impetus to arts and crafts under the T'ang, potters devised all manner of innovations.

Discovery of fragments of Chinese ceramic wares at the site of the ancient Mesopotamian city of Samarra, unoccupied after 883, proved beyond doubt that true porcelain was first made in China under the T'ang dynasty. Other fragmentary wares were also unearthed, including green and yellow dappled ware, which therefore cannot have been made solely for mortuary use, as was at one time believed. A flourishing trade existed between China and Western Asia by the ninth century leading to artistic and cultural connections between the Chinese and peoples to the west and accounting for the presence of Chinese pottery in Mesopotamia.

T'ang techniques acquired in the development of vitreous white stoneware, but more especially in regard to translucent white porcelain, gave the Chinese potters superiority in ceramic manufacture which potters in countries to the west of China failed to emulate with any degree of success for hundreds of years.

The key to the remarkable achievements of T'ang potters in their production of smooth white clay bodies lay in the special care they gave to selection of materials. Their mastery of processes was accomplished through their expert technical knowledge. The method of mixing *kaolin* with suitable amounts of feldspar, which at great heat causes the clay to fuse and vitrify in an approach to translucence, was of paramount importance. In manufacture of whitewares the utmost precautions were taken during preparation of materials in order to exclude iron-bearing substance which would discolour the body. While it may be advisable to point out here that white T'ang vitreous stonewares and porcelains were never of such pure whiteness as was obtained in wares made under later dynasties, T'ang wares possessed undeniable beauty and for their period represented a notable advance in technical skill and knowledge.

The glaze usually applied to T'ang wares was composed of clay, limestone, feldspar and quartz, which owing to careful selection of materials and controlled firing processes, imparted superiority to the methods of T'ang potters and their predecessors. Variation in texture and colour tones of the glaze was obtained by altering the proportions of ingredients or the actual ingredients in the glazing mixture and firing at different degrees of heat. T'ang transparent glazes possess exceptional purity of colour and the manner of application contributed in no small measure to the beauty of the finished product.

The Chinese custom of placing pottery figures of servants, animals and household goods in tombs with the dead originated with an ancient barbaric custom of immuring live people in tombs. By the middle of the Chou period (1122–256 BC) the practice was dying out and by the end of the period it had become customary to substitute models for live people and animals. Tomb figures dating from the Chou dynasty are rare. The Chinese believed that as far as means allowed the deceased needed to be provided with everything necessary to ensure their well-being in the life to come. Servants and animals, considered essential for comfort and enjoyment in the after-life, were provided in numbers according to the rank of the deceased person. Furthermore, it was considered essential to provide amusement for the dead in the shape of entertainers, dancers, acrobats and, in the case of a man, a company of beautiful women.

Recognisable human figures were not placed in tombs until the late Chou period. Early figurines found at Chang-sha, in the Yangtze valley, include specimens in lacquered wood with painted decoration. Third-century-BC Chou tomb figures were crude prototypes of figures placed in tombs during subsequent Han and T'ang times. Han and T'ang clay tomb figures were usually produced from moulds. At first only wealthy families could afford to place figurines in the tombs of dead relatives, but with the Han dynasty even the poorer classes were able to purchase cheap figures usually made of greyish clay dipped in white slip and decorated with black or red pigment.

Han tomb figures are invested with vitality and artistic quality absent from Chou examples. A well-ordered society, increasing affluence and zest for life, are reflected in the best Han tomb figures. Earthenware was first used for tomb figures in Han times. The early commonplace type were fashioned from grey or red clay covered with a dark-green glaze, with occasional variation in yellow or brown glaze. After burial for a long period this type of earthenware has acquired a delicate

4 SHALLOW BULB BOWL. 'Numbered' Chün-yao. Sung/Early Ming dynasty, Chinese. *D 10in*

iridescence which is now much admired. Naturalism is the essential characteristic of Han tomb figures. From this period onwards the ceramic art of China developed along naturalistic lines.

Despite constant repetition of types, Han figures were endowed with extraordinary animation. Horses were a favourite animal under the Han and were portrayed hunting, drawing carts and carriages, with riders mounted on their backs and caparisoned for war. Superb modelling, a characteristic feature of T'ang horses, is curiously absent from most Han examples, considering than Han potters were gifted modellers capable of rendering figures of animals with brilliant realism.

Tomb figure art attained its zenith under the T'ang dynasty, largely due to Chinese technical developments in ceramics. Although most T'ang pottery is of high quality, in the production of tomb figures potters really excelled. Clay used was usually grey or pinkish in colour, in the early period often covered with a thin monochrome glaze, yellow, blue or green being the most common colours, though other colours were sometimes used. The striking beauty of finely modelled T'ang tomb figures, richly decorated with beautiful glazes in vivid monochrome or polychrome, can hardly be imagined. Few ancient Chinese ceramic objects are more arresting than T'ang tomb figures. Larger figures were frequently hollow and faces were seldom enamelled.

An intriguing fact concerning T'ang tomb figures is the number of foreigners portrayed, particularly Semitic merchants. Foreign trade expanded rapidly under the T'ang, as has already been noted, and traders from all parts of Asia and the fringe of Africa visited China. Women were frequently depicted mounted on horseback, as dancers, or dressed to attend court or social functions, with graceful

23

5 EWER. White, early Ming, Chinese. *H 13in*

bodies in elaborate costume, their hair extravagantly dressed and ornamented. T'ang horses are almost invariably astonishingly true to life, ranking among the finest examples of T'ang ceramic animal art. A galaxy of figures, as fascinating as they are varied, includes priests, actors, warriors, jugglers, dancing girls, huntsmen, merchants, beggars, carriers, dwarfs, camels, wrestlers, servants, officials, musicians, and many more, all modelled with extraordinary attention to detail. T'ang mastery of expression, care for detail and obvious enjoyment of life expressed in potter's clay never fail to arouse admiration and curiosity. The passion of the warrior, the voluptuousness of women, pride and humility are depicted with moving realism. The master craftsmen who created T'ang tomb figures worked free of convention, obviously enjoying the opportunity to exercise their originality. Even inferior figures, reproduced in moulds, are today regarded as minor masterpieces. Surface cracks, or crazing, which tended to develop in T'ang coloured glazes during centuries of burial in tombs, scarcely impair the compelling beauty of the figures.

In addition to the important ceramic manufacturing centre at Yüeh Chou which flourished under the T'ang dynasty, it is clear, judging from ancient records, that pottery and porcellanous wares were being manufactured in other parts of China during the period. By the eighth century pottery-making in China was mainly concentrated in three areas, in Chihli and Honan in the north, where potters specialised in the production of white, buff and creamwares, eastwards in Chekiang, noted for greenwares, and to the south in Kiangsi, where white and buff porcellanous wares were made. Surviving records do not indicate that pottery was made in the west of China at the period. In noting the colours and kinds of wares particularly associated with these districts it is perhaps advisable to point out that potters in various localities apparently did not confine themselves to the production of one type of ware.

T'ang white stoneware and porcelain were made by following similar techniques, differences resting with the relative thickness or thinness of the body, the fine texture of porcelain being achieved by refinement of materials and newly developed firing processes. Although the refinement and pure whiteness so admired in porcelains produced in later centuries was lacking in the T'ang body, which tended towards grey or buff-colour, the progressive condition of Chinese ceramic production at the period was of the utmost significance. Superficial decoration was never applied to T'ang whitewares, their unique attraction stemming from the harmony achieved by purity of colour and beauty of form. During the T'ang period the beauty of Chinese ceramic wares was in large measure due to superb modelling combined with quality of paste and glaze.

T'ang potters evidently expended considerable time and energy in developing glazing techniques. The technique of applying green glaze to wares, widely used under the Han dynasty, was apparently discarded in T'ang times, probably due to scarcity or high cost of materials during the unsettled period of the Six Dynasties. Green-glazed wares continued to be made under the T'ang dynasty, but the colour was of different tone, deeper and of richer quality. Authorities have long disagreed on the question of whether or not the green-glazed tradition of Han wares did in fact survive into the T'ang period. However, obvious differences between authenticated Han and T'ang examples indicate changes in materials used and production techniques.

While Chinese potters were always prepared to use new ideas and learn new techniques from foreigners, especially potters of the Near East, development of porcelain in China owed nothing to outside sources. Probably the technique of using colouring oxides in lead glazes was learned from Near Eastern potters, but the extensive range of coloured glazes developed by the Chinese potters during the T'ang period was far superior to any known outside China. A beautiful amber-yellow, a sombre brown, violet-tinted blue, leaf-green and greenish- or brownish-black were T'ang innovations. T'ang potters used lead glaze more sparingly than their Han predecessors, applying thin coats over a hard body. Perhaps due to age, T'ang glazes on authenticated examples usually display slight crazing – although this may not be due to age but may have been deliberately caused during firing as decoration. When objects were dipped the glaze was often left to run down the sides and gather at the base, forming an irregular line round the foot, part of which was left unglazed.

Streaked and spotted glazed effects were devised by the application of stained glazes or by dusting metallic oxides on the body prior to firing. Monochromes are among the most beautiful lead-glazed T'ang wares, with the glaze applied over a creamy-white or buff-coloured body. White glaze was also improved in texture and tone and in consequence became popular, especially when applied to the exquisite straight-sided cups which are considered by many to be the most beautiful ceramic wares ever created. So-called *san ts'ai*, a 'three-coloured' lead-glazed ware, is attractively dappled and streaked, combining beauty of form and lavish decoration. According to personal taste, these may not be regarded as more entrancing than a variety of other attractive wares including handsome dishes on three feet enriched with splendid design and colouring, blue, brown, yellow, with stylised birds, flowers and rosettes, the incised outlines governing the flow of the glazes, a technique which continued in use for centuries. Lead glazes were also employed in a marbling technique, later adopted by English potters with charming results. Marbling was achieved by mixing different coloured clays in order to produce a variety of stoneware to which cream-coloured glaze was applied.

The Sung period (AD 960–1279) has become noted for the perfection of its ceramic wares, in particular its high-fired stonewares and porcelain. Sung culture, characterised by acute refinement of taste and intense interest in the arts supported by the possession of great wealth by the upper classes, led to a marked change in ceramic styles and methods of production. Comparative political stability was established and an atmosphere of tranquillity and fulfilment pervaded the empire, contrasting with the energetic enterprise of T'ang times. Pottery, in common with other products, assumed a serene character expressive of the mood of the age. Tranquillity may indeed be a term applicable to Sung art in all its forms. In ceramics, potters who enjoyed imperial patronage found inspiration and encouragement to produce some of the most serenely beautiful wares the world has ever seen.

Glazing techniques were further developed under the Sung, with a range of new colours, including soft opalescent greens as lustrous and smooth as jade. Certain wares were made exclusively for the emperor and members of his court in factories established by imperial command. Every new design and change in techniques had to be approved by the master potter in control appointed by the emperor. Sung rulers became noted for their unrivalled collections of ornamental pottery and porcelain. Under the Sung a wide variety of ceramic wares was acquired by all classes.

Types of wares produced in respective factories depended largely upon the kind of materials available locally. In Sung times many kilns operated which owed success and imperial favour to the all-round knowledge and experience of the master in control. It became normal practice for a potter and his descendants to manufacture a particular type of ware for which a good market was established and to continue making the same type of ware over an extended period, sometimes for centuries, with little modification of process or design.

Sung pottery is notable for dignity of form and a subtle relationship of body, colour and glaze. Forms are often so deceptively restrained and simple a novice may imagine it an easy matter to imitate them. Many have failed utterly in the attempt. Unsurpassed beauty, harmony of form and colour were achieved by superb mastery of style and technique. Sung potters selected their materials carefully and gave close attention to the vital process of refining and blending clays. Development of new techniques proceeded by 'trial and error' which gave the potter greater insight and understanding of materials.

Sung pottery may be classified according to characteristics and the purpose for which it was made. The finest wares were invariably made for the imperial court. Celebrated collections housed in the royal palaces for centuries (including numerous deceptive copies made at a later date) leave no doubt on the score of the superior quality of Sung ceramic wares. Imperial wares are the work of potters of high repute who enjoyed favour at court and found opportunity to exercise their utmost skill in the creation of the most superb objects. Among the known kilns which produced wares for the emperor and court were the so-called 'classical' kilns, which included Ju, Ting, Kuan and Ch'ai. The famous Chün, Yüeh and Lung-ch'uan factories are also thought to have made pottery for the imperial court.

Sung wares are admired principally for subtle form, restrained use of coloured glazes and avoidance of the extremism in shape and decoration which imparted flamboyance to T'ang pottery. It was left to artistic Sung potters, working quietly without aiming at novel effects and drastic changes in techniques, to modify and refine old styles and endow their productions with a unique serenity and harmony in composition never previously achieved in Chinese ceramic wares. Variety in form and mode of decoration were unlimited, but almost always excellent taste prevailed.

Ting wares are certainly among the most beautiful of Sung productions. An imperial kiln which operated at Ting Chou in Chihli province was founded early in the Sung period, fine white or ivory-tinted wares becoming a speciality in the early twelfth century. Manufacture was interrupted in 1127 when the imperial court fled south, with a number of Ting potters included in the emperor's entourage who were destined to later set up factories in Kiangsi province. Well-authenticated examples survive to prove that Ting whitewares continued to be made in the original factory under the Tartar dynasty which ousted the Sung rulers in the north.

The Ting ware body is of remarkable quality, free of impurities, smooth to the touch and translucent. All Ting ware is exceptionally thin and delicate, the decoration generally consisting of incised designs. To prevent warping in the kiln Ting whiteware was often placed on the rim whilst being fired. A metal band fitted after firing to the unglazed rim also served as a decorative feature which enhanced the beauty of the object. Variation in texture and tone of body and glaze was obtained by control of heat during firing. An oxidising atmosphere during firing resulted in

6 SEATED BUDDHA. *Blanc-de-chine*. Tê-hua, Fukien province. Ming-Ch'ing dynasty, seventeenth century, Chinese. *H 6¾in*

the production of ivory-tinted wares. Whitewares were probably fired in reduction. In addition to *Pai Ting*, the highest quality wares made, other less fine Ting wares were made, whiteness sometimes being obtained by application of a white engobe to a coarser body. Other types of Ting wares, notably those made in Kiangsi province after the removal of the imperial court to the south, are covered with creamy or yellowish glaze over the porcellanous body which is translucent in thinner paste. Ting ware, known as Ch'u Chou ware after the district where factories engaged in the manufacture sprang up, has always been admired for the beauty of incised decoration in freehand patterns of flowing lines. Moulded decoration was also applied, while other examples are left devoid of ornament, but the most attractive wares are delicately incised in traditional line designs.

The development of celadon glaze reached its peak during the Sung period. Lung-ch'uan celadon is of superlative form and quality, its rich sheen one of its most striking characteristics. Glaze was invariably applied thickly over the dense porcellanous stoneware body. As a rule, Lung-ch'uan glaze is found crazed, which increases the attraction of wares. The glaze is of a distinctive, somewhat cloudy bluish-green, with an incised pattern showing faintly through.

Chün wares, which have long interested collectors of Chinese ceramics, are among the best known and most attractive of Sung pottery. Several types of wares were produced, none of which were particularly esteemed by Sung emperors. Wares of similar type were produced in several other districts besides Chün Chou where it originated. Chün stonewares, usually of a fine-grained buff or grey-coloured body, are thickly covered with an opaque glaze in varying tones of green and pale lavender, bluish-tinted and sometimes splashed with a rich plum colour. Coloured glazes were allowed to mingle as they ran, creating a pleasing decorative feature on moulded wares. Perhaps the most attractive glazed Chün ware is a type covered with monochrome blue-green glaze. A peculiarity of Chün glaze is variation in tone from lavender to a clear soft blue. Chün glaze splashed with red markings is richly opalescent, evenly applied over the exceptionally smooth surface of the body. The blue Chün glaze cannot easily be successfully imitated. The rich colour was probably derived from iron. That Chün potters were already endeavouring to develop red glazes seems fairly conclusive from the presence of copper in the glaze, whether by accident or intention. After a lengthy experimental period peach, *flambé* and ox-blood glazes, all greatly admired by the Chinese, were derived from copper. The characteristic blue colouring of Chün glaze was obtained by the use of a small proportion of iron, while the occasional presence of small amounts of copper in the glaze, which resulted in red blotches, cannot readily be explained unless we accept that experiments were in progress.

Ju and Kuan wares resemble Chün wares in certain respects but are much more refined, being supplied to the imperial court. Few examples of these wares survive. Shapes of Ju and Kuan wares are often unusual and reminiscent of ancient Chinese bronze sacrificial vessels. The majority were slab-constructed, following a somewhat primitive pre-casting technique. It is the characteristic, thickly applied high-fired glazes of Ju and Kuan wares, always very smooth and dense, and of exceptional refinement and luminosity, which are their chief attraction and place them among the 'classical' Sung wares.

Wares made in the locality of Tz'u Chou – where it is interesting to note in passing that pottery production has continued uninterrupted from the Sung period into modern times – principally consisted of stonewares, glazed and decorated by the use of various processes. A notable feature of Tz'u Chou wares made under imperial patronage is fine decoration in the form of brushwork patterns composed of lines. Colours of wares are quiet tones of brown, grey, black and white. Tz'u Chou potters were also masters of the wheel. They did not hesitate to make large pieces, usually vigorously modelled, with an evident command of techniques. Many potters working in the locality produced wares of similar type. It is therefore not unreasonable to conjecture that a single large communal kiln may have been erected by a group of potters who shared its use in a concerted effort towards more economical operations. Tz'u Chou wares were in 'traditional' style. Each potter or group of potters added their individual touches to wares.

Brush decoration, painting with coloured slips and pigments, on Tz'u Chou wares was of high order, almost calligraphic in character, boldly applied with swift decisive strokes clearly defined beneath a transparent glaze. One type of ware was covered with light-coloured slip and decorated with red pigment under a translucent feldspathic glaze. A carved slip-glaze technique employed in the decoration of Tz'u Chou wares was somewhat complex to carry out. Objects were first coated with a brown or black slip glaze before firing, the glaze incised with a linear design or cut away to disclose the unglazed coloured clay beneath. The attraction of the ware depended not upon the glaze alone but also upon the charming colour contrast of glaze and body.

Although dedicated in their endeavour to achieve perfection of form and develop a superior porcelain paste, Sung potters were conscious of tradition. At first, elegance and dignity were sustained in form and the colouring of wares was restrained. But as time passed an inevitable slackening of standards occurred with a debasement of quality, principally due to over-refinement.

Dark-glazed Sung Chien wares, chiefly comprising tea bowls, which have survived in large numbers, were probably a type of household ware made for an extensive market. The sombre Chien glazes ranged from black and brown in varying tones to other drab colours. Tea bowls were covered with dark slip glazes, applied thickly over the smooth surface. Chien ware will be found to be less finely finished than most other Sung pottery. The glaze was allowed to run freely and gather at the foot which was generally left unglazed. A basic ingredient of Chien glazes was ordinary fusible red clay in which impurities were present that during firing in an oxidising atmosphere caused the resulting slip to boil. Bursting bubbles caused bluish-black or brown streaks to appear in the glaze of a type known as 'hare's fur', or 'temmoku'. The effect was greatly admired in Japan where the ware found high favour with eminent masters of the tea ceremony.

7 (*outside*) PAIR OF FIGURES OF IMMORTALS. Porcelain. *Famille verte* decoration.
H 6in; (*centre*) RHYTON. Porcelain. *Famille verte. H 6¾in*. Both K'ang Hsi, Chinese

'Hare's fur' glazed wares were also produced in Honan, along with other wares of various kinds. 'Mirror-black' Honan wares are covered with an almost flawless smooth black glaze. 'Oil-spot' glaze, obtained by a special firing technique which involved creating blisters on the surface of the glaze, exhibit silver or brown spots on the smooth black surface. Other decorative effects include leaf patterns in blurred outline in grey or brown on a black ground. The appeal of these wares lies in an exquisite use of decorative glaze more than in beauty of form.

Decorative brush painting on ceramic wares, popular during the Sung period, was of such high order that it calls for consideration at this point. Artists worked with great accomplishment, skilfully using their brushes and painting in fired colours to a degree of perfection rarely attained under the T'ang.

In the early Sung period the Chinese potter remained content to decorate his wares with black or brown pigment, covering his designs with clear glaze. Later, turquoise-coloured glaze applied over black or brown brush painting became a favourite mode of decoration. It is surmised that the introduction of painting on wares was the natural outcome of Chinese admiration for Persian brush-decorated wares. Certainly on the earlier painted Chinese wares the designs closely resemble those seen on Persian wares of about the twelfth century.

At Tz'u Chou, where the majority of brush painting on wares was executed in black or brown, a Persian type of design was favoured, the motif carried out with great precision in what may be regarded as the Sung tradition. Whilst through a long period painting under a turquoise-blue glaze in the Persian manner found favour with Chinese potters, from the beginning they sought variety of colour. The eventual introduction of brush painting in red and green overglaze colours was a momentous step forward. With the establishment of Ming rule the techniques of painting ceramics assumed increasing importance, with the result that the character of painted decoration underwent considerable change.

Under the Ming dynasty (1368–1644) imperial interest in the production of porcelain led to the establishment of numerous important kilns where experiments were conducted and fine wares were produced under the emperor's patronage. The first Ming emperor, formerly a Buddhist monk, who ascended the imperial throne as Hung Wu, was undoubtedly too occupied with restoring the empire and consolidating his imperial power to devote much of his time to artistic pursuits and interests. Under his successors, however, a long era of peace gave China the opportunity to develop arts, trade and commerce. All crafts and manufacture benefited. Imperial interest in translucent white porcelain produced in the factory established by Hung Wu at Ching-tê-chên in 1369 gave pottery-making great impetus. As the fourteenth century passed porcelain became much in demand throughout China. Blue-painted wares were favoured more than celadons, especially in the growing export trade. Love of colourful decoration on wares led to potters forsaking the Sung taste for subdued tones and simplicity in design.

Ching-tê-chên became the most important porcelain manufacturing centre in China and was destined to remain so for centuries. Work was conducted on well-organised lines, the number of workmen employed amounting to hundreds. Inevitably, the extent of operations, producing porcelain wares in huge quantity to meet an ever-increasing demand, led to a decline in quality. Even decoration suffered. Moreover, standardisation developed as a result of the division of labour in production, each man fulfilling his allotted task, with the adoption of what were virtually mass-production methods.

First in the important developments in manufacture and decoration of ceramic wares that occurred under the Ming dynasty was the great popularity and prodigious production of blue-and-white wares. It may be fairly assumed that cobalt ore, the source of blue colouring, was first imported into China by way of the Near East where it had long been employed in blue underglaze painting. The Chinese originally followed the Persian method of preparation which, due to the presence of impurities in the ore, imparted a greyish tint. In the reign of Hsüan Tê (1426–35), blue-painted porcelain became immensely popular and was exported in vast quantity. Under Hsüan Tê the underglaze painting technique was perfected and a much more definite blue was developed. While the cobalt process was being improved to obtain a more satisfactory blue the quality of the porcelain body also received attention, with the result that by the fifteenth century Ming blue-and-white porcelains had become magnificent. Ming porcelain was even more translucently white and more finely glazed than the Sung porcelains.

8 (*left*) PUNCH BOWL. Porcelain. Enamel decoration, *famille verte* and powder-
blue. Imari style. D *14in*; (*right*) OVAL DISH. Porcelain. 'Tobacco'-leaf shaped,
famille rose enamel decoration. D *16in*. Both Ch'ien Lung, Chinese

Unfortunately, eagerness to take advantage of opportunity in the great foreign
demand for blue-and-white wares led the Chinese potter to a debasement of the
quality of his wares. Quality was neglected for the sake of producing quantity.
While it is true that incomparably fine blue-and-white was made almost throughout
the entire Ming period – the beauty of the wares captivates us today – it is nevertheless possible to trace the slow decline in quality from the early to late periods. In
quite a short time the serenity and grace of Sung forms were wholly lost.

Throughout the Ming and Ch'ing dynasties the technical side of production received close attention from potters. Whiteness of the body became ultra-important,
with constant striving after yet greater achievement. Earthenwares, stonewares and
porcelains were all subjected to experiment in efforts directed at improvement of
paste. Among the colours introduced the beautiful monochromes were perhaps
the most outstanding. Under the Ch'ing dynasty monochrome glazes in sombre
tones of brown and rust appeared, their rather austere beauty very different in
mood and effect from the velvety-toned Ming monochromes.

Perhaps the most important and interesting Ming wares, apart from blue-and-
white, are the wares decorated with coloured glazes in the so-called three-coloured
or *san ts'ai* tradition. The best of Ming three-coloured wares belong to the fifteenth

33

and sixteenth centuries and the finest of these, albeit the most striking in appearance, must assuredly be richly decorated ornamental wares upon which a deep purplish-blue and brilliant turquoise predominate. The mode of decoration was not confined to porcelain; it was also applied to stoneware.

Three-coloured, 'cloison' decoration, as applied to the finest Ming wares, required great patience and skill. Designs were composed of raised, moulded slip outlines which kept the glazes divided as they flowed. Occasionally incisions were made as ornament and to prevent glazes flowing together. Sometimes carved open-work added charm and interest. Glazes were usually medium-fired, the palette including a rich aubergine, a clear turquoise and an opaque dark purplish-blue, the so-called 'three-colours', used in conjunction with colourless glaze, amber yellow, brown and dark-green. In similar wares of later date the colours were improved, with the aubergine (produced from manganese) almost of amethyst hue. The glaze of later wares displays a tendency to craze. Designs applied are principally floral motifs, featuring the lotus and chrysanthemum. Floral patterns composed in the 'three-colours' appear on all types of wares but more especially on bowls and vases. Engraving, when featured, was always carried out with great delicacy and refinement. The cloison decoration technique, resembling cloisons in enamelled decoration on metalwares, probably evolved in the early fifteenth century and continued to be used over a long period.

At the commencement of the Ming period, when the imperial factory was still endeavouring to improve the quality of porcelain, the almost pure white body, fine-grained and of silky smoothness, continued to be marred by a greenish-blue tinge. A coarsening of texture in the paste towards the close of the important long reign of Chia Ching (1522–66) is said to have been due to the exhaustion of the kaolin deposits in the Ma-tsa'ang hills adjacent to the imperial factory, when material had to be procured from other sources. In general, Ming white glaze is dense and somewhat greasy in appearance, but its quality and character were not consistent throughout the period due in part to experiment and changes in basic materials. The Ching-tê-chên potters composed their porcelains of equal parts of petuntze and kaolin.

Under Yung Lo (1403–24) porcelain manufacture greatly increased owing to popular demand. The quality of the finest wares was incomparable. The majority of Yung Lo porcelain is coloured, often monochrome, frequently ornamented with incised patterns and painted in white slip under the glaze in the so-called 'secret decoration' technique, the design being scarcely visible until the object is held up to light. At this stage in development Chinese porcelain attained a 'heavenly' whiteness, serene and pure as never previously achieved in the centuries of striving towards perfection. Thereafter, although earthenwares and stonewares continued to be made, it was through their creation of superlative porcelain that the Chinese potters sought the highest expression of their art and skill.

Notwithstanding the immense popularity of blue-painted wares throughout the Ming period, underglaze red-painted wares became fashionable, particularly in the reigns of Hsüan Tê and Chia Ching. It is not known for certain how the technique of underglaze painting in copper-red pigment evolved in China, but it is improbable that Chinese potters acquired the technique from the Near East, for the reason that it is not known to have been practised other than in China and Japan until centuries later. It is reasonable to conclude that because he wished to use a red pigment to decorate his wares the resourceful Chinese potter set about searching for a substance that would provide him with the desired colour. As is evident from the red blotches on Chün ware, caused by the presence of a copper ingredient in the mixture, the Chinese potter was already aware of the value of copper in developing a red glaze considerably earlier than the Ming period, when painting in copper-red was first attempted on an extensive scale in the reign of Hsüan Tê. A brilliant red was devised which required firing at a higher temperature than blue pigment with the result that where examples are found with perfect red decoration the blue is impaired, and in examples displaying a clear blue fired at the correct temperature the red is invariably poor. The finest underglaze painted copper-red belongs to the reign of Hsüan Tê. According to legend, the secret of the copper-red process was lost after the reign of Chêng Hua (1465–87) but there is little doubt that red-painted wares were still being produced in Chia Ching's reign half a century later. From surviving records it appears that Chinese potters always regarded red-painted ware as difficult to produce. The techniques of making both red glaze and pigment were evidently never developed to complete satisfaction.

With red and blue monochrome glazes potters at work in the time of Hsüan Tê found themselves on much firmer ground. A beautiful blue glaze known as *chi ch'ing* first appeared in Hsüan Tê's reign. Also from the reign of Hsüan Tê there gradually developed a style of painting which achieved great popularity in the reign of Chêng Tê (1506–21). The style of decoration featured designs of robust character amidst lotus springing from thick sinewy stems. In addition to lotus and vine there appeared the type of scrolls and arabesques referred to as 'Mohammedan' frequently seen in later Chêng Tê wares.

Ming porcelain decorators also excelled at painting over the glaze in enamel colours. Mastery of a most complex and exacting technique was attained during the reign of Chêng Hua (1465–87). Indeed, such a high standard of skill and artistry was never surpassed in overglaze enamel decoration. The technique evolved over two centuries. Success depended upon preparation of the enamels and manner of painting on biscuit or over the glaze, which might be white or coloured. Firing had essentially to be of low temperature. The fashionable style of decoration embodied flowers, foliage and figure subjects, with lotus-scroll work and occasionally arabesques. Designs were applied in dark-blue outlines contrasting with the brighter colours used for filling in.

In the late sixteenth century brighter colours came into use and a noticeable coarsening in both materials and workmanship occurred. It is true to say that the colours employed in enamel decoration were more attractive due to intensity, though oddly enough the blue commonly used tended to become weaker and even

9 PAIR OF PHOENIX FIGURES. Porcelain. *Famille rose* decoration. Ch'ien Lung, Chinese. *H 20¼in*

greyish in tone with passing time. Under Wan Li (1573–1619) shapes and workmanship showed a general decline that became more marked by the middle years of
the seventeenth century which witnessed the fall of the Ming dynasty and the
establishment of the Ch'ing dynasty.

Chêng Hua enamelled porcelain made expressly for the imperial court was
decorated in the style known as '*tou ts'ai*' or 'painting in contrasting colours',
which embodies outlines in exquisite soft underglaze blue, contrasted with gleam-
ing coloured enamels applied in thin washes. The porcelain body is invariably of
fine quality, often only of eggshell thickness.

Chêng Hua enamelled porcelain set the style and standard of such wares for a
long period and was extensively copied in subsequent centuries. In the reign of
Chia Ching enamel painting on porcelain attained great beauty and was executed
with extraordinary skill and sensitivity. An attractive tomato-red enamel came into
use, possibly as a substitute for underglaze copper-red, the secret process of which
is said to have been lost at the period. Probably copper-red was discarded in favour
of red enamel painting. The new red served as a background for reserve panels
decorated with floral and figure subjects. Gourd-shaped vases were made at the
period decorated with green lotus-scrolls painted in enamel over a tomato-red
enamel ground.

An outstanding ceramic innovation of the Ming period was the exquisitely beautiful
so-called *blanc-de-chine* ware made by the Tê-hua potters in Fukien province. It is
believed that manufacture began under the Sung, but it was not until the seventeenth
century that the Fukien potters produced their *blanc-de-chine* masterpieces in fine
white porcelain covered with a thick white glaze. From their absence it may be
concluded that use of coloured glazes and enamels was never considered. The body
was eminently suitable for modelling graceful figures. Kuan-yin was foremost
among a host of deities and characters portrayed.

The pure whiteness and velvety smoothness of *blanc-de-chine* ware is unique
among Chinese ceramic achievements. It was instantly admired and marvelled at
when the first examples appeared in Europe and today it is still considered by many
to be the most beautiful porcelain ever made. Certainly Fukien figures are incomparably fine. *Blanc-de-chine* wares may possibly have inspired European
potters working in rococo style, as has been suggested. The soft flow of draperies
was never more sensitively and realistically imitated than in Ming *blanc-de-chine*.
Perfected techniques in the preparation of materials which apparently vitrified
without warping, and the unsurpassed skill of master craftsmen were combined in
the creation of wares of incomparable brilliance and beauty. Tê-hua wares continued to be produced under the succeeding Ch'ing dynasty (1644–1912) but were of
an inferior quality and style that is at once apparent when Ming and Ch'ing examples are placed side by side for comparison. Authentic Ming *blanc-de-chine*
emanates a rosy glow when held against light. *Blanc-de-chine* wares produced in

modern times are dead white and almost invariably lack the velvety texture of the old ware.

Unfortunately, many Western potters attempted to imitate original *blanc-de-chine* wares, which led to the production of inferior figures that continue to deceive the inexpert. Not invariably, but quite often, old *blanc-de-chine* wares carry incised seal marks beneath the glaze on backs or bases, but of course reproductions will bear such a mark. Authenticity is therefore not established by the presence of a seal mark.

A fine stoneware was made at Yi-hsing in Kiangsu. Red and brown stonewares produced at Yi-hsing probably inspired Western potters in manufacture of similar wares. The kiln may have been much older, but wares of the type first appeared towards the end of the Ming period. It seems fairly certain that the red and brown pastes composed of blended clays which easily vitrified in firing were closely imitated by Johann Böttger in Germany, Ariz de Molde in Holland and the Elers brothers in England, all active experimentalists in the search for a porcelain formula. Yi-hsing ware was usually left unglazed, its faint surface sheen possibly being due to reaction during firing or produced by polishing immediately after cooling. Very rarely, a thin bluish glaze was applied to Yi-hsing stonewares, said to have been the secret process of a potter named Ou Tzū-ming. Enamels were also applied, but infrequently. According to tradition, Kung Ch'un, who devised the first Chinese teapot, established a teapot manufactory at Yi-hsing in the early sixteenth century. Teapots are said to exist bearing his signature. Kung Ch'un was succeeded by other makers of teapots, including Shih Ta-pin, the most celebrated, Hui Mêng-chên, a late Ming potter, and Ch'en Ming-yuan, said to have worked as a master potter at Yi-hsing in the reign of Wan Li. Yi-hsing teapots were exported to Europe in quantity.

At the fall of the Ming dynasty the imperial porcelain factory at Ching-tê-chên experienced disaster when the town was destroyed during rebellion. The establishment of the Ch'ing dynasty and the rebuilding of the imperial factory in 1681 ushered in an era of unprecedented artistic achievement and prosperity at Ching-tê-chên. Emperor K'ang Hsi (1662–1722) proved to be a wise and enlightened ruler, an enthusiastic patron of the arts who was, moreover, closely concerned with the development of native crafts and industries. Twenty years after he ascended the throne K'ang Hsi appointed a member of his household named Ts'ang Ying-hsüan as director of the imperial porcelain factory. Ts'ang Ying-hsüan was the first of several eminently successful directors of the imperial porcelain factory at Ching-tê-chên under the early Ch'ing emperors.

In the reign of K'ang Hsi potters favoured Ming styles. A marked preference for decorating wares with monochrome glazes prevailed and the use of copper-red was resumed. Enamel painting in Ming 'five-colours' continued, but with a change in the underglaze blue technique and a less profuse use of turquoise-blue.

The exquisite rose-pink colour, derived from gold and first used in Chinese porcelain decoration late in the reign of K'ang Hsi, and which subsequently became

10 PAIR OF FIGURES OF KNEELING BOYS. Perhaps Europeans. Porcelain. *Famille rose* decoration. Ch'ien Lung, Chinese. *H 8¼in*

known as *famille rose* decoration, originated in Europe. Up to that time the enamel palette had been dominated by the rich green which gave its name to the *famille verte* mode of decoration. In the succeeding reign, that of Yung Chêng (1722–35), *famille rose* decoration became exceedingly popular, largely superseding *famille verte*.

When Nien Hsi-yao succeeded to the post of director of the imperial porcelain factory in 1726, he appointed as his assistant and eventual successor a potter of outstanding talents named T'ang Ying. In 1736, when Nien Hsi-yao retired, T'ang Ying assumed complete control of the factory and supervised production for almost twenty years, raising the quality of the wares yet higher and introducing techniques and styles of decoration of unprecedented refinement and beauty. It is recorded that T'ang Ying constantly associated with the potters and artists employed in the factory and that his knowledge of materials and mastery of all techniques rendered him unique among directors at Ching-tê-chên.

Directors at the imperial factory concentrated energy and experiment in the continuous improvement of the porcelain body. In general, it was exquisite Ch'ing period porcelains that European potters admired and endeavoured to copy throughout the eighteenth century. Under the emperors K'ang Hsi, Yung Chêng and Ch'ien Lung, by their creation of shapes of superlative beauty and grace, with exquisite use of decorative motifs and colouring, the Ch'ing potters attained mastery of techniques that was never to be surpassed. Inevitably, as had happened before, over-refinement and concern regarding materials brought a decline in form and increasing carelessness in decoration. For a long period, however, *famille verte*, *famille rose* and *famille noire* decorated wares were superb and these, together with monochrome wares decorated with coloured glazes, rank among the finest porcelains produced in China. K'ang Hsi white porcelain of the type known as *chiang t'ai*, containing the ingredient *hua-shih* or 'slippery stone', mistaken for steatite or soapstone by European potters, has a soft-paste body which is opaque, fine-grained and slightly crazed upon the surface. It was probably not made outside the imperial factory.

Glazes occupied the attention of T'ang Ying throughout his years in control at Ching-tê-chên. *Sang de boeuf* (ox blood) and *flambé* glazes derived from copper, peach-bloom and apple-red were developed and used in a variety of ways which included applying the glaze by a spraying technique. The first director of the imperial factory, Ts'ang Ying-hsüan, is said to have invented a method of spraying on glaze through a bamboo pipe covered with gauze at one end. The technique was used to spray cobalt-blue glazes on monochrome wares. Delicately beautiful soft lavender-blues applied to Yung Chêng monochrome wares were, according to tradition, the invention of the imperial factory director Nien Hsi-yao. Lustrous black glazes of superb richness, embellished with *famille verte* decoration belong to K'ang Hsi's reign. Kingfisher-blue, or 'peacock-green' as it is known to the Chinese, is derived from copper with an alkaline flux and is said to belong to the range of beautiful glazes developed at Ching-tê-chên by Ts'ang Ying-hsüan. He also invented a somewhat rare brownish-olive-coloured glaze known in China as 'eel-yellow'.

In K'ang Hsi's reign the imperial factory revived the late Ming decorative style *san ts'ai* – 'three-coloured' painting. Aubergine or manganese-purple, yellow and leaf-green on a greenish-white ground were a favourite combination. Attractive dappled green glazes were used, also soft greens and yellows of fine texture mainly serving as ground colours. A taste developed for drawing outline designs in black or brown before applying a green enamel wash.

Porcelain wares manufactured at Ching-tê-chên were in later periods sent elsewhere to be decorated. Canton eventually became the principal centre for the decoration of Ching-tê-chên porcelains outside the imperial factory. Painting on 'egg-shell' porcelain wares became a speciality of Cantonese ceramic artists. Wares of the type known as 'ruby-back' were finely coloured crimson or rose-pink in enamels on the reverse side. From almost the middle of the eighteenth century the decoration of porcelain amounted to an industry in Canton. Huge quantities of export wares were decorated, a great deal in European taste. Black came into more general use both in outline drawing and as a ground colour.

With the turn of the century the quality of Chinese pottery and porcelain entered upon a period of rapid decline. Chinese potters active in the early nineteenth century retained their unrivalled technical knowledge but originality vanished. During the reigns of Chia Ch'ing (1796–1820) and Tao Kuang (1821–50) few wares were produced that were not wholly imitative or derived from ancient styles. Nonetheless, tradition and inherent skill endured. In the twentieth century Chinese craftsmen continued to turn out excellent ceramic wares of utilitarian character. It appears improbable that China will ever again know conditions that will allow her potters to create masterpieces of the superlative order of those which remain to captivate us with their timeless beauty.

CHINESE DYNASTIES AND EMPERORS MENTIONED IN THE FOREGOING TEXT

DYNASTIES:

Shang-Yin	1765–1122 BC
Chou	1122–249 BC
Ch'in	221–206 BC
Han	206 BC–AD 220
The Six Dynasties	220–589
Sui	589–618
T'ang	618–906
The Five Dynasties	907–960
Sung	960–1279
Yüan	1280–1368
Ming	1368–1644
Ch'ing	1644–1912

EMPERORS:

Huang Ti	3rd millennium BC?
Hung Wu	1368–1398
Yung Lo	1403–1424
Hsüan Tê	1426–1435
Chêng Hua	1465–1487
Chêng Tê	1506–1521
Chia Ching	1522–1566
Wan Li	1573–1619
K'ang Hsi	1662–1722
Yung Chêng	1723–1735
Ch'ien Lung	1736–1795
Chia Ch'ing	1796–1820
Tao Kuang	1821–1850

KOREA AND JAPAN

Korean art has been strongly influenced by Chinese elements, but the assertion that Korean art is merely a provincial extension of Chinese art is debatable. From the remote past the Korean peninsula served as a natural bridge between China and Japan for the transmission of cultural and artistic ideas and developments, and in the process Korean art was much more exposed to influence from her great neighbour China than happened in Japan. Nevertheless, in certain aspects Korean art exhibits concepts and forms which are wholly indigenous.

For convenience, Korean pottery is usually divided into three groups named after dynasties, namely Silla (57 BC–AD 936), Koryo (936–1392), and Yi (1392–1910). Almost all Korean pottery shows affinity with Chinese wares. Authenticity of many examples of wares considered to be Korean has been hotly disputed by authorities who believe them to be of Chinese origin. Considerable uncertainty has arisen from the fact that quantities of Chinese wares were imported into Korea over the centuries which were widely copied by Korean potters. Certain types of Korean pottery were quite unknown and never made in China, proving that Korean craftsmen did not lack enterprise and imagination and were capable of more than emulation.

Korean ceramic wares of the Silla period were of extremely primitive type, the earliest known being stonewares of porcellanous character with an ash-grey body usually left unglazed. Feldspathic glazes were used later in the period. The ware was fired at a sufficiently high temperature to obtain vitrification. First grey, then greyish-white, cream-coloured, brown and black glazed wares made their appearance. The most important development was the production of a type of celadon ware with a greyish-green glaze clearly derived from early Chinese celadon. Among various specimens excavated in Korea it has proved extremely difficult, if not impossible, to distinguish indigenous from Chinese imported ware. Apparently content to make slavish imitations of Chinese wares, Korean potters of the Silla period displayed slight inclination to advance their techniques and create original wares. Korean wares of the Silla period show close affinity with T'ang pottery, as in a characteristic style of decoration embodying lines and trefoil designs, incised or impressed.

Contrasting with the crude Silla wares are the beautiful wares of the Koryo period, including some of the finest pottery made in the Far East. The Koryo period in Korea was contemporary with the Sung in China. There is little doubt that techniques of the Sung potters were closely studied by the Koreans who modified them to suit their own tastes and needs. Of such glorious colour were Koryo wares that more than one Chinese traveller in Korea wrote enthusiastic accounts of their beauty. Hsü Ching, a writer travelling in the entourage of the Chinese envoy to Korea in 1123, wrote of green-coloured wares of incomparable quality. He noted a melon-shaped wine-jug as being original, but commented that most of the wares he saw were derived from Ting prototypes. The typical green Koryo wares of the time were referred to by the Koreans as 'kingfisher-coloured'.

Koryo wares were developed through four successive periods of which the first may be regarded as a transitional period commencing in the tenth century when the low-fired greenish-brown glazed wares of Silla origin were still being made. Towards the end of the same century the prototype of Korean celadon appeared, but this early type of olive-coloured celadon ware possessed slight attraction compared with magnificent Koryo celadons which were to follow.

The second period in the development of Koryo pottery began about the end of the tenth century and lasted for about 150 years. Chinese influence grew stronger once more, particularly in the art of celadon. The beautiful Koryo celadons vary in colour and tone from light-grey to brownish-green, with a grey porcellanous stoneware body that appears slightly tinged with red in places, and is covered with mouse-grey, putty, greyish-green or brownish-green glaze that is frequently found crazed. As time passed, the celadon glaze became extremely beautiful, with the soft, lustrous sheen that is the principal attraction of Koryo celadons. Foot-rings and bases are usually found glazed all over. In late examples the foot rim was left unglazed, with the red-tinged body exposed. Korean potters of the period became renowned for their mastery of modelling techniques and good design. In fine modelling and incised decoration the Korean potters of the second Koryo period had few equals in the Far East. They were highly accomplished in varied, sometimes complex, decoration of celadons, generally favouring incised designs or carving, painting in slip or black pigment, moulding, and inlaying wares with white or black slip following an exacting technique. Although Chinese influence is apparent in some decorated Koryo wares, the celadons belong to an exclusive category, being essentially Korean in character, beauty of form and manner of embellishment.

In the third period of Koryo ceramic art Korean potters no longer looked towards China for inspiration and practical guidance but proceeded to develop a purely native style. The unique and extremely beautiful inlaid design technique first began to be used in the decoration of celadons, as far as is known, in the reign of King Uijong (1147–70) and continued in use until the Yi period. Opinions differ, but it is generally conceded that the finest Korean inlaid wares, notable for quality of form, glaze and decoration, were made between about the middle of the twelfth century and the end of the thirteenth century. Decoration was mainly in naturalistic style, direct and simple in line, the designs depicting clouds and cranes, ducks and other birds, willow trees, grasses, flowers, fruits and vines. It may be that a similar form of decoration was on rare occasions used in China, but the inlay technique as practised in Korea should be regarded as an indigenous development. Inlaying was

11 WINE EWER.
Porcelain. Greyish-green
celadon glaze over white
inlaid decoration against
brown ground. Koryo
dynasty, Korean.
H 13 7/16 in

but a natural progressive step from incising and impressing wares to filling lines with coloured semi-liquid slip. Copper-red colouring was effectively used in contrast with black and white slip at the end of the Koryo period. Beauty of coloured design was sustained, but after the close of the fourteenth century workmanship showed carelessness in application and finishing processes. Designs composed of radiating lines and stylised flowers on a brownish-grey or reddish body became coarser and were more boldly though less finely executed.

The fourth period of Koryo wares may be considered as one of decline, continuing from about the beginning of the fourteenth century until the end of the dynasty. Chinese influence was strong and inevitably a trend towards imitation of Chinese wares prevailed. The quality of white porcelains and blackwares declined, but degeneration was most evident in the celadons. Despite the general decline, the introduction of painting on pottery gave brief impetus to design and for a short period arrested degeneration. Korean painting on pottery is thought to have been inspired by the Tz'u Chou wares of China but, if so, the Korean potters considerably modified the technique to suit their own preferences and purposes. Exquisitely painted decoration was applied to celadons in characteristic composition of incised lines over black pigment. Brushwork was almost invariably applied with great skill and regard for effect, sometimes in a series of delicately executed radiating lines or alternatively in swift, broad strokes. A somewhat coarser style of painting became common about the end of the fourteenth century.

The inlaying technique in the decorating of porcelain by Korean potters was devised by them. The technique, mainly applied to porcelain, involved incising the design and filling the lines with black or white slip. After wiping away excess slip the object was fired once at low temperature then, in the case of celadons, wares were removed from the kiln and covered with glaze, to be returned to the kiln for a second firing. It is feasible, as certain authorities maintain, that wares were subjected to only one firing and that all decoration was applied before wares were submitted to the kiln. The earliest known Korean inlaid ceramic wares date from the mid-twelfth century, but their advanced technique suggests that the technique evolved perhaps sometime around the end of the previous century or even earlier, though this is only conjecture. Certainly by the middle of the twelfth century potters had added copper oxides to their materials which resulted in a reddish colour after firing. Iron oxides similarly used produced a rust colour. Less frequently, a different, more complex inlaying technique was followed which involved the decoration of the inside of a vessel entirely in white inlay, providing a ground for the design, this reversal of technique showing how advanced Korean methods eventually became. In the second half of the twelfth century Korean potters were producing elaborately inlaid wares of very superior type and they continued to work without diminution in standards of craftsmanship and design until the end of the fourteenth century.

The porcellanous wares of the Koryo period in Korea may be classified according to type. Celadon wares of plain type were either without surface decoration or

45

ornamented with lightly executed designs in relief or incision. As celadon became very popular in the early Koryo period, large quantities of less elaborately decorated wares were produced in kilns operating in different parts of the country. Early Korean celadons clearly show affinity in decorative style with similar Chinese wares of the period. At first the sombre brownish-green colour prevailed. The attractive 'kingfisher-coloured' ware, covered with a distinctive bluish-green glaze, appeared towards the end of the tenth century and continued to be made until the commencement of the Yi period in 1392. In addition to conventionally shaped vases and bowls with impressed or incised decoration, early Koryo potters also produced notable celadons in human and animal form.

Painted celadon wares, derived from the Tz'u Chou porcelains of China, began to be made in Korea late in the thirteenth century. At the period the Koryo celadons were declining in quality. A similar glaze to that used at Tz'u Chou was applied to Korean painted celadons, the dark-green colour tinged with yellow.

Excellent modelling is one of the most striking decorative features of Koryo celadons which were invariably executed in masterly style. It was usual to surmount covers of vessels with stylised animals, including tortoises and lions. Birds and plants were also represented in a stylised manner. The incised or carved decoration on early celadons was usually carried out with a pointed tool or a knife, certain designs being produced by using a very fine point. Designs of vine and lotus were particularly favoured by highly accomplished craftsmen who executed extremely fine decoration that in its simplicity, remarkable delicacy and clarity is wholly characteristic of Korean work of the period.

Early Koryo white porcelain undoubtedly derived from Sung whitewares imported into Korea. For a long period in its development Koryo white porcelain either exhibited a bluish tinge or was really ivory-coloured. There has been considerable argument among authorities on the question of whether the early white porcelains of Korea were in fact of native origin or were made in China, but from examination of excavated examples in unfired state there now appears little doubt that Koryo white porcelains were an indigenous product. Incised and impressed decoration was generally applied, occasionally varied with inlay or attractive open-work. Gilding is known to have been used, but only rarely.

Some striking blackwares were made, surviving examples of which leave no doubt as to the versatility of the Korean potter when he wished to make other than celadon wares. The ordinary Korean iron-black ware, which should not be mistaken for black-glazed ware, was made from the same grey clay as the celadon body. A coat of iron pigment was applied before the glaze, which was of celadon type, with the result that the black was often greenish in tone. Plain examples are uninteresting compared with decorated specimens which have an incised pattern cut into the iron pigment revealing the grey body underneath. The pottery usually designated 'black-glazed', covered with a thick black or dark-brown glaze, is of the type called by the Japanese *temmoku*, closely resembling a similar type of ware made in Honan province and elsewhere in China. The ware was probably

12   JAR. Decorated underglaze blue-and-white. Yi dynasty,
Korean. *H 16¾in*

made in Korea at an early period and continued to be produced until about the end of the fourteenth century.

Red and brown iron-glazed wares were also made in the Koryo period, their colour obtained by the use of a large proportion of iron oxide in the glaze mixture. While most of this type of ware is found plain, devoid of incised or any other form of decoration, a few examples are extant decorated with simple designs cut into the body and filled with white slip. Of the origin and subsequent development of Koryo celadons there is no doubt. Most authorities are agreed that the Koryo potters devised their own peculiar techniques in manufacturing celadons which only superficially resemble northern Chinese celadons. Concerning other Koryo wares doubt and speculation continues. Many are still believed to be importations from China despite their characteristically Korean shape and mode of decoration.

In 1392 the Koryo dynasty came to an end and was succeeded by the Yi dynasty which lasted until 1910 when the Japanese annexed Korea. Almost immediately following the change of dynasty the style of Korean ceramics underwent a change. As happened to Chinese ceramic wares after the fall of the Sung dynasty, bringing new elements, in Korea the refinement and grace of Koryo wares were superseded by the simple directness in shape and decoration of Yi wares that at the beginning of the Yi period were not without some degree of coarseness. Although the shape and appearance of Korean wares altered considerably in the first century of the Yi period, Korean potters were as conservative and bound by tradition as their Chinese counterparts. Thus the same type of wares made from the same blending of clays and decorated in the same style continued to be produced in Korea over centuries. Often a family specialised in a single type of ware and manufactured it for generations. During the first century of Yi rule the pottery industry expanded as never before, especially in South Korea where many important kilns were erected, including state-operated concerns, of which those at Chinjou, Kory Ong, Kyeryöngsan and Sangju became the most renowned.

Blue-and-white wares were being made in emulation of Chinese prototypes soon after the establishment of the Yi dynasty, but the art of blue-and-white flowered in Korea in the period 1659–1868. For a long period Korean blue-and-white wares were made exclusively at Punwôn. Manufacture of such wares remained in government hands until 1883 when the factory was sold. Korean techniques almost certainly derived from Ming blue-and-white wares which were imported into Korea from the early fifteenth century onwards. Until cobalt ore was discovered in Korea in 1464 the cobalt needed in order to decorate in underglaze blue was obtained from foreign sources. Most Korean blue-and-white wares extant are dated subsequent to the disastrous Japanese invasion of Korea, led by Shogun Hideyoshi, which devastated the country. The factory at Punwôn prospered exceedingly as Korea recovered from the effects of the invasion. Blue-and-white wares became a speciality. Owing to cobalt being very costly, it was used sparingly. King Yôngjo prohibited the use of blue-and-white porcelain in 1754, except by his court and the nobility.

The most common, and characteristically Korean, ceramic product of the Yi period is that now known as *punch'ông* ware. This was made from a grey clay similar to that used in production of Koryo celadon, but of coarser texture. The surface was partially or completely coated with white slip applied in strokes with a brush or by dipping.

Ornamentation of *punch'ông* wares greatly varied. Sometimes the white slip coating was incised or stamped with a design composed of dots or floral motifs in a style derived from Koryo inlaid or incised work on celadons. Occasionally the decoration consisted of incised and inlaid patterns used conjointly, embodying peonies and aubergines. A type of *sgraffiato* decoration was sometimes used in which designs were made to stand out by scraping away the white slip. In nearly all examples the decoration of *punch'ông* ware is markedly inferior to that on Koryo celadons from which it derives. Nor is the inferior quality of the body and glaze concealed by the use of white slip and lavish decoration.

After the Hideyoshi invasion of 1592 *punch'ông* ware was little used by Koreans. The ware became popular with the Japanese, however. Eventually manufacture was restricted to the kilns at Pusan specially constructed for making export wares for Japan. *Punch'ông* ware is known as *mishima* in Japan.

As a result of the Hideyoshi invasion, when many kilns were destroyed and numerous potters were carried off by the invaders to work in Japan, the Korean pottery industry suffered a severe set-back. Owing to the destruction of kilns the court found it difficult to obtain supplies of wares, which prompted the government to set up a large state-owned pottery-making centre at Punwôn near Seoul. Pottery manufacture continued at Punwôn from the seventeenth to the nineteenth century. In 1883, due to economic difficulties, the Korean government sold the factory to a private firm who promptly employed Japanese potters to reorganise and operate the concern.

White porcelain remained as much a favourite ware throughout the Yi period as it was in earlier times. Despite the fact that the ware was made in large quantity due to its popularity it was always admired and treasured. White porcelain was made at a number of kilns but the best was produced at the Punwôn kiln. In the early Yi period Korean white porcelain assumed a robust character when the potting became somewhat heavy. The most important change from the Koryo period was a greatly improved whiteness achieved by the elimination of blue or ivory tones. In the period roughly extending from 1495 to 1659 a further subtle change of colour tone occurred, probably due to a slight change in ingredients, resulting in the reappearance of a bluish tinge, the 'clear water' tone, as it has been designated. Other coloured Yi porcelains included fine wares painted in underglaze colours, copper-red and iron-brown predominating. Copper-red and blue were occasionally used together.

Painted decoration applied to fine Korean white wares invariably arrests the eye. Bold brush strokes, the balanced yet free distribution of curving and radiating lines over the surface, the abstract character of simple designs, may well inspire modern artist potters.

In common with the other Far Eastern countries, Japan owes much of her art and cultural development to China. As already noted, the ancient decorative arts of the Chinese, their inventions, techniques and styles, usually reached Japan by way of Korea which, stretching out from the Asian mainland towards the Japanese islands, formed a bridgehead between the great cultural centre of China and the archipelago inhabited by one of the most intelligent and artistically gifted races on earth.

It will be advantageous to know something of the successive periods into which Japanese art history is usually divided before embarking on a study of the techniques originated or developed by Japanese potters. Here are the respective periods briefly outlined in relation to ceramic production.

NEOLITHIC PERIOD: 4500–250 BC

Phallic worship prevailed, as is evident from excavated objects. Considerable quantities of primitive Jomon pottery objects have been excavated revealing an extensive range of shapes and varied decoration. The period was also notable for its clay figurines.

BRONZE AND IRON AGES: 250 BC–AD 300

So-called *yayoi* pottery appeared, largely made on the wheel, but in limited variation of form compared with Jomon pottery. *Yayoi* pottery is notable for painted red decoration of which the so-called 'running-water' motif is most striking.

PROTO-HISTORIC PERIOD: 300–645

The period when *haniwa* or tomb pottery attained a high level of technical excellence. Human beings were modelled in clay, also houses. Models of houses and large erect figures were placed round the outsides of enormous tombs. It is surmised that the practice of making *haniwa* mortuary pottery was introduced into Japan by immigrant Korean potters who originally acquired the technique from the Chinese.

NARA PERIOD: 710–94

A brief era of transient artistic advancement when art forms and techniques evolved by artists and craftsmen in distant Asian countries were imitated by the Japanese. The court was re-established at Nara which became a centre of the arts.

HEIAN PERIOD: 794–1184

All branches of Japanese ceramic art advanced rapidly during the four centuries covered by the period. Pottery assumed great refinement, with forms in softer outline than previously. Celadon wares were greatly admired, but it is believed that celadons used to adorn palaces and homes of the aristocracy were chiefly imported from China. It is doubtful if celadons were produced in Japan at so early a period. Pottery made in the Heian period was commonly coated with ash-glaze (*haigusuri*) over a hard grey body frequently pitted by sand grains.

KAMAKURA PERIOD: 1184–1333
Mainland influences strongly affected Japanese ceramic design. Korean and Chinese designs and techniques were imitated by both native and immigrant potters.

MUROMACHI PERIOD: 1397–1573
Many potteries destined to become famous were established. As the tea ceremony grew more important the wares used in ritual became finer. Tea ceremony wares made by master potters of high repute were greatly in demand. Wares decorated with *temmoku*-type glazes resembled vessels made in China under the Sung dynasty. Seto – the classical pottery centre of Japan – became pre-eminent in production of tea ceremony wares which superseded the simple tea bowls and other vessels the Japanese had previously been content to import from Korea. The Wabi school of the tea ceremony, which gradually became very influential, insisted that all wares used in ritual should be extremely simple in form. This explains why so many tea ceremony vessels of the period displayed imperfections. Wares purposely lacked finish in order to comply with the tastes and ruling of Wabi tea masters.

MOMOYAMA PERIOD: 1575–1600
Tea masters not only governed the tea ceremony but exerted strong influence in social life. They virtually dictated pottery styles, insisting on simplicity though countenancing the use of improved glazes. Pottery production in consequence made little advance technically and styles were slow to change.

EDO PERIOD: 1600–1868
Two-and-a-half centuries of vital development carried Japanese ceramics to their highest peak of artistic and technical perfection. Brilliant craftsmen worked in potteries which became celebrated for the beauty of their productions. Potters of the calibre of Ninsei, who initiated the final break with Sino-Korean traditions, freed Japanese ceramic art from mainland influence. A recognisable native Japanese style emerged during the seventeenth century and many potters no longer looked to Korean sources for inspiration. After some thousand years of domination by China and Korea in arts and crafts Japanese craftsmen became interested in a revival of native tradition which, in so far as ceramic production was concerned, brought a dramatic change in styles and techniques although continental influence was not entirely eradicated. Admiration and emulation of Chinese ceramic art continued, but on a diminished scale and with less slavish imitation. A number of Japanese potters of the period went on producing copies of Chinese wares and never forsook Chinese tradition in design.

During the Edo period the aspiration of outstanding Japanese potters rose with

13   PAIR OF EWERS. Imari ware. Decorated underglaze blue, iron-red and gilt.
Seventeenth century, Japanese. *H 12in*

their increasing technical ability. Increasing skill engendered a desire to create porcelain as beautiful as the Chinese product. Japanese porcelain makers attained a high degree of skill and artistic achievement – we have only to consider examples of superb Hirado or Nabeshima porcelains to realise the extent of Japanese talent – but the truth quickly becomes clear, that no Japanese potter acquired the degree of technical skill required to produce porcelain comparable with the finest Chinese wares. Nonetheless, just as Chinese porcelain is unsurpassed in quality and sublime beauty and belongs to a class of its own, so does Japanese pottery. Inasmuch that they failed to surpass or even equal the achievements of the Chinese in the creation of incomparably fine porcelains, the great Japanese potters created pottery far superior to the finest made in China or Korea. This important fact is not even yet generally realised in the West.

As the foregoing chronological summary indicates, pottery of a primitive type was being made in Japan long before the initial period generally accepted by historians. Certain Japanese historians refer to Oosiu-tsumi, a maker of clay pots nearly seven centuries before the beginning of the Christian era, but there are no proven facts.

The earliest recognised Japanese ceramic style is that of *yayoi* pottery, known as *hajinoutsuwa*. Though undergoing modification with passing time, the style prevailed until about the middle of the fifth century when a more refined ware called *suenoutsuwa* appeared. *Suenoutsuwa* originated in Korea and required employment of different techniques from those hitherto known in Japan. Korean potters used a wheel differing from the Japanese type. They also fired their *suenoutsuwa* wares at high temperature in large kilns erected on open hillsides. *Suenoutsuwa*, as made in Japan, was a much harder type of ware than any previously produced in the islands. It was thickly glazed over a close-grained body.

White, green and yellow glazes were developed during the Nara period, but some uncertainty exists as to whether or not wares decorated with the glazes were actually produced in Japan. It has not been conclusively established if wares thus decorated were of utilitarian or religious use. Glazed wares of the type are thought to have been made in Owari province – possibly at Seto – as early as the Nara period. If this is so they were exceptional, for the reason that although kilns were certainly in existence in the province at that time by far the greater proportion of wares made were of primitive character.

The arrival of Kato Shirozaiemon (Toshiro I) at Seto in or about 1225, following his return from China where he spent several years training as a potter, marks the beginning of significant advancement in Japanese pottery production. Toshiro's discovery at Seto of the clay he needed to commence manufacture proved to be a major event in the history of Japanese ceramics. Principally due to Toshiro's introduction of *temmoku* ware, which he had learned to make in China, Seto became known as a pottery centre. The character of wares used in the Japanese tea ceremony was finally established at Seto. For a long period thereafter *temmoku* tea ceremony utensils produced at Seto were regarded by eminent tea masters as the most desirable of their kind.

On his return from the victorious campaign in Korea in the late sixteenth century Toyotomi Hideyoshi brought in his train a number of skilled Korean potters whom he established in Japan to instruct native potters in their advanced techniques. Shogun Hideyoshi was particularly interested in production of fine tea bowls and was responsible for the establishment of the Korean potter Ameya at Juraku, Kyoto. Ameya's son Chojiro received a gold seal from Hideyoshi engraved with the character *raku*, meaning 'enjoyment'. The character was afterwards impressed on the *raku* ware which the potter usually made entirely by hand. Tea bowls in this somewhat coarse stoneware, covered with gritty brownish-black glaze, were highly favoured by the tea masters and in consequence were generally considered superior to all others.

From the eighth century onwards native Japanese potters apparently rarely experimented in techniques, preferring to follow traditional methods used by previous generations of potters. As already stated, Korea long remained the principal source of Japanese technical knowledge and design.

Japanese potters displayed a natural aptitude for working with clays, but their inherent penchant for imitation long delayed the development of a truly native Japanese style. Following Hideyoshi's campaign in Korea, which initiated an influx of Korean immigrant potters into Japan, Sino-Korean influence predominated in Japanese ceramic art. Both native and immigrant potters in Japan produced similar types of wares during the late sixteenth and early seventeenth centuries. Korean styles were imitated with a cream or greyish-white glaze often used to cover the coarse body, the glaze occasionally decorated with painted designs in blue or brown. Grey-green celadon ware, decorated in white, was also produced in the period. During the seventeenth century copies of Chinese prototypes appeared. The volume of production increased with passing decades. As a rule, Japanese copies were much inferior to the Chinese originals. The Seto potters were the most accomplished and successful at the period although potteries established at Karatsu, Satsuma, Takatori and Hagi, were operated by potters of great talent whose work ultimately made the kilns famous. No potteries in existence in Japan at the period turned out such a quantity and diversity of wares as the flourishing concerns in and around Kyoto.

Early in the sixteenth century – probably between 1510 and 1516 – the potter Gorodayu-go Shonsui travelled to China for the purpose of studying the technique of porcelain manufacture. Shonsui probably spent some time in various potteries in turn, possibly in the pottery-making province of Fukien, at Foochou or at the celebrated imperial factory at Ching-tê-chên. He remained in China until he had learned all the essential techniques. When he was confident that he could return to Japan and teach potters there how to make porcelain he left China and subsequently established his first kiln at Arita in Hizen.

Shonsui carried home to Japan a supply of requisite materials sufficient to meet his production needs for several years. He mastered the art of mixing pastes of various kinds, learned to decorate in underglaze blue and, more importantly perhaps, acquired great skill in the process of firing at *grand feu* temperatures. Shonsui imitated Chinese blue-and-white porcelain during his early years at Arita, but in most respects his copies lacked the grace and beauty of the prototypes. In his later period he enamelled over the glaze. Shonsui continued making porcelain at Arita until his supplies of materials were exhausted. His productions decorated in underglaze blue emulated Ming porcelain and were embellished with naturalistic bird and floral patterns. When Shonsui died in about 1550 his factory had already entered upon a period of decline despite efforts made to manufacture porcelain successfully using only materials obtained locally. A further century or so passed before Arita porcelain acquired the quality for which it ultimately became celebrated throughout Japan. Through several decades following Shonsui's death decoration applied to Arita porcelain was, even at its best, poor.

At about the time that Shonsui and his successors at Arita, including the famous potter Ri-sanpei, were striving to perfect their porcelain, other potteries that had been operated by Koreans for centuries produced only earthenwares and stonewares. Korean potters working in Japan never made porcelain. Both Korean and native Japanese potters created splendid pottery. For example, scarcely any ceramic ware made elsewhere in the world has transcended the delicate beauty of the early finely crackled, pale-yellow or cream-coloured ware made for the princes of Satsuma. In the finest Satsuma ware we see the ultimate perfection in pottery as achieved by a group of master potters at work under princely patronage.

Characteristic of some early Japanese ceramic wares is a certain lack of symmetry and restraint in decoration which distinguish them from Chinese productions. The latter, needless to say, are seldom marred by similar faults. Even the finest Japanese porcelains include examples exhibiting fault in form or decoration, usually the latter, which detracts from otherwise admirable work.

The development of ceramic art in Japan is, as we have seen, rooted in remote antiquity. Even when her art was under the domination of Korea the Japanese native tradition in style and techniques was never completely extinguished. Early Japanese potters manifested an acute sensibility towards nature, as is obvious from extensive naturalistic decoration on different types of wares. In general, design was balanced and rather formal, while even in the decoration of the most ordinary objects forethought usually ensured satisfactory construction of design. Normally, decoration was carried out with great sensitivity, especially in use of the brush. New skills and technical invention were speedily mastered by intelligent Japanese craftsmen. Their inherent gift for copying, allied to a natural flair for good design and colour arrangement, gave them important advantages. However, it will be clearly discerned from study of specimens, that on the whole Japanese potters could not easily emulate, much less exceed, the simplicity and harmony in form and colour which the Chinese achieved with their porcelains and in a lesser degree the Koreans achieved with their finest pottery. Yet there were remarkable exceptions, for the celebrated Japanese master potters of later centuries were supreme in their individual accomplishment, combining high artistry with technical ability. The superb, daringly original work of Ninsei and his followers, for example, allowed full expression of artistic sensibility which endowed fine wares with a unique vitality and character.

For a long period Japanese pottery was strongly influenced by Buddhism, mainly in respect of ceremonial wares. It would not be an exaggeration to state that in matters of style and decoration early Japanese pottery owed its character to the dictates of Buddhist tea masters, the natural successors of the Zen priests who initiated the tea ceremony in Japan. By far the greater quantity of ceramic wares produced in Japan in the centuries when Buddhism influenced every facet of Japanese life were intended for ritual use in the tea ceremony.

Probably the earliest pottery ceremonial vessels used in Japan were of Chinese origin and made during the T'ang period. Archaic, green earthenware tomb figures and funerary vessels made in Japan had no counterparts for use in everyday life. Pottery-making as a craft cannot be said to have commenced in Japan until the almost legendary Toshiro I returned from China early in the thirteenth century and began production of the brownish-black-glazed *temmoku* tea ceremony wares for which his factory at Seto became renowned.

The genius of the Japanese potter, his unrivalled ability as a copyist, his inherent technical skill and artistry in the use of materials and his flair for creating unusual forms and designs, eventually won him superiority over all other Oriental potters except the Chinese. Only in the manufacture of porcelain were the Japanese potters outclassed by the Chinese.

To reiterate, although unmistakably inferior to the finest Chinese porcelain, the quality and beauty of certain Japanese porcelains, such as the productions of Nabeshima and Hirado, are beyond question. The latter ware, though of superlative quality, undoubtedly falls short of the claim made for it by an enthusiast – 'old Hirado porcelain shows the highest degree of excellence and perfection to which the ceramist ever attained'.

From the early sixteenth century, when Shonsui made his Ming-style blue-and-white porcelain at Arita, to the mid-nineteenth century when fine porcelain was still being produced at Mikawachi exclusively for the princes of Hirado, the great Japanese artist potters created exceedingly beautiful porcelain wares. Japanese productions generally emulated Chinese prototypes, it is true, but outstanding wares also appeared that were purely Japanese in concept, their form and decoration owing nothing to Sino-Korean inspiration, expressing in their graceful style and attractive decoration the vital spirit of Japanese traditional ceramic art.

Shonsui's activities and achievements are shrouded in legend. Perhaps more reliance should be placed on the assertion that materials suitable for the manufacture of porcelain were discovered on Izumi mountain in Hizen province by a Korean potter searching in the neighbourhood in the early seventeenth century, resulting in the establishment of a pottery at Arita. So-called Imari export wares made at Arita were very inferior to early wares from local kilns. Gaudy colouring, crowded designs and garish gilding characteristic of this class of Imari ware were not in true Japanese taste of the period, the ware being produced expressly for the European market.

With Sakaida Kakiemon, at work in the mid-seventeenth century, and his followers, Japanese porcelain entered upon a new phase of development. Enamel decoration, embodying the most delicate brushwork, came to the fore. Kakiemon-style porcelain was extremely graceful in form, decorated sparingly in green, turquoise-blue, yellow, and a beautiful soft red, greatly admired by Western connoisseurs. European potters attempted to imitate Kakiemon wares with varying degrees of success.

Kutani porcelain tended to be coarse in texture, but it was usually vigorously decorated in bold designs, the palette including an exceptionally rich eye-arresting green.

Nabeshima porcelain may appear to be almost too fragile, with delicate colouring too weak, the decoration principally composed of thin washes applied over outlines of soft underglaze blue. In its finest period, during the seventeenth century, charming floral designs were painted on Nabeshima porcelain.

To complete a brief survey of the evolution of Japanese ceramic production, although the Japanese potters retained their traditional skill and peculiar techniques when Japan was opened up in 1848 to trade with the outside world, vital changes were destined to occur. Unprecedented demand for Japanese ceramic wares in foreign markets led to a general debasement in quality. Typical Japanese wares of the later nineteenth century were notable for ingenious design and over-brilliant decoration. Some 'egg-shell' porcelains of the period were not altogether devoid of attraction but the majority, especially wares decorated in Tokyo, were in appallingly bad taste.

The amazing variety of Japanese ceramic wares is bewildering, while authentication of examples is often rendered almost impossible due to the incessant copying of wares made by the great potters over a long period up to the present day. For the interest and guidance of readers, concise accounts of the more important potteries follow, with notes concerning the careers and wares of various famous potters associated with particular kilns.

ARITA (HIZEN, IMARI, KAKIEMON)

Prince Nabeshima, feudal overlord of the province of Hizen, is reputed to have brought a Korean potter, by name Ri-sanpei, to settle in Japan in the sixteenth century. Ri-sanpei was put in charge of the prince's pottery at Taku. The district around Arita thereafter became a centre for immigrant Korean potters.

According to legend, Gorodayo-go Shonsui returned from China early in the sixteenth century with the secrets of porcelain manufacture and a supply of materials and established the first porcelain factory in Japan in Hizen province where the village of Arita subsequently developed. By the end of the century Shonsui's factory was in a state of decay. When Ri-sanpei discovered the long-sought feldspathic rock (*kaolin*) near Arita, together with equally vital white clay (*petuntze*), he lost no time in establishing himself at Arita and revitalising the old factory.

To avoid possible confusion in the minds of readers, it perhaps needs to be pointed out here that Arita, Hizen and Imari wares are basically the same. Arita was the village in the province of Hizen and Imari an adjacent seaport. Kilns operating in the district during the early period turned out almost identical wares, mostly inferior imitations of Chinese blue-and-white porcelain. The same basic ingredients were used in the manufacture of Arita and Imari wares, also in the production of wares at Koshida, Matsugaya, Okawiji, Shida, Shiraishi and Yoshida.

While immigrant Korean potters established in Hizen apparently did not begin to prosper until the second half of the sixteenth century, the making of pottery in Hizen had been continuous in centuries prior to Shonsui's arrival. An ancient kiln at Karatsu is believed to have been constructed as far back as the seventh century. Few examples of old Karatsu wares – *Ko-Karatsu* – are known to exist. Several types of wares were produced at Karatsu. At the beginning of the seventeenth century the factory commenced making stoneware decorated with somewhat

14 JAR WITH COVER.
Imari ware. Porcelain.
Decorated with
underglaze blue and
overglaze enamels in
red, green and gold.
Edo period, seventeenth
century, Japanese.
H 5½in

crudely painted scrolls in Korean style. Imitations of early Korean wares, principally tea bowls, with a reddish-brown-coloured body covered with dull yellowish-brown or pinkish glaze are known as *Oku-Korai*. The ware known as *Karatsu-yaki* belongs to the period 1600–54.

As previously noted, some authorities contend that it was not Shonsui but a Korean searching for materials in the seventeenth century who discovered suitable clay and rock on Izumi mountain which led to the establishment of the first Arita factory. Without further evidence forthcoming it does not appear that the truth will ever be established.

During the period of Ri-sanpei's control of the old factory at Arita it began to compete seriously with Karatsu in quantity of output. Ri-sanpei was ambitious and eager to create porcelain as beautiful as the Chinese productions but he failed in his efforts, producing nothing more important than an inferior type of porcelain painted blue under the glaze.

Ri-sanpei emulated Shonsui, perhaps even to the extent of using the seal character *fuku* (happiness) for a mark, as did Shonsui. Despite his efforts, Ri-sanpei made little advance on Shonsui's techniques. It is feasible that both Shonsui and Ri-sanpei were acquainted with enamelling on ceramic wares without succeeding in mastering the techniques of application. All that Ri-sanpei is known to have achieved in decoration was ability to paint in blue on biscuit ware, the use of glazes, and firing at *grand feu* temperature.

At about the time that Korean potters in Hizen were seeking new ways of decorating their wares a resourceful potter named Higashi-shima Tokuzaiemon resolved to visit China in order to learn the techniques of decorating in coloured enamels. He arrived in Nagasaki on the first stage of his journey in 1648. According to tradition, he chanced to learn the secrets of the enamel-decorating process from the captain of a trading vessel in Nagasaki harbour, which made his proposed voyage to China unnecessary. Tokuzaiemon returned to Arita where he proceeded to instruct others in the use of enamels. First results proved disappointing. The enamel dulled and designs derived from old styles lacked spontaneity. Further experiments brought success with the introduction of brilliant enamels and a more attractive range of designs.

The accomplished Sakaida Kakiemon, member of a famous family of Arita potters, is probably the Japanese potter best known in the West. He is known to have worked with Tokuzaiemon and may possibly have been the first potter in Japan to decorate wares with vitrifiable enamels embellished with gold. The Japanese usually credit Kakiemon with the introduction into Japan of Chinese techniques in polychrome enamelling. Kakiemon wares – the majority of extant specimens were made in the late seventeenth century – are quite distinctive in style, the enamels applied in soft shades of blue, green, turquoise, red and yellow. The ware was extensively copied by European potters. Kakiemon-style decoration inspired ceramic artists at Worcester, Chelsea, and other English factories. Rather than novel materials and methods it was styles that Kakiemon evolved, notably his version of a local style featuring chrysanthemums and peonies executed in blue, red and dull gold. So-called Imari ware, similarly decorated, was supplied in quantity to Dutch traders who took over at Deshima in 1641 following the expulsion of the Portuguese. Crates of Imari ware were shipped to Holland from Nagasaki. Delft potters quickly began successfully copying the Japanese product which became immensely popular throughout Western Europe.

Kakiemon's finest ware, invariably superbly decorated, was quite different in appearance from and much more delicately embellished than the Imari product popular in Europe. A soft though brilliant glaze was applied to white porcelain of superior quality and decoration consisted of floral medallions in blue, red and green, the colours glowing yet delicate on the pure white ground. Subjects depicted within the medallions were in great variety, including blossom, dragons, ho-ho birds and diaper designs, to name a few. Only a limited range of colours was used. The graceful shapes of the finest Kakiemon wares were never surpassed in Japan. All are simple in style, with little in the way of relief decoration or moulding, the sublime beauty of each piece emanating from the perfection of Kakiemon's work in enamels and the purity of the porcelain body to which the colours were sparingly applied. This particular type of Kakiemon ware has long been greatly admired by European connoisseurs. German potters and artists at Meissen enthusiastically copied Kakiemon designs but with a heavier hand. French potters at Chantilly followed suit. Kakiemon's distinctive blue is removed from the harsh violet-blue used in combination with vivid red and gold in the familiar chrysanthemum and peony design on later Imari wares. It may hardly be necessary to add that it was the decoration on late Imari ware which inspired the English Crown Derby pattern known as 'Imari', so popular in England in the late nineteenth century.

AWATA

The celebrated master potter Ninsei carried out important work during his time spent at the Awata factory, which was established during the second decade of the seventeenth century. Originally, the Awata paste was very inferior, so much so that while at Awata Ninsei experienced difficulty working with such poor materials. Early Awata faience had a coarse, hard body and the creamy or greyish-white semi-translucent glaze, though not completely devoid of lustre, was not on a par with most other fine glazes used in Japan at the period. Decoration of a heavy kind was lavishly applied over the crackled surface. Among other defects, raw edges showed, a fault never to be found on finer Japanese crackled wares.

Mention is called for of Kuzaiemon, a talented potter who endeavoured to emulate the brilliant Ninsei with whom he worked for a time at Awata. Kuzaiemon painted his wares in striking combinations of rich colours and black. Occasionally he experimented with enamels.

In the early eighteenth century the gifted artist potter Kenzan worked at Awata and eventually succeeded in improving the quality of the paste. His efforts to improve the glaze also bore fruit, resulting in the creation of a lustrous creamy glaze over which coloured enamel decoration could be applied with admirable effect. Kenzan's overglaze enamel decoration on Awata pottery was extremely attractive, with restrained use of deep-blue and grass-green, contrasted with brown and black touched with red, the whole embellished with fine gilding. Other colours Kenzan favoured included yellow, purple and silver, but these appeared less frequently on his work. His brushwork was bold and sweeping in the execution of his favourite abstract designs. Copies of Kenzan ware have been produced in Japan over a long period, not only by potters claiming to be his descendants but also by others.

Ninsei worked only a short time at Awata, but Kenzan passed much of his working life in the factory. Kenzan's improved Awata ware was undoubtedly superior to the early faience decorated by Ninsei. Kenzan's unusually hard biscuit body admirably lent itself to decoration in coloured enamels.

BANKO WARE: GOZAIEMON

Gozaiemon, 'Banko' (1736–95), the originator of Banko ware, was a wealthy amateur potter of Kuwana in Ise province. He was also an addict of the tea ceremony. Increasing interest in pottery manufacture led him to commence production of tea ceremony vessels. Wealth and influence enabled him to study techniques in important factories and to obtain supplies of the best materials when he established his studio-workshop. At first he merely copied the common Japanese *raku* wares and Korean wares. Later he imitated Ninsei's decorative style and Kenzan's designs. Recognition of his talent came in 1785 with a first important commission from the Shogun Iyenari. Gozaiemon so delighted the shogun with his work that he was commanded to set up a pottery to supply the court.

Gozaiemon entered upon his best period after the shogun obtained a secret formula for making porcelain, together with supplies of materials, from the imperial factory in China. He imitated red and green late Ming export wares, but was more brilliantly successful with his copies of Chinese polychromatic wares. The erstwhile merchant of Kuwana proved himself an able and accomplished copyist in ceramics – he even imitated Delft ware – but his enduring fame rests upon his superb technique, characteristically Japanese, in applying floral decoration over brilliant glazes. He was also a master in the use of enamels.

Only members of the aristocracy at the shogun's court were privileged to commission Gozaiemon to execute work for them, with the result that even during his lifetime his wares were relatively scarce. By the time he died at Kuwana his beautiful wares had brought him fame, though few people outside court circles owned specimens of his work. His secrets were safeguarded as he instructed no pupils and his productions remained principally in the possession of an exclusive class. But for a chance occurrence Gozaiemon's techniques might have been lost to the world for ever.

Some thirty years elapsed from the time of Gozaiemon's death until his written

15 TRAY. Kyoto ware, by Kenzan. Stoneware with dark brown decoration under the glaze. Edo period, seventeenth century, Japanese. W 8 9/16 in

formulae for decorating in coloured enamels passed into the possession of a curio dealer who gave them to his son Mori Yusetsu, a potter. Yusetsu, who worked in Kuwana, knowing the reputation of Gozaiemon, immediately perceived the importance and value of the dead potter's formulae. After obtaining the original Banko stamp from Gozaiemon's grandson, Yusetsu launched into production, boldly copying Gozaiemon's original designs. Yusetsu had already achieved a reputation early in his career for making pottery finished with finger or thumb before firing, a method which left an impression on the wet clay. When he commenced reproducing Gozaiemon's wares he used moulds in the making of certain pieces in the manner of Chinese potters. It appears probable that Yusetsu modelled his pieces from the inside.

Gozaiemon-style wares, whether rare original examples or Yusetsu's nineteenth-century reproductions, are usually very attractive. A finely crackled, cream-tinted ware is among the most outstanding, richly decorated in underglaze blue, with overglaze panels painted in reserve, depicting scenery. Diaper designs were also favoured by Gozaiemon.

Yusetsu's reproduction Banko wares, also a range of objects attributed to his younger brother, Yuyuki, a talented ceramic artist who worked with him, were well modelled and decorated. Relief moulding in representation of dragons, storks and mythological creatures was skilfully executed, as were arabesques in coloured slip on green and red grounds.

The name Banko appearing as a seal mark on Gozaiemon's wares means 'everlasting'. Alternatively, the word *fuyeki* – 'changeless' – was sometimes used. The same Banko marks were also used by later potters who emulated Gozaiemon's techniques.

BIZEN

Admirers of Johann Böttger's early red wares produced at Meissen during his experimental years which preceded the founding of Augustus the Strong's porcelain factory, and of the pleasant red wares made by the Elers brothers in England, will note their resemblance to beautiful old red Bizen ware. This is explained by the fact that certain Japanese potters who worked at Imbe in the sixteenth century, Böttger and the Elers all succeeded in imitating Chinese redware.

The earliest ceramic wares made in Bizen province comprised three types, unglazed, glazed and marbled. Dramatic changes were effected in the body at the close of the seventeenth century when two new pastes were developed. The first, known as *Ao-Bizen*, was a fine, hard, slate-coloured or brown stoneware ornamented with excellently modelled mythological figures. Next appeared the new red paste often used by Bizen potters in making charming figures. The thin glaze was enhanced by its distinctive metallic sheen, the brown body showing through and creating a pleasing bronze-like effect. White Bizen ware was a rare product which was left an unusually long time to bake in the kiln in order to achieve complete

16 DISH. Kutani ware.
Porcelain with overglaze
enamel decoration in
yellow, green and brown.
Edo period, seventeenth
century, Japanese.
D 13⅛in

fusion of paste and glaze. A peculiarity of Bizen ware, the absorption of the glaze
into the paste, may be due to prolonged firing.

Bizen potters made a variety of objects but became noted for figures. Divinities,
human beings, and animals were excellently modelled. Old Bizen stoneware figures
have the appearance of being salt-glazed, though salt-glazing of wares in the English
manner was a technique unknown, or at least little, if ever, practised, in Japan.
The glaze was extraordinarily fine and translucent, usually completely fused with
the paste.

FUJIWA

A feudal Prince of Fumai established a private kiln at Matsuye in Idsumo, where the
little known Idsumo wares were first produced. The Fujiwa paste was composed
of easily worked clay which during firing assumed drab, grey, red and buff tones.
Good quality glazes were applied to Fujiwa ware in a colour range which included
white, brown, brownish-red, buff, yellow, sea-green and sage-green. Overglaze
decoration comprised flowers on white slip, gilded or painted. Streaks of blended
colour also served as decoration.

As Fujiwa ware resembles Idsumo ware and both exhibit characteristics of Hagi
ware, a note of explanation is advisable. The early eighteenth-century Korean potter
Rikei settled at Hagi after his arrival in Japan, changing his name to Korai Saiemon.
Hagi ware is also known as Saiemon ware. In common with other Korean potters,

17 JAR. Kakiemon ware. Porcelain with overglaze enamel decoration in
red, blue, yellow and green. Edo period, seventeenth century,
Japanese. *H* 15 ⅝ *in*

Saiemon cut a triangular space out of the raised edge on the base of his wares. Fujiwa, Idsumo and Hagi wares, though varying in quality, show affinity chiefly in colour, ranging from light-brown to rich chocolate, with an excellent crackled glaze.

At a later period the Fujiwa factory imitated Satsuma wares, supposedly due to the influence of Kobori Masakutsu, one of Japan's most venerated tea masters.

HIRADO (HIRATO)

In about 1600 a Korean potter founded what was destined to become a renowned pottery at Mikawachi (Mikawa-uchi-yama, the hill between three rivers) in Hizen. For many years only underglaze blue decoration was applied to wares. It is not thought that porcelain was produced at the factory until about 1712. A period of decline was halted when Matsura, Prince of Hirado, gave his patronage to the factory which thenceforward made wares exclusively for the prince and members of his court. By mid-century the factory was again flourishing. As occurred at Meissen, and at the Elers factory in England, work at Mikawachi was conducted in great secrecy. Workmen were placed under surveillance and no wares could be removed from the factory without Matsura's consent. Few productions were sold. Almost all objects made were either distributed among Matsura's relatives and friends or presented to prominent personages in the Tokugawa's court at Yedo (Tokyo).

Old Hirado porcelain has serene beauty and technical perfection almost equal to Chinese porcelain, which it resembles. Japanese connoisseurs regard Hirado porcelain as the highest achievement in Japanese ceramics, if not in the world. An enchanting soft, clear blue is, with rare exceptions, the only colour used in decoration, applied with amazing delicacy over the lustrous milk-white glaze. The finest Hirado porcelain, which is not marked, was produced in the peak period 1750–1830 when the white body remained exceptionally pure in quality due principally to rigid selection and control of materials used. Old Hirado blue, of surpassing loveliness, was never matched by the most brilliant copyists working in the later nineteenth century. Relief ornament and decoration in gilt and enamel executed by nineteenth-century copyists on reproductions of old Hirado porcelain was of high standard but still fell short of the splendid originals.

On the exquisite blue Hirado porcelain of early date almost the only other colour used, if any at all, was brown. Hirado blue is different from any other blue found on old Japanese ceramic ware. The nearest approach to Hirado blue is the serene Nabeshima blue, which is less compelling in tone than that of Hirado.

Hirado ware became a source of inspiration to eighteenth-century European potters. Meissen modellers and artists not only copied the wares in entirety, but drew on design for other wares. This is particularly true in regard to open and relief work, floral and bird designs. In England, where Oriental ceramic wares have always been admired, examples of Hirado porcelain inspired the raised shell

65

and seaweed decoration found on Plymouth, Bristol and Worcester porcelains.

KENZAN

The Sansei family included two brilliant brothers, both trained as artists. Korin, the elder, became a celebrated artist in lacquer. The younger brother, Ogata (1660–1743), one of the most brilliant Japanese ceramic decorators, as well as a noted painter of screens, adopted the studio name Kenzan and achieved renown as a potter. His work at the Awata factory has already been considered.

When Kenzan realised where his strongest interest and talent lay he abandoned his artist's studio and commenced studying the potter's craft at first hand, working in a number of potteries until he developed great skill in all known techniques. He was an exceptionally proficient clay manipulator and the creator of exquisite glazes of the finest texture. Moreover, he was a supremely talented decorator of ceramics, scarcely surpassed in his dexterous use of the brush in the execution of highly original designs. Kenzan's training as an artist stood him in good stead in the ceramics of beautiful designs. He vigorously applied boldly conceived decoration on both Awata and *raku* wares, many of his abstract designs being derived from plants and landscapes. Kenzan usually preferred to work in sombre colours, heavy inky blues, browns, contrasting black and white and a distinctive dense green. He worked in a number of Kyoto potteries and at Irya in the vicinity of Tokyo, soon developing his individualistic style. At a later stage in his career he concentrated on applying enamel and gilt decoration on pottery. Most of the time he worked in harmonious colour combinations of black, golden-brown and blue in the tonal arrangement known as *shibu-ye*. Kenzan also decorated wares in a charming native Japanese tradition, in all respects an impressionistic style embodying sketchily drawn blossoms, birds in flight or perched on branches and flowers as depicted in early Japanese paintings. The exquisite delicacy and simplicity of Kenzan's impressionistic style of decoration rendered it outstanding if not virtually unique. With a few deft strokes of his brush he sketched prunus blossom, birds in foliage, or the misty outline of a distant hill with unerring mastery of style. Undoubtedly, Kenzan's finest work in the vein was executed on Awata wares.

As a decorator of ceramics Kenzan had few equals in Japan during his lifetime. Although imitators of his techniques were numerous they hardly succeeded in equalling his skill. Kenzan's son and grandson, following after him, contrived to emulate his style with considerable success, but their wares did not exhibit the grasp of techniques associated with the first Kenzan. Boldness of design and execution, originality, his artistic genius expressed in swift strokes and delicate working of his brush imparted sublime beauty and character to Kenzan's finest work.

Kenzan produced excellent work at Shigariki where poor clays were used which apparently did not deter Kenzan from applying fine decoration to the coarse body. In his later years at Yedo (Tokyo) he carried out experiments which resulted in an entirely new concept of ceramic decoration. When he arrived in the Imado district

18 DISH. Nabeshima ware. Porcelain with underglaze blue and overglaze green enamel decoration. Edo period, late seventeenth to early eighteenth century, Japanese. *D 8⅝in*

Kenzan found that the limited materials available only allowed production of pottery to which coloured glazes could be applied. He proceeded to experiment once more and devised his own revolutionary technique for the practical application of brilliant glazes to an inferior clay body. He founded the Imado pottery and became successful in the use of new decorative techniques.

As already noted, Kenzan's son and grandson inherited his talents in a lesser degree. An expert eye can easily distinguish the work of the master from that of his successors. Authenticated examples of the first Kenzan's work are extremely rare and very valuable. Kenzan's descendants frequently made use of a vivid emerald-green enamel in conjunction with more subdued colours. Massed colour is the characteristic of later Kenzan ware which also closely followed the original decorative style of impressionistic sketches. Almost invariably, the body of Kenzan ware is coarse.

KISHIU

Pottery – and perhaps also porcelain – is known to have been produced from two kilns established by the Prince of Kii at Wakayama in Kii province. The amount of wares made is believed to have been very small since few examples have been identified with any certainty. It appears probable that the potter Zengoro Hozen – Eiraku – improved the body, but curiously little is known about the factory or its wares. Ornamentation principally consisted of floral patterns executed in low

19 (*left*) ONE OF A PAIR OF STANDING LADIES. Imari ware. Decorated enamels.
H 19in; (*centre*) As left. *H 21in*; (*right*) FIGURE OF A STANDING LADY. Arita ware.
Decorated underglaze blue and the Imari palette of red, green and gold, auber-
gine enamels. *H 16in*. All three Edo period, seventeenth century, Japanese

relief, the space between embellished with coloured glazes, purple, yellow and blue, with occasional use of white and green. The rich green Kishiu glaze veined with purple, decorated with medallions in contrasting colours, was considered extremely beautiful. The paste varied considerably in colour and texture. The first Eiraku, who produced some fine wares at Wakayama, is believed to have made several examples of all his wares from which he selected the most perfect and destroyed the remainder.

KIYOMIZU

The Kiyomizu factories established at Kyoto gave the city considerable importance as a ceramic production centre. Ninsei executed his finest work at Kyoto. At Kiyomizu, in the Seikanj district, the celebrated Takahari Dohachi executed the brilliant work which made him famous throughout Japan. Various coloured wares originated at Kiyomizu including a buff-coloured ware and a yellowish type, the former produced from about 1800 and the latter appearing some two or three decades later. During the early nineteenth century Kiyomizu potters copied old Arita ware, using a similar rich underglaze blue of great beauty. Enamel decoration applied over a greyish crackled glaze was another Kiyomizu speciality inspired by a type of Arita ware. Kiyomizu wares are placed among the finest ceramic wares made in the Kyoto neighbourhood.

KUTANI

At about the middle of the seventeenth century porcelain production began attracting the same amount of attention among the feudal princes of Japan as was to occur a century later among European princes. The powerful Prince of Taichoji erected a kiln at Kutani-mura, a village situated in the mountain range in the province of Kaga. Conflicting accounts are given of the early years of the pottery. The most reliable records tell how in 1664 or 1668 young Prince Toshiaki, who shared his father's enthusiasm, sent a capable potter named Goto Saijiro to Arita to learn the techniques of porcelain manufacture. When the potter returned to Kutani, well versed in the art of porcelain production, the prince lost no time in establishing a new factory at Kutani-mura for the sole purpose of manufacturing porcelain which, as it proved, was to be quite different in character to that made at Arita.

Owing to the poor quality of the paste made from local clays, which rendered it impossible to make anything but coarse pottery, it was decided to procure essential materials from Imari. Even when this was done, for a long time, in spite of continuous experiment, the Kutani body remained unsatisfactory, with faults that could not be concealed even when lustrous glazes or brilliant enamels were applied. Attempts to develop a fine body were ultimately abandoned in favour of obtaining white biscuit ware from outside sources which Kutani artists decorated.

The foremost designer at the factory was Kuzumi Morikagé who was revolted by the gaudy Imari floral mode of decoration. Morikagé preferred to paint scenes from nature executed in a simple direct style. Morikagé established the high standard of Kutani decoration which was maintained for a long period. Kutani artists were particularly fond of depicting children at play as in Chinese *karaku*. The finest early Kutani ware was frequently decorated with medallions enclosing symbols, scrolls and diaper patterns. Figure subjects were also favoured, but not to the same extent as conventional stylised designs comprising formal motifs and symbols. Early wares were decorated in a quite different style to late nineteenth- and early twentieth-century wares when an extensive range of new subjects appeared including flowers, principally chrysanthemums and peonies, birds, especially peacocks, and figures of graceful women and saints.

A peculiar soft, waxen glaze was a unique attraction of Kutani porcelain, enhanced by brilliant enamel decoration applied with the unerring skill of Kutani decorators who worked in the Morikagé tradition. Inevitably, as time passed,

20 BALUSTER JAR. Arita ware. Enamelled in Ko-Kutani style, in iron-red, yellow and green. With panels of peony sprays surrounded by fish-net design between formal geometric borders. Genroku period, Japanese. *H 9½in*

artists employed at Kutani ceased to maintain the high standards of design and decoration set by Kuzumi Morikagé. From about 1780 until 1800 increasing decadence became evident. During the last decade of the nineteenth century the master potter Yoshidaya and the artist Shozo associated in an attempt to restore the declining technical and artistic quality of Kutani porcelain, but for nearly another three decades little important work was done in the factory.

In or about 1840 the famous Zengoro Hozen – descended in the direct line from the celebrated Eiraku – assumed direction of the Kutani pottery where he immediately set about instructing artists in the decorative style known as *kinranté*, featuring designs in imitation of scarlet and gold brocade. Patterns bore some similarity to the much earlier *ao-kutani*, one of the old factory's major successes in design. Zengoro Hozen imitated brocade weaves, diapered, or with Greek key ornament, scrolls, lozenges, stars, scales, flowers and trellis.

During the nineteenth century other factories were erected in the vicinity of the original factory. Productions from these concerns bear no comparison with fine wares made during the seventeenth and eighteenth centuries in the old factory. Heavy gilding on bright red enamel grounds was favoured by later Kutani potters. Compared with the delicately enamelled wares of the mid-eighteenth century, the later wares appear garish. Kutani porcelain of the best period dates from about 1670 to not later than 1770.

A word concerning the Kutani paste and clays used. The pure white translucent body is most likely to be found made from materials obtained from outside sources during the nineteenth century. Early Kutani porcelain, the rarest and most valuable type, was made from local dark red clay. A greyish-white clay was also used in the early period, but it was procured from an outside source. Stoneware and porcelain were manufactured at Kutani.

KYOTO

The ancient Eiraku family, a title bestowed on them by a Prince of Kii, were active as potters from a remote period and enjoyed high repute as craftsmen at the end of the sixteenth century when they settled in Kyoto.

Zengoro Hozen, eleventh in the direct line of descent from his illustrious ancestor, the first Eiraku, rose to prominence in the nineteenth century as a master potter. He was fortunate at the outset of his career in attracting the attention of Harunori, Prince of Kishiu, and in due course entered his service. Prior to his association with the prince, Eiraku, as he became better known, concerned himself with the manufacture of tea ceremony wares. He consulted tea masters on suitable designs. Eiraku showed taste and great skill in blending different coloured clays. He eventually became noted for his excellent copies of old Korean faience.

As he progressed, Eiraku developed a consuming passion for porcelain. He devoted his skill and energy to production of superb underglaze blue-and-white porcelain and fine celadons. When Prince Harunori appointed Eiraku manager of his pottery at Nishihama in 1827 it was the feudal prince's purpose to send the finest porcelain as tribute to the ruling Prince Iyenari at Kyoto.

After his appointment Eiraku concentrated upon the creation of new wares to delight Prince Harunori. Eiraku's much admired *oniwa-yaki*, which imitated a type of Chinese ware, though beautiful and successful, lacked the rare quality of the prototype.

Zengoro Hozen remained in Prince Harunori's employ for about nine years. The factory continued in existence until 1844 when Prince Harunori died.

The potter Takahari became better known as Dohachi. Later in his life he assumed the name Ninami which appeared on his wares of the period. Of several talented members of his family he was without doubt the most brilliant and successful. Almost from the commencement of his career, which began in Kyoto in 1825, his work won high praise and was extensively copied. Rival potters endeavoured to emulate Dohachi's brilliant glazing techniques. His outstanding artistry rendered all his productions attractive. Dohachi often looked to the work of early Korean potters for inspiration, as is evident, for example, in his wares decorated with a matt white glaze tinged with pink and closely resembling the Korean glazed ware known as *gohan* or 'pattern-ware'. Examples of this ware by Dohachi are extremely rare and are now highly prized in Japan.

Following the example of numerous master potters who preceded him, Dohachi became an instructor associated with a number of factories in the Kyoto area. Within five years of commencing his career in Kyoto he gained high repute as a brilliant artist potter. It was considered a great privilege to receive instruction from him. Dohachi is regarded as the first Japanese potter to merge the elements of Korean and Japanese traditional style in ceramic decoration. Dohachi's finest works, executed during middle age, are usually stamped with his name. In most respects the productions of his later years, marked with his adopted name Ninami, lack the originality and fine finish of his earlier wares.

NABESHIMA

Porcelain was made exclusively for Nabeshima, Prince of Hizen, who established a factory at Okochi-yama in about 1660. Korean potters were employed in early years and at first all materials were obtained from Arita. As with Hirado porcelain, the paste and glaze of Nabeshima porcelain are distinctive, unlike any others used elsewhere in Japan. Blue was the colour most favoured, darker than that of Hirado ware. Also on Nabeshima porcelain greens and reds were occasionally used to offset the predominant blue, a characteristic decorative treatment never seen on Hirado porcelain. In time Nabeshima porcelain reached a high degree of technical perfection. Soft underglaze blue outlines were enhanced by washes of delicate green, red and yellow. Floral designs predominated, applied with admirable restraint.

In 1710 the factory was transferred to Okawachi (Okochi). Wares made for presentation to the shogun and the imperial court at Yedo (Tokyo), including ornaments and vessels, carried a blue mark, actually a decorative motif, resembling the teeth of a comb. This presentation type of ware came to be known as *kushite* – comb-teeth ware – and has always been coveted by collectors inside and outside Japan. The factory also produced celadon wares in imitation of Chinese prototypes.

NINSEI

Nomura Seisuke, whose studio name was Ninsei, ranks high among the great Japanese master potters. Ninsei used the elements of Chinese, Korean and Japanese ceramic art and devised a new type of pottery that was unmistakably Japanese. After learning enamelling techniques from Hizen potters he settled at Omuro where he produced his first wares. While working in the vicinity of Kyoto in the latter half of the seventeenth century, successively at Iwakura, Awata and Mizuro, he developed his individual styles and techniques to such a remarkable extent that his work influenced that of all potters in the neighbourhood and far beyond. His unsurpassed skill as a decorator, particularly in his ingenious use of gold and silver in conjunction with superb enamelling, invested his wares with enthralling beauty that no other Japanese potter of his time could emulate. Ninsei was also a skilful modeller. The variety of wares attributed to him attests to his versatility and technical knowledge. His crackled wares, light and dark buff or cream-coloured, were remarkable for their uniform, circular crackle of unique character, which rendered them superior to all other similar wares made in Japan at the period.

Ninsei's paste varied according to the places he worked in and the period of production. A yellowish-grey, close-textured body was characteristic, although the most common type was a durable close-grained red body. His most admired wares were of crackled type with enamel floral decoration in green and blue embellished with gilt. Furthermore, Ninsei was eminently successful in his use of monochrome glazes including honey-brown, chocolate, buff, a lustrous white and black upon green, used as grounds for floral decoration touched with gilt.

RAKU

Differing accounts of the origin of this ware are somewhat contradictory, but as far as Japanese ceramic wares are concerned there appears little doubt that the first *raku* ware made in Japan was produced by a Korean potter named Ameya who settled in Kyoto about 1560. *Raku* ware was originally known as *juraku*. In about 1580 Ameya's son Chojiro began making tea ceremony wares from a porous, low-fired clay body, occasionally worked with a piece of bamboo and sometimes thrown on the wheel, but more often shaped entirely by hand. Vessels were lead-glazed.

Chojiro's *raku* wares soon attracted attention and won high praise. Shogun Hideyoshi presented Chojiro with a seal with which to mark his wares. Thereafter, through successive generations, the descendants of Chojiro, always using the *raku* character as a seal mark, continued to manufacture *raku* ware. Eventually numerous other potters imitated Chojiro's wares, using an almost identical paste. From the earliest period two types of *raku* were made, the red-glazed *raku* ware lightly decorated with coloured slip under the glaze and the coarser black *raku* ware coated with dark-brown or black glaze. The word *raku*, meaning 'pleasure' or 'enjoyment', was first applied to the ware by the greatly venerated Japanese tea master Rikyu, through whose good offices Chojiro received his seal from Hideyoshi.

Raku wares became immensely popular in Japan. *Raku* was subsequently produced by amateur potters working in their homes and gardens. The simplest type of *raku* ware requires little technical knowledge and skill in production.

SATSUMA

Old Satsuma wares take their place among the most beautiful Japanese ceramic productions. Not the garishly decorated Satsuma ware shipped to Europe in large quantities in the late nineteenth century, a gaudy ware calculated to appeal to Western taste at the period, but the alluring old Satsuma which is exceedingly rare. It is believed that certain extremely rare types of Satsuma ware have never been seen outside Japan.

In their disgust upon discovering that the Satsuma ware they proudly displayed in their homes was altogether different from and very much inferior to genuine old Satsuma ware, Europeans reacted unfavourably towards Japanese ceramic wares in general, no doubt feeling cheated and deceived. In fact, no massive vases and other large ornaments were made in the old traditional Satsuma style, early items for the most part being small. The ground colour of old wares varied in tone from an attractive lustrous cream to deep ivory, over which the enamel and matt gold decoration was carefully applied with exquisite delicacy. The texture of the early ware so admired by the Japanese was hard and the crackle invariably minute.

Returning from Korea in 1598, the Prince of Satsuma brought in his train a group of skilled potters whom he subsequently set to work at Chiusa. Early wares were usually decorated with yellow, green or black glazes over a fine body. Eventually Prince Mitsuhiso of Sasshiu erected a kiln in his palace grounds. He employed highly accomplished ceramic artists to decorate his wares with vitrifiable enamels. It is believed by Japanese authorities that the celebrated artist Tangen designed some of the fine Satsuma ware produced in Prince Mitsuhiso's pottery. Moreover, it is asserted that the finely enamelled objects designated Satsuma-Tangen are the actual work of the master.

Towards the end of the eighteenth century the original Satsuma factory flourished under the patronage of a later Prince of Sasshiu named Yeiô. After workmen who were sent to Kyoto to learn new techniques returned with information concerning certain processes production rapidly expanded. The most popular decorative style

21 DISH. Banko ware. Stoneware with overglaze enamel decoration in red, blue, green, aubergine and yellow. Edo period, late eighteenth to early nineteenth century, Japanese. D 9⅛in

featured landscapes, flowers, diapers and various mythological animals and birds. No wares produced for Prince Yeiô were allowed to be sold.

An extremely rare type of early Satsuma ware was decorated with coloured enamels and gilt upon the hard white body. The 'splashed' variety, commonly coloured olive-green touched with chocolate-brown or mustard-yellow, had a hard body approaching the density of stoneware. Monochrome glazes were only seldom used on old Satsuma. It is asserted that painted figures will never be found on authentic examples of early Satsuma ware.

So-called 'mushroom' Satsuma ware was devised, with a unique, somewhat peculiar, circular crackle with creamy-brown outlines, resembling a bed of mushrooms. At Chiusa, in the province of Satsuma, the old factory produced a type of ware known as *ko-chiusa*, best described as resembling the shell of an ostrich egg in colour and texture, with the most delicately applied decoration.

Designs painted on old Satsuma wares were never crowded, and mainly comprised floral sprays or flowering branches outlined in gold. A form of panelled decoration included diaper and other motifs painted in enamel colours touched with gilt. 'Brocade' wares were a nineteenth-century innovation introduced with a regard for export opportunities.

Satsuma potters operated the wheel with the left foot, unlike Japanese potters in general who work with the right foot, in consequence the spiral goes from left to right in Satsuma ware and not in reverse as is usual.

The *flambé* glazes used by Satsuma potters were distinctive, if not unique, usually applied over a red body, both red and white paste being used. Satsuma *flambé* glazes resembled 'shot' silk, in colour blends of red and violet and violet and blue. It may be that coloration was first produced accidentally, though obviously a process was devised to produce coloration as desired.

SETO

In addition to Seto, a village in the province of Owari, kilns were in operation at other places in the neighbourhood at a very early date, including Shino and Oribe, the wares produced generally being named after the nearest village. Seto became the centre of production in the vicinity when one of Japan's most celebrated early potters, Toshiro, settled there in the thirteenth century after his return from China.

Early Seto ware was a reddish-buff-coloured stoneware covered with a streaked brown glaze. The curious concentric ring marks on the base of stonewares were left by the thread used in detaching objects from the wheel.

Brown-glazed pottery known as *temmoku*, said to have been copied from bowls brought back from China by Japanese workers, was produced at Seto from about 1220 onwards. Other Chinese wares inspired the Seto potters. The Japanese cylindrical or oviform tea jar was originated at Seto, together with a variety of other vessels used in the tea ceremony. Both T'ang and Sung influence may be observed in the shape of vessels, the glazing techniques and manner of decoration. Early Seto stonewares were completely unsophisticated in style.

Ko-Seto wares, as a prized range of tea ceremony vessels made at Seto were called, were greatly admired and even in Toshiro's lifetime became valuable 'collector's' items. Toshiro imported certain clays from China in order to make his beautiful *Karamono* ware which was even more prized. His descendants of the second, third, and fourth generations working after him at Seto, continued in Toshiro's tradition.

Ki-Seto ware, a buff-coloured, yellow-glazed stoneware, was the product of another factory. At first only a very thin, transparent glaze was applied. The glaze later became opaque, with green spots, and flame-red and green decoration. *Haku-an*, made in the fifteenth century, was an early type of *Ki-Seto* ware. A more common type of *Ki-Seto* ware, made in the seventeenth century, displayed considerable variation in the tone of its yellow glaze.

The famous potter Tomikichi worked at Seto early in the nineteenth century, after training at Arita. *Sometsuké* ware, an attractive fine porcelain painted blue under the glaze, is associated with Tomikichi.

Seto became renowned for the high quality of its wares and for centuries remained pre-eminent in the production of tea ceremony vessels. Its fame as a pottery-making centre has continued until the present day.

WESTERN ASIA AND ISLAM

It would be futile to attempt to catalogue in the space of a few pages the many varieties of beautiful, unique wares produced through the ages by potters in Western Asia. The region offers an extensive, though somewhat complex field for study and research; for as yet, even concerning the comparatively late sphere of Islamic ceramics, our knowledge is not extensive and many mysteries remain unsolved. Continuous excavation and study of examples of ancient pottery brought to light at Near Eastern sites strengthens the opinion that pottery-making was truly an art in the region long before Islam. At least as far as the Old World is concerned, a conviction that the potter's craft originated in the Near East is widely shared. To suggest precisely where making pots had its beginnings in the Near East must be mere guesswork, although there are strong indications that potters first worked clay on the central plateau of Iran. It is known for certain that potters were at work in Iranian villages in about 5500 BC and it is feasible that pottery was being produced in the plateau region even much earlier. In the following pages devoted to a brief survey of the development of pre-Islamic and Islamic pottery a few of the more outstanding achievements of Western Asiatic potters are described. The ancient, beautiful ceramic wares of the Near East are worthy of praise and deserving of greater attention than they have hitherto generally received.

Anonymity among ancient Near Eastern potters confounds us once more as when considering the development of ceramics in China. A few names of Islamic potters have come down to us, but it is virtually impossible to say who invented techniques or gave the lead in changes of style. Techniques which evolved over thousands of years were commonly practised among potters who passed them down from one generation to another. All that is known for certain is that brilliant master potters worked and died through the centuries, leaving their work in the form of improved techniques or wares produced in adventurously conceived new shapes and decorative styles, the introduction of which vitally changed processes and fashions. Undoubtedly, less inspired and enterprising craftsmen turned out indifferently made pots that were soon broken or discarded. However, pottery-making ultimately became such a highly sophisticated art in the Near East, and more so with the rise of Islam, that besides innumerable humble potters who made commonplace wares for ordinary use there were brilliant masters in clay who fashioned beautiful objects for the adornment of the palaces of the high and mighty.

It is generally conceded that the potter's wheel was an Egyptian invention, although some authorities support the assumption that it first appeared in the Near East and that potters in Western Asia developed the art of making symmetrical

22 BOWL ON RING FOOT.
Transoxian or Eastern
Iran. Simple leaf
decoration with Kufic
inscription. Black-brown
and dark brick-red slip
with green spots on
white slip under
colourless glaze.
Nishapur, tenth century,
Persian. H $4\frac{7}{16}$ in, D
$15\frac{1}{16}$ in

vases with walls of uniform thickness. The use of the wheel spread across Asia to the Far East and westwards into Europe. As it was with the wheel, so with the kiln, which in all probability was also an Egyptian invention. The construction of the kiln initiated an important stage of development for ancient potters, offering infinite possibilities by means of new production techniques. When firing processes evolved, making it possible to apply painted decoration and durable glazes on hardened clay in biscuit state, the potter's craft can be said to have truly commenced.

Near Eastern potters discovered how to glaze earthenware at a very remote period. Glazes were invented that served to decorate wares besides meeting practical requirements. In Mesopotamia and Iran potters commonly used an alkaline glaze composed of quartz mixed with a sodium and potassium flux. Use of an admixture of coloured metallic oxides, chiefly lead, followed later. Chinese potters could not claim to be inventors of coloured glazes, although they improved on original Near Eastern glazing techniques to such an extent that in due course their methods and finished wares differed entirely from Near Eastern productions.

Each region in Iran had its potters who followed a conventional style, but when in later development it became the practice to decorate wares with simple designs, ornamentation was individualistic according to the craftsman's taste and capabilities. The quality of the pottery produced largely depended upon that of local materials available.

Perhaps the most important and attractive early Iranian wares belong to a class

78

designated Chalcolithic painted wares, examples of which have been excavated in several areas of Iran and are believed to have originated on the central plateau and in mountain regions to the west. Decoration of abstract character consisted chiefly of geometric patterns, painted and impressed. At about the same period, in the important pottery centre of Tepe Sialk, a distinctive type of decoration, abstract in character, came into use. Examples have been excavated on the site showing a buff-coloured slip serving as a ground for delicately executed panel patterns.

Painted pottery, one of the glories of Iranian ceramic art, appeared at a very early period, with varying forms and application techniques, and continued to be produced until the establishment of Islam. The Mesopotamians may have learned techniques for painting pottery from Iranian potters. With the rise of Sumerian civilisation very little painted pottery was produced in the region. When painted wares reappeared in Mesopotamia in about 1500 BC decoration was usually applied over the glaze. So-called Mittanian pottery, made in the Mesopotamian pottery centre of Mittania, was a richly glazed ware with impressed decoration in the form of stylised plant motifs, the colouring carefully applied. In the central plateau region of Iran, not only at Tepe Sialk, but in other pottery-making centres, painting on pottery rose to a high artistic level. Abstract and geometric designs and painted animal figures continued popular into the Sassanian period (AD 226–641). Not until the Islamic faith and way of life became firmly established in Iran and elsewhere in Western Asia were representations of humans and animals excluded from decoration. Contrary to general belief, figures of animals never entirely disappeared from pottery decorated in Islamic regions.

During the Halafian period in Mesopotamia, when the influence of Iran was very strong, Tell Halaf pottery became renowned for its outstanding quality and attraction. Even the earliest Halafian wares were well shaped and profusely decorated in a naturalistic style in which animal figures and plants predominated. Towards the end of the Halafian period potters in the Tell Halaf region turned to the production of fine glazed monochrome wares. The wares closely resembled examples found at Samarra where Iranian influence was always strong.

Moulded wares were apparently never as popular or made in such quantity in Iran as in Mesopotamia where techniques were highly developed. A somewhat coarse red clay was used in the production of moulded pottery, usually well glazed in a limited range of colours including brown, green, blue, yellow and cream. Broad painted bands of colour were favoured in the decoration of these moulded wares. Early Iranian moulded pottery forms which survived into the Sassanian period, or were revived by Sassanian potters prior to the advent of Islam, were conceived on graceful, pleasing lines and were usually vigorously executed. Moulded decoration was applied on brilliantly glazed wares combined with incised and pierced ornamentation into which coloured glaze was left to run.

Techniques in applying painted decoration on pottery culminated in the beautiful painted wares produced in the flourishing pottery centre of Susa, where it is believed earthenware vessels were produced as early as 6500 BC. Susanian pottery

23 PLATE. Opaque cream-white stanniferous glaze. Painted in gold lustre with iridescent reflections. Kufic inscription and potter's mark. Egyptian Fātimīd period, tenth to eleventh century, Egyptian. D 15⅝in

comprised a variety of types of excellent standard, included among the best ceramic wares produced in the ancient Near East. Remarkable Susa painted wares showing panelled animal designs were an impressive achievement and are considered to be the finest early ceramic wares produced in the region. Susa has become noted for the exceptionally beautiful large goblets with painted decoration which are now regarded by many as the most striking objects devised by Near Eastern potters.

The prophet Mohammed died in 632. Within thirty years of his death the first capital of Islam was established at Damascus under the Omayyad caliphate. With the birth of Islam and the spreading of Islamic doctrine throughout Western Asia dramatic changes occurred in all branches of arts and crafts. In about 800 the first Chinese stonewares and porcelains to reach Islam so captivated the potters of the time that they immediately began emulating Chinese wares in so far as available materials and their limited understanding of techniques allowed. At that period Islamic civilisation, under the domination of the Omayyads (661–750), was closely linked with Eastern Mediterranean cultural centres. After the Abbasid family superseded the Omayyads they established a new caliphate at Baghdad from which time Islamic culture assumed a definitely Asiatic character. When the Abbasid caliphs ruled in Baghdad the capital of Islam became the flourishing art centre of Western Asia where pottery attracted renewed interest and increasing favour.

From emulation of Chinese wares Islamic potters gradually introduced their own shapes and decorative styles. Chinese influence on Islamic pottery endured for about a century. T'ang and Sung wares are thought to be the first Chinese wares seen by Islamic potters. White porcelain fascinated the potters of Islam and they were entranced by its serene beauty. They vainly directed tremendous effort towards successful emulation. When it was realised that true porcelain could not be produced owing to lack of suitable materials they came to terms with the situation. Instead of endeavouring further to create translucent white porcelain they first invented a white glaze which when applied to the surface of wares gave the illusion of being porcelain, and three centuries later they developed a white paste to which the white glaze could be applied with more satisfactory results. The white tin glaze developed in Mesopotamia was basically the same as that used in Italy by makers of maiolica a few centuries later. The paste obtained from mixing white clay and ground quartz produced soft-paste porcelain, known in France as *pâte tendre*.

The amount of Islamic pottery made for ornamental use was negligible. Early wares were not crude as a rule though they were of simple character. Restrained decoration was applied, stamped, moulded or painted. Unglazed domestic vessels were made of whitish or buff-coloured clay, the porous walls keeping the contents cool by surface evaporation. For some five centuries following the establishment of the Omayyad caliphate at Damascus almost without exception clays used by Islamic potters were of a common variety which could only be low-fired in order to produce a buff or reddish body covered with lead glaze that became very fluid in the kiln.

The true flowering of Islamic ceramic art occurred with the appearance of exquisitely painted wares which are considered to be unsurpassed in their magnificent design and colouring. Materials, also to a considerable extent the techniques of Islamic pottery painting, were derived from Mediterranean sources, principally Greece, and not from Asian sources to the east as may be supposed. Perhaps the most vital technical achievement of Islamic potters was their ability to combine the practical application of durable glazes with painted or relief decoration. The most active region was Mesopotamia from whence potters in regions to the north and east acquired knowledge of techniques and copied modes of decoration. Even the resourceful and inventive Iranian potters did not exhibit such ability to improve techniques and evolve new forms as later Mesopotamian potters.

Until the mid-ninth century the Mesopotamians used alkaline glazes, which continued to be used in Syria but were superseded in favour, almost everywhere else in Islam, by lead glaze. The serious fault of lead glaze lay in its extreme fluidity in the kiln during firing which necessitated the use of only earthy pigments in painted decoration in order to avoid smearing. Development of underglaze painting on pottery was therefore delayed for some three centuries until potters rediscovered the advantages of using the old Egyptian alkaline glazes.

Lead-glazed wares of the *sgraffiato* type represent a considerable advance in decorative techniques. Wares at first resembled the Chinese stonewares that inspired their creation. Red-bodied vessels were coated with white slip over which a transparent yellowish glaze was applied, with added splashes of brown, green and purple. Sometimes, prior to glazing, designs were scratched through the white slip to expose the red body of the ware in the so-called *sgraffiato* style. Attempts to apply underglaze painted decoration were seldom successful owing to smudging caused by the fluidity of the lead glaze during firing. Lead-glazed relief-decorated wares were an attractive innovation copied by the Mesopotamians from Egyptian prototypes. Mesopotamian wares of the type were rendered much more striking by the introduction of glazing with metallic pigments. The ware was fired once then coated with metallic pigment and returned to the kiln. When the vessel was drawn out again the metallic pigment had fused to the surface, spreading over in a smooth, golden layer. In this manner the admirable Islamic lustre technique evolved, which in subsequent phases of development, with infinite variation, was to predominate in the embellishment of Islamic pottery for a long period.

Almost certainly, the practice of decorating pottery with painted lustre designs originated in Egypt where the technique was primarily used in decoration of glassware. The pigment was basically composed of sulphur in various forms mixed with silver and copper oxides, the former producing a yellow stain on glaze and the latter creating the lustrous element. Yellow or red ochre was added to obtain the desired colour. During the second firing in a reducing kiln the metallic particles were deposited on a film which spread over the surface of the ware. In the intense heat of the kiln the pigment completely burned away leaving only the metallic film and the ochre vehicle adhering to the surface which, in order to obtain an effect of depth and richness, had to be glassily smooth.

Until the twelfth century the history of the development of Islamic pottery centres upon Egypt, Syria and Mesopotamia. For centuries Iranian potters, who in pre-Islamic times retained the lead in pottery styles and techniques, apparently remained content to follow the fashions set by potters working in Baghdad for the caliph and his court. With the opening of the twelfth century Iranian potters entered upon an extraordinary new phase of productive activity, taking over the lead from potters elsewhere in Islam as well as the important pottery centre which had developed in Samarkand to the north. In the remote past Iranian potters transmitted new ideas and technical developments to Chinese potters. Now it became the turn

24 BEAKER. Decorated
in turquoise and black.
Damascus, thirteenth
century. *H 5½in, D rim
4in*

of Iran to borrow from China. At the beginning of the ninth century when Chinese
porcelain first appeared in Western Asia, the potters of Iran were captivated by
its beauty and became envious of the powers of the Chinese to produce such exquisite wares. As occurred in other Islamic states, Iranian potters endeavoured
to make true porcelain, but were prevented from doing so mainly through the lack
of supplies of *kaolin*. As in Mesopotamia, Iranian potters ultimately resorted to
counterfeiting by using a white glaze applied over a coarse earthenware body and
later in applying the glaze to an artificially composed white body.

Evidence indicates that it was from Iran that the use of the white glazing technique spread across Islamic regions northwards as far as Anatolia. A Kashan potter
named Abulgasim, a member of a renowned Iranian family of potters, left an account of how white Iranian ware was created from an artificial paste. The process
scarcely differed from a similar technique first used in Egypt and later modified for

83

use by Mesopotamian potters. The paste used in Iran was composed of proportionate parts of powdered quartz, a frit and white plastic clay. Resultant quality of wares depended upon the quality of materials used, while the advantage of the glaze and body being basically composed of the same materials made complete fusion of glaze and body practically certain. As in Mesopotamia and Egypt, in Iran tin oxides were used to render the glaze opaque. Brilliant glazes were applied over relief or painted decoration. At Kashan, where potters specialised in the production of whitewares, at first closely imitating Chinese porcelains, the latter wares became increasingly original and eventually purely Islamic in character.

The painted, so-called *minai* (enamel) wares of Iran, produced from the twelfth to the fourteenth century, are considered by some to be the most attractive Iranian ceramic wares. Whether or not they are the finest Iranian wares, *minai* painted wares are the most brilliantly colourful. When the fashion for polychrome painted wares was revived Iranian potters were confronted with the problems of fixing enamels exposed to the heat of the kiln. A satisfactory method allowing use of low temperature colours had to be devised. It became general practice to submit wares to successive firings according to the nature of the enamels used. Where an extensive palette was in use the range included the few colours that could withstand great heat and many others that were less stable and could only be fired at low temperatures. Firing was always a hazardous, complicated process, no doubt considered worthwhile in view of the splendid results achieved.

Often layer upon layer of brilliant colour was used in the *minai* technique which marked the apogee of Iranian polychrome ceramic decoration. Glorious reds, blues, purples, lilacs, glowing chestnut, shining black and exquisite leaf gilding were employed with dazzling effect, ornamentation being so thickly applied to the body of wares they were to all appearances sheathed in metal. The shapes of wares ornamented in the *minai* style were less heavy and on the whole more elegant than most other Iranian wares of the period.

In Islam generally, however, the unique beauty and lasting perfection of lustre-painted wares was the supreme glory in ceramic achievements. The technique was scarcely attempted anywhere beyond the confines of Islamic territories. If, as appears doubtful, Far Eastern potters were versed in the technique of lustre painting they refrained from practising it. Italian potters interested themselves in the technique during the Renaissance but production was never more than limited and wares bore no comparison in quality with the splendid lustre-decorated wares of Islam.

2

EUROPE

GREECE

The ceramic art of ancient Greece can be traced back to Neolithic times when, during the period of the so-called Sesklo culture, female clay statuettes, standing, sitting or crouching, were made in representation of the Great Mother who was worshipped throughout the Aegean region at the dawn of Greek civilisation. The simplicity and stark realism of these primitive Greek clay figurines appeals to modern taste.

Early in the second millennium BC a foreign race invaded the Greek island of Crete and established the first great Aegean civilisation, which we now refer to as Cretan-Minoan. Evidence exists to support a theory that the Minoans were of eastern origin. Greeks of later ages probably derived their predilection for art in miniature – including ceramic statuettes – from the Minoans. Examples of Minoan ceramic figure art include 'Snake-Goddess' figures in faience, fascinating to most people as much on account of their slightly sinister character as their unconventional attire, which consists of a full flounced dress with tight-fitting bodice leaving the ample breasts bare. Clay figurines of bulls taken from tombs indicate that a bull cult existed.

What are referred to as the 'archaic' periods of Greek ceramic development began with the ages of pre-history, continuing through the Neolithic Age and the successive civilisations of the Minoans and Mycenaeans and terminating at about the end of the sixth century BC. Following the Dorian invasion, Greek culture remained at a low ebb for some four centuries until the early eighth century BC when what is now known as the geometric style evolved in Greek art. During the ensuing six centuries Greek ceramic production continuously expanded and progressed, culminating in the development of a unique form of painted pottery.

One of the major differences between Greek pottery and that of the Egyptians, Mesopotamians and Iranians is that Greek potters never covered their wares with heavy glaze. It has been suggested that the Greeks refrained from using glaze to enhance their wares because they wished to avoid obscuring the finer details. They preferred to embellish the surface of wares with a beautiful sheen, employing materials and methods that, due to present limited knowledge, we can only guess at. Almost all Greek pottery made in the heyday of Greek civilisation is beautifully shaped and usually adorned with fine painted and relief decoration.

In briefly considering the techniques used in Greek ceramic art the importance of painted decoration immediately becomes apparent. Painted pottery, specimens of which have been excavated at Athens, Melos, Corinth and other centres, consisted of primitively fashioned wares painted black or brown on a greyish drab ground.

25 JUG. Geometric style. Greek, c600 BC. *H 8¼in*

Important technical advancement followed the discovery of suitable cream-coloured clay from which were produced wares painted red and white, with occasional touches of black. Towards the end of the late archaic period it became customary to depict the female figures on pots in white paint to distinguish them from males usually shown in black or red.

In the great period of Greek ceramic art, extending from the sixth to the fourth century BC, a style of decoration entailing the use of clay slip was skilfully executed by artists versed in the technique. Ornamentation composed of moulded slip in different colours was applied to surfaces previously marked with a design drawn in freehand. Gradual decline in the practice of this and other techniques occurred during the early fourth century BC. Decadence in the second century BC took the form of pretentiousness when over-ornate wares came into favour. Towards the end of the century the production of painted pottery practically ceased.

Basic materials used and methods of production varied little between Greek pottery and that of adjacent countries, but clearly, in its peculiar characteristics and forms, the pottery of ancient Greece owed little to outside influence. Existing remains of Greek kilns do not lead us to presume that the techniques of pottery-making in Greece were unique. The important difference lay in a distinctive mode of decoration and even more emphatically in the beautiful lustrous sheen produced on the surface of wares.

Greek ceramic art reached its apogee of technical refinement during the late sixth and early fifth centuries BC, when potters and ceramic artists working in the Attic region combined their powers in the production of masterpieces, superbly modelled and ornamented. So-called 'red-figure' pots were the most common type, produced from the local clay which was dug up and left to weather prior to use. It is not known if Greek potters practised the technique of mixing clays. The clay was first washed then left to stand until coarse particles sank away. After the water was poured off subsequent evaporation produced a paste of the right consistency for working, which commenced with kneading. The red colouring of the common clay was due to the presence of ferric oxide. Large wares were produced on the wheel and were usually made in sections joined up with thin slip before the ware hardened. Pottery was generally fashioned entirely by hand until Hellenistic times, which explains why the shapes of vases and other objects are sometimes disproportionate.

The fine gloss on Attic pottery and similar wares made in other Greek pottery centres still baffles us concerning the formula and method of application. Not the least mystifying feature is that the sheen appears strong on black-painted surfaces and weaker on red-toned unpainted surfaces. It is erroneous to refer to the gloss as varnish, nor can it properly be regarded as glaze. Modern experts have reached the conclusion that the unique sheen can be attributed to the presence of fine illite or a similar clay mineral in a weak solution applied thinly to the surface of wares. It has also been noted by experts that illite vitrifies at a temperature around $900°–1000°C$, the temperature normally reached in firing by Greek potters. It appears probable that illite in a stronger solution was mixed in the black 'paint' used in the decoration of wares.

When decorating in the red-figure style the artist normally first drew an outline sketch on the ware, using a sharp instrument. Some of the artist's marks still remain visible on pots that have survived through thousands of years. If pigment was used in the execution of a preliminary sketch it presumably burned away during firing. Marks left on surfaces from sketching with a hard instrument have not been found on extant black-figure painted wares.

It is surmised that before commencing to paint the artist applied a thin coating of illite in weak solution to the surface of the ware which instantly dried, leaving a soft sheen. The painter used the clay solution in strong concentration as a medium and proceeded to work with the brush in broad, firm strokes, using a quill or finer brush in the execution of delicate line designs. The artist probably worked in a conventional routine, first painting over the sketched outline then filling in the black-

painted areas. Purple and white ornamentation was sometimes applied, also incised and relief decoration carried out with an engraving instrument. A deeper
wine-red colouring was occasionally added to painted decoration for effect, applied,
it is conjectured, before the firing process.

Strength and density of the solution used to cover the surface of a pot determined
its colour after firing. In other words, the colour scheme of black-painted decoration
on the red surface was obtained by control during firing. Purple and white pigments
used in decoration did not acquire sheen, nor did they altogether satisfactorily
adhere to the body of wares. White was obtained from a fine solution of pipe clay.
Purple was probably derived from powdered red ochre in solution.

Firing methods governed the alternative production of red- or black-surfaced
wares, arising from the density of ferric oxide in the clay. Ferric oxide being un-
affected by an oxidising atmosphere, the clay retained its natural red colour. In a
reducing oven, however, oxygen was absorbed, thereby converting ferric oxide
into dense black iron oxide. Moreover, when exposed to an oxidising fire black
iron oxide absorbed oxygen and turned red. Greek potters were thus able to produce red or black wares as required by simple control of firing processes. Wares
were normally fired in a temperature around 900°–1000°C, left to cool in the oven
and when removed and wiped were immediately ready for use.

Greek potters practised their traditional techniques through centuries with little
change in methods or styles. The development of the gloss applied so effectively
to wares, and black colouring, were innovations of sixth-century Attic potters.
Attic styles remained popular into the Hellenistic epoch but with increasing diminution of elegance and beauty. In the final phase of decadence potters omitted to produce the sheen which is characteristic and one of the principal attractions of fine
Attic painted pottery.

Dated somewhat earlier than the extensive range of Greek black-painted and
relief-decorated wares are striking dark-painted wares with pleasing ornamentation
consisting of a formal arrangement of white and purple narrow stripes usually
appearing round the body or on the lips of vessels. An impressed style of decoration
popular during the seventh and sixth centuries BC comprised bands of impressed
and painted designs encircling vases and jugs. The style evolved in Athens and continued in use in Greece and Rome for upwards of ten centuries. A noted ceramic
artist, Sotades, is known to have been the first Greek to paint in the style. Impressed
and incised ornament was executed on wares before they were fired. For several
centuries designs remained uncomplicated and free from over-elaboration, small,
simple decorative motifs obviously being preferred. In the late Hellenistic period
impressed decoration was applied with diminishing concern for finish, the traditional
but gradually coarsening patterns including carelessly executed palmettes and other
classical motifs.

Relief decoration did not really gain popularity with Greek potters until the
Hellenistic period when painted pottery became outmoded and vase painters no
longer worked at the high artistic level sustained throughout the two preceding

26 CUP. Red-figure decoration by so-called Elpinikos painter. Attic
Greek, fifth century BC. *H 2⅝in, D of bowl 7⅝in*

centuries. So-called Megarian bowls of the period were outstanding productions
made by a number of potters in Greece and the Greek colonies. A hemispherical-
shaped bowl was lavishly decorated on the outside with relief ornamentation depicting human beings and animals. Designs were often executed in abstract manner.
Early Megarian bowls were particularly richly decorated. Bowls were usually
produced in moulds and the relief pattern was applied by stamping. After the
initial firing, when cool, the bowl received a coat of dark paint and was refired,
following the same process as in firing ordinary black-painted wares. Techniques
employed in the decoration of Megarian bowls continued to be used in the production of later wares, the decorative style remaining popular until well into the
second century AD.

The names of many Greek makers and decorators of pottery are known to us
through the custom of signing wares, although it is often difficult to determine
whose signature appears on a particular ware, that of the maker, the artist who
decorated it, or even perhaps the merchant who sold it. Greeks first began signing
pottery in the late eighth century BC but the practice did not become relatively
common until some three centuries later when it was no doubt recognised as a
means of advertisement. Signatures are found painted, stamped and incised. For

27 AMPHORA. Black-
figure decoration.
Herakles hurling the
Erymanthian Boar upon
Eurystheus. Attic Greek,
c510 BC. *H 20¾in*

obvious reasons, only signatures applied to wares before firing are accepted without
question by modern collectors suspicious of forgery.

Independent one-man pottery-making concerns existed in relatively large number
in the Greek states during the sixth and fifth centuries BC when the industry
flourished. The number of Attic potters and decorators at work at any given period
is believed to have amounted to hundreds. The potter did not invariably undertake
the decoration of his wares nor were numerous accomplished artists, including a
number celebrated and fashionable in their day, always concerned with the making
of the pots they decorated. Possibly the most talented and highly paid artists worked
freelance for various potters who desired their wares to be skilfully decorated by
a well-known painter in order to ensure a ready sale. Schools of painting were
established in the major pottery centres, as at Athens and Corinth, where students
learned techniques which perhaps in their turn they passed on to assistants employed in potteries where they eventually worked. An artist naturally studied and

usually adopted the style of his particular school. A reputable painter of figures on pottery commanded considerable respect within the industry and was regarded as an important individual – perhaps even more so than the maker of pots.

Among potters and artists known to us is Nikosthenes, one of the most celebrated potters at work in Athens at the end of the sixth century BC. He made a varied range of amphorae which were distributed over a wide area, as far distant as Etruria, and is also credited with having introduced a white ground technique into Athens. Euphronios was a noted Attic pottery painter working at the end of the sixth century BC. Praxias first painted vases in red-figure style in a rather fussy manner but subsequently changed to painting black figures in a more robust style. In the fourth century BC the Athenian brothers Kittos and Bacchius owned a thriving pottery where wares were produced that sold throughout Greece and the colonies. Sophilos is the first Attic vase painter known to us; an artist who painted in the Corinthian style and favoured the use of white paint, particularly when depicting the flesh of women, also draperies. Timonidas of Corinth was associated with the development of styles and techniques.

The ceramic art of Greece can hardly be referred to without mention of the Greek tradition in terracotta. The terracotta art of ancient Greece was extraordinarily rich and varied. Of all Greek terracottas the figurines of Boeotia – especially the productions of master potters working in terracotta in the small Boeotian town of Tanagra – are the finest and the most interesting. Terracotta figurines were fashioned by the earliest inhabitants of the Greek mainland, but in the seventh century BC, in Boeotia, modellers in terracotta developed unprecedented skill and produced figurines of compelling charm and beauty. Early, so-called bird-faced Boeotian figurines are characteristically naïve, with narrow faces and wearing a unique type of head-dress. These figures are sometimes erroneously ascribed to an earlier period than the sixth century BC to which they belong. Nearly all bird-faced Boeotian terracottas were hand-modelled, although examples have been found, particularly in Cyprus, with cylindrical trunks shaped on a potter's wheel and hand-modelled heads.

As Boeotian modellers developed greater skill their terracotta figures assumed more character and animation. Judging by numerous ancient moulds found it is evident that the use of moulds became general practice. Colouring was applied to most figures after firing, usually either black, white, blue or red, or various combinations of these colours.

Tanagra terracotta figurines, which are so universally admired today, were mainly produced after the destruction of other important ceramic production centres in Boeotia during the Macedonian attacks of 338 and 335 BC. Only Tanagra survived to keep the industry alive. Tanagra speedily became the thriving principal pottery centre where skilled modellers in terracotta produced some of the most attractive figurines ever made in Greece. The finest Tanagra figurines date from the

28 KYLIX. Red-figure decorated with an owl and two leaves. Greek, c400 BC.
H 7¾in, D rim 3¾in

late fourth century BC and the third century BC. To whatever extent Tanagra terracotta figures may be considered deficient in quality the fault is more than compensated for in their clear-cut lines, vigorous realism and spontaneous artistry, which is surprising, perhaps, considering that the majority were produced from moulds. The most striking productions are figures of serene, graceful women wearing the flowing robes and broad-brimmed hats of their day, standing or seated in dignified attitudes, sometimes clasping a child. All are painted in various colours.

As has often been noted, the simplicity of Tanagra terracotta figures is much more subtle than is at first realised. Many examples have been found in tombs. While the precise significance of this circumstance is open to speculation, it is not generally believed that the figures had any special religious or funerary connections.

Terracotta figures were made in quantity in Greece throughout the Hellenistic period. For an inexplicable reason, actors were apparently popular subjects with modellers, as surviving examples indicate. Hellenistic modellers frequently imitated earlier works. Late reproductions are usually easy to distinguish from originals by their lack of finish after removal from the moulds.

ITALY

There evolved in Italy during a brief period of about fifty years commencing in the last quarter of the fifteenth century a distinctive type of painted earthenware known as maiolica. The term was once applied to all earthenware of a certain type but it now usually signifies the characteristic painted earthenware produced in Italy during the Renaissance. Italian maiolica indirectly owes its origin to Chinese porcelain. In their endeavour to superficially emulate porcelain by their use of white tin glaze over a coarse clay body Near Eastern potters produced the colourful wares which later inspired Italian potters in production of maiolica. A type of painted earthenware was produced in Italy in Roman times. It is believed that the painted earthenware which the Italians called maiolica was inspired by the Hispano-Moresque lustre-decorated wares of Spanish origin introduced into Italy by Majorcan traders. The word 'maiolica' is an Italian corruption of the name Majorca once applied to all kinds of tin-glazed earthenware. With their inherent artistic talent, being naturally accomplished in the use of the paint brush, Italian potters found no difficulty in applying painted decoration on wares and developing their own peculiar techniques. Within a few decades they succeeded in evolving a distinctive, elaborate style.

Techniques were traditional, commencing with either throwing clay on the wheel or pressing it into hollow moulds. Wares were fired once to obtain a buff or brown body. The biscuit ware was then dipped in a glaze composed of tin and lead oxides and a silicate of potash. When dry, the opaque glaze provided a surface suitable for decorating. By means of a second firing, which took place after painted decoration had been applied, the white glaze was fixed to the body while the pigments fused into the glaze and also became fixed, the colours thereby permanently retaining their brightness. In order to add brilliance to the wares, before the second firing they were frequently dipped in a translucent lead glaze composed of oxide of lead mixed with salt, sand and potash. It was sometimes necessary to fire wares at low temperatures in a muffled kiln, especially when certain enamels and lustre pigments were used in an all-over painting technique. Successful application of metallic lustre pigments depended upon sound knowledge of the vital techniques. Owing to their extremely volatile character, lustre colours had to be applied to wares after firing and fixed by a third firing at low temperature in a special type of kiln.

From the end of the Middle Ages the manufacture of maiolica in Italy became concentrated in a number of leading centres, developing from a purely utilitarian craft into fine art. At that period pottery was gradually becoming more important in daily life. Italian craftsmen introduced new shapes and devised variations in decoration completely different from anything known previously in Italy where

29 JUG. Maiolica. Painted in greenish-yellow lustre and blue on white ground. Deruta, c1540, Italian. *H 7½in*

pottery styles had scarcely changed since Roman times.

Vasari was wrong, of course, when he asserted that Luca della Robbia invented the enamel tin-glazing process. Della Robbia made clever use of an already developed process to embellish his works. He was eminently successful in his use of white and blue enamels, although both his own later works and the decorated terracottas of others who emulated him lacked the vigour and spontaneity of his early works. Luca della Robbia, his nephew Andrea and Andrea's son Giovanni raised the production of decorated pottery to a high artistic level, although the somewhat mannered style of the latter's work detracted from its appeal. Terracottas decorated in relief with festoons, flowers and fruits painted in enamels, created by Andrea della Robbia's sons and others who imitated their technique, including Santi Viviani, Filippo Paladino and Benedetto Bugliani, were less successful both in design and use of colour.

To the della Robbias and their followers may be attributed the introduction of the human figure into maiolica decoration by Italian potters working in the last quarter of the fifteenth century, chiefly in the workshops of Emilia and Florence. Luca della Robbia was primarily a sculptor who turned to the maiolica technique as a means of colouring his compositions. While his work undoubtedly gave fresh impetus to Italian potters, in Faenza especially, Luca's important work also manifestly raised maiolica production from a craft to an art. The erstwhile general utilitarian character of even better-class Italian pottery underwent transformation. With the universal adoption of developing techniques and the swift expansion of maiolica production Italian pottery took on an entirely different character. In some quarters the change was only gradual, for despite the wide influence of della Robbia's work, not all potters rushed to abandon time-honoured methods and traditions. Nevertheless, within two decades the revolution was complete. The *stile severo* (severe style), mainly practised in the school of Tuscany, survived until the end of the fifteenth century, but with gradual slackening of rules and principles, the school ultimately countenanced inclusion of human figures in designs.

For a period Florence and neighbouring Faenza led the way in production and technical developments, their flourishing workshops conducted by forward-looking craftsmen who vied with each other in innovation. Style was no longer held in restraint by tradition. It became the principal aim of designers and decorators to introduce new forms and modes of decoration whereby techniques and an increasing palette might be employed to the fullest extent. Plates, dishes and albarelli (drug jars), the principal wares made, were freely decorated in an imaginative version of the style known as 'floral Gothic', embodying a profusion of flowers and foliage, and in its later phase included portraits.

From Faenza, the centre of the rebirth of the Italian pottery industry at the end of the fifteenth century, emanated new ideas that stimulated production in practically every other pottery centre in northern Italy. At Faenza there evolved a style of decoration that fired the imagination of potters and created enthusiasm for production on an unprecedented scale. This style, known as *istoriate*, entailed decorating wares with narrative subjects of religious or historical character, or from nature and Greek mythology. Pictorial designs entirely covered the surface of the ware to the exclusion of border motifs. Almost all important Italian workshops began to produce wares decorated in the new style. In its later development, the *istoriate* style reached its apogee at Urbino.

During the second half of the fifteenth century, for the first time in Italy, painters began to be employed in potters' workshops on a regular basis in much the same way that artists in ancient Greece collaborated with potters in the creation of finely decorated wares. It is thought that Florentine potters were the first to avail themselves of artists' talents in this way. Within a short space of time artists trained in the leading schools were employed to full capacity in the workshops of Faenza, Deruta, Gubbio and numerous other centres. Artists naturally looked to the masters for inspiration. Painters at Deruta and Urbino favoured the Raphaelesque style, whereas in Florence the prevailing style was Botticellian. The human figure was given prominence as never before, represented in a stylistic manner, surrounded by or set against naturalistic plant motifs. Engravings were a common source of design, including the prints of Marcantonio, Mantegna, Dürer and many others.

The *istoriate* style imparted a cultural aspect to pottery, raising finely decorated maiolica to the level of high art. Two classes of ware were made, the high quality wares, principally comprising jugs, plates, and dishes, splendidly decorated for display in palaces and villas, and vessels of ordinary character intended for every-day use. Maiolica became enormously popular. As was inevitable, large amounts of inferior wares were produced, obviously with no attempt at emulation of the ex-travagantly conceived, magnificent objects which issued from celebrated workshops.

A variation of style which originated at either Florence or Faenza and was suc-cessfully adopted by leading potters in both centres consisted of leaving white reserves in the centre of plates upon which were executed landscapes, portraits, heraldic devices and coats of arms, painted in brilliant colours. The style remained popular until shortly after the end of the fifteenth century when that of the 'Masters' was introduced. The serene, so-called 'style of the individual Masters' was ex-ploited to the full at Faenza in magnificent compositions executed in a spontaneous, original manner by artists known to us only by their superb works, namely The Master of Selene, The Master of St John, The Master of the Resurrection, The Painter of the Assunta and others. At Faenza several progressive workshops gave the lead to lesser establishments. Giuliano and Sebastiano Manaru and Piero and Paolo Bergantini were eminently successful masters. The Pirota workshop specialised in plates richly adorned with *istoriate* subjects, abstract patterns and grotesques on a brilliant blue enamel ground, the arrangement of the decoration indicating Chinese influence. Zoan Maria worked at Faenza for a time before moving on to found the celebrated Casteldurante (Urbania) school. Master Benedetto trained at Faenza and later became a leading exponent of the school of Siena.

Nicola Pellipario, who worked brilliantly in the *istoriate* style, is believed to have been born at Casteldurante in the late fifteenth century. At all events, he spent much of his working life in Casteldurante workshops. After his removal to Urbino in 1528, where his family assumed the surname Fontana, his son Guido and later his grandson Orazio conducted the celebrated Fontana workshop. One of Pellipario's best-known works was a magnificent service decorated for Isabella d'Este. Due to his inclination towards eclecticism Pellipario found inspiration in the classics and in a number of instances drew upon engravings for his designs, principally from Francesco Colonna's *Hypnerotomachia Poliphili* published by Aldus in 1499 and other engravings in the style of Raphael. Pellipario's classical trend became more pronounced after about 1521, as is clearly seen in designs on his plates. He was

30 DEVOTIONAL ROUNDEL. Maiolica. With figures of St Francis of Assisi,
St Bonaventura and St Louis. Dated 30 August 1550 (Venetian?),
Italian. D 12½in

among the first to use the brilliant yellow associated with the Urbino masters.

The dukes of Rovere patronised the Fontana workshop where artists of the Urbino school studied techniques. Among the most brilliant masters of the Urbino school was Francesco Xanto Avelli di Rovigo who formed his early style on that of Pellipario but later developed his own distinctive style with the use of a much more extensive palette. His figures were principally copied from engravings and adapted to serve as imaginary portraits, or in some instances used as representations of real personages. Avelli's extensive use of engravings as a subject source was emulated by many of his contemporaries, bringing about a further development in the *istoriate* style. The engravings of Marcantonio were among the most popular which inspired potters.

At Cafaggiolo, the traditional maiolica production centre of Tuscany, craftsmen

31 PAIR OF ARMORIAL JUGS. *Istoriate* decoration. Twin snake handles with satyr masks below, decorated in the Fontana workshop. Each jug has the arms of Salviati in an oval cartouche of strap-work below the spout. Urbino, c1555, Italian. H 15½in

were slower in adopting the *istoriate* style. With the arrival from Montelupo of Pietro and Stefano Fattorini early in the sixteenth century design and production received fresh impetus. Pier Francesco de Medici had become eager to see the workshops of Cafaggiolo restored to their former prosperity and by means of the fine productions of the Fattorinis, which inspired other potters in the vicinity, this was achieved. Cafaggiolo artists worked with richer colours and a greater sense of style than was usual at Faenza where maiolica decoration was on the whole more spontaneous due to its free, impressionistic character.

Deruta, near Perugia, became one of the foremost centres in the production of maiolica. Some of the finest wares of the type made south of the Apennines issued from Deruta workshops. Colour schemes were usually harmonious in effect, executed in attractive tones of deep orange, blue, pale violet, yellow and bluish-green. Figure subjects were a speciality of Deruta painters, some artists becoming skilled in a difficult technique involving scraping away the white enamel and thereby exposing the buff-coloured body to simulate flesh tint.

There appears little reason to question a tradition that the first Italian lustre-decorated maiolica was produced at Deruta. Potters working with lustre pigments emulated the lustre-painted wares of Valencia. Metallic lustre pigments were in use at Deruta as early as 1501. A characteristic early lustre was derived from silver, first as a pale-yellow metallic pigment and later much richer toned. Although ruby lustre was invented after experiments with copper it was very inferior to the glowing red lustre used later at Gubbio. Deruta potters ultimately mastered a difficult lustre-painting technique derived from that developed long before by Islamic potters.

At Gubbio, in Umbria, the art of lustre painting on earthenware attained its highest pinnacle of achievement in Italy. Master Giorgio – Giorgio Andreoli – was probably the most accomplished exponent of the technique to work in Gubbio where he became renowned for his splendid wares embellished with glorious ruby-red lustre. Evidently, besides decorating his own wares in his workshop, such was the fame of Master Giorgio that wares were sent to him by other potters to be lustre-decorated, often from far distant places.

From the early sixteenth century potters and artists began moving from one workshop to another, spending varying periods of time working in different styles and following the techniques of the several schools within whose sphere of influence they happened to be. It was not unusual for a potter to seek the services of a reputable craftsman or painter. In consequence, a single workshop employing craftsmen and artists from distant places might turn out wares varying in form and manner of decoration according to the training or taste of those concerned in its production.

It is generally conceded that the finest Italian maiolica was produced well before the end of the sixteenth century. Baroque taste and the enduring traditions of maiolica decoration were not always compatible, but in the transitional or early baroque period some Italian masters in maiolica contrived to produce excellent wares decorated in such a manner that they combined the milder elements of baroque design with traditional form. The Urbino school continued to exert influence upon other schools in northern Italy throughout the sixteenth century and well into the following century. This is especially true of the Ligurian school and of the production of Agostino Salamone in particular. At Albissola, in the workshops of Salamone, Levantino Grosso, Seirullo and others, potters specialised in the production of drug jars and table services decorated in brilliant colour.

The school of Savona became noted for its characteristic linear or calligraphic style of decoration. Savona workshops were among the first in northern Italy to produce wares inspired by the beautiful Genoese silverwares of the period. At Savona and Albissola artists developed an attractive free style of painting in baroque taste. The renowned Chiodo family adopted an increasingly popular sketchy style in the decoration of their pottery which was remarkably original in concept and finely modelled. Light-blue became a characteristic Chiodo background colour. Numerous Savona and Albissola potters were inspired by the fine whiteware originated by Faenza potters in the early seventeenth century.

At Genoa the Guidobono family attained high repute and prosperity as master potters engaged exclusively in the production of maiolica. Giovanni Antonio Guidobono and his sons Nicola, Bartolomeo and Giovanni Bartolomeo specialised

32 SPOUTED DRUG JAR.
Maiolica. Savona, c1670,
Italian. *H 7in*

in superb dishes painted in enamel colours in which a pleasing light-blue predominated. Relief designs executed on large dishes were very ornate, enhanced by
the beauty of the painted decoration, sometimes in filigree reminiscent of a Faenza
style, though more often featuring cherubs and shells within medallions. Numerous
potters emulated Guidobono maiolica wares which are among the finest produced in
Liguria during the seventeenth century. The Corrado family made free use of
forms and decorative techniques originated by the Guidobonos in the modelling
and decoration of their wares. When the Corrados removed to Nevers in France they
continued working in an Italianate manner obviously derived from Guidobono
techniques.

At Angarano, near Bassano, the Manardi brothers conducted an important
workshop established in 1649. For a period the principal wares made were in
emulation of Faenza whiteware. As a result of becoming influenced by the Savona
school, the brothers later changed their style. Besides shapes which obviously
derived from silverware the Manardi became celebrated for their extremely beautiful
maiolica plates that varied little in form but were exquisitely decorated by highly
accomplished artists in an astonishing variety of designs based on pictorial representation. Manardi plates were usually embellished with pictorial designs derived
from engravings, notably those of Marco Ricci, comprising landscapes, ruins and
houses standing amidst trees. An unusual feature of the decoration of these plates
is the manner in which the 'picture' covers the surface of the plate from centre to

edges, eliminating the conventional border. Colours are usually subdued, in soft tones of green, blue, yellow and mauve.

Maiolica was produced throughout Italy, but the productions of the south were generally poor in comparison with the splendid wares made in northern centres. An important exception among the merely imitative potters of the south was Carlo Antonio Grue who, with members of his family, produced fine maiolica during the late seventeenth and early eighteenth centuries. The Grue workshop was situated at Castelli in the Abruzzi. Grue undoubtedly owed the continuing prosperity of his business to the brilliant specialist work of his four sons, Francesco, Anastasio, Aurelio and Liberio. In earlier years the Grue palette comprised orange, light-green, a warm yellow and rich blue. A later cooler palette of soft colours proved eminently satisfactory in the decoration of high quality wares. As time went by, however, the style of the artists became monotonously repetitive, causing Grue maiolica to lose its popularity.

With the passing of the eighteenth century and the development of pottery and porcelain manufacture in Germany and France the Italian maiolica industry entered upon a period of decline. A number of prominent workshops continued to prosper early in the new century but enterprise and invention gradually diminished. Many factories survived only by imitating French styles. The Coppellotti family of Lodi were among the first to forsake tradition in this way.

In about 1745, in his workshop in Milan, Felice Clerici began manufacture of attractive vases copied with remarkable exactitude from Japanese Imari originals. Clerici's decoration in Oriental taste caused a stir and it was not long before his productions were being extensively copied in Italy. A celebrated Modenese potter, Geminiano Cozzi, owner of a porcelain factory at Venice, produced good quality maiolica wares. At Le Nove in the Veneto at the turn of the eighteenth century the potters Pasquale Antonibon and Giovan Battista made excellent maiolica decorated in rococo taste.

But for Italy the great era of maiolica production was over and the glory departed. Ceramic design and manufacture gradually became centred north of the Alps in France where faience assumed new styles and imitated porcelain in an endeavour to arrest the decline in popularity of ornamental earthenware.

The so-called *sgraffiato* technique, practised in Italian workshops before the fifteenth century, reached Italy via the Near East where potters had long used it extensively. Most probably the technique originated in China. After further development of the technique by Italian potters in the sixteenth century wares decorated in *sgraffiato* vied in attraction and popularity with maiolica wares. Bologna and Padua became noted centres for *sgraffiato*-decorated wares. Fine quality wares of the type were made in the late seventeenth century by Antonio Maria Cuzio working at Pavia.

Sgraffiato or 'scratched' technique entailed creating scratched or cut designs on red or buff earthenwares glazed with ordinary transparent lead glaze. Usually the glaze was yellow-toned due to the presence of iron in the lead ore. Sometimes the glaze was stained brown, green or copper. After the first firing, wares were dipped in white clay slip to obtain a light-coloured surface upon which a dark pattern could be produced. In working out his design by scratching or cutting away the white slip surface to expose the red or buff body the artist produced a pleasing effect of contrast. In more elaborate decoration the artist added colour to the design by applying touches of underglaze pigments. The ware received a coat of lead glaze and a second firing completed fusion. Lead glaze tended to run in the kiln, blurring the pigments, but often, where running of colours due to heat was not too excessive, the effect was not unattractive.

The following brief account of the more important early Italian porcelain factories principally touches upon directors, modellers and artists working in Italy during the eighteenth century. More specific details of techniques followed in the making, modelling and decoration of porcelain, as developed at Meissen and emulated by the Italians, will be found in the ensuing section concerning masters at Meissen.

With the exception of Medici porcelain, early Italian porcelain largely owed its character and development to the influence of the Meissen factory. Marquis Carlo Ginori, Charles of Bourbon and others depended upon foreigners, principally Germans, for the design and decoration of wares produced in their factories, which could scarcely have operated successfully without their presence. Considerable time elapsed before Italian workmen and artists acquired sufficient technical and artistic skill to allow their being left to work without supervision by foreign specialists. This situation existed in porcelain factories established in Italy during the first half of the eighteenth century.

Documents and traditions survive that indicate the possibility of porcelain having been produced in Italy prior to the appearance of Medici porcelain which, wherever truth lies, must be regarded as the first soft-paste porcelain made in Europe.

Francesco I de Medici, Grand Duke of Tuscany (1574–87), was responsible for the fitting up of the workshops in the Boboli Gardens adjoining the Grand Ducal Palace (now the Pitti Palace) in Florence where the first Medici ceramic experiments were conducted. The porcelain which resulted was somewhat poor in quality, with many flaws in its composition owing to the vitreous substance of which the paste was mainly composed reacting uncertainly to heat during firing. Nevertheless, the ware, which is rare and precious today, is not devoid of beauty. Had production continued, with eventual improvement of materials and techniques, very splendid wares might have been made in the taste and spirit of the Renaissance.

Vasari's pupil, Bernardo Buontalenti, later famous as an architect, was also talented in several arts and crafts. He controlled activities in the grand ducal workshops and took charge of porcelain experiments. It is probable that the original Medici porcelain formula originated in the Near East and may have reached Buontalenti and his master, the grand duke, by way of Greece. Francesco I is

33 LARGE DISH.
Maiolica. Painted in
brown, showing Mars
conversing with Cupid,
against coloured
landscape background.
Angarano, Italian.
D 18½in

reputed to have searched for a porcelain formula for ten years before obtaining sufficient practical information on the subject to enable him to venture into production. No doubt Buontalenti designed many of the shapes of wares which issued from the Medici factory. Others with technical knowledge were more closely concerned with mixing the paste and the firing process, among them Flaminio Fontana, a member of the celebrated family of potters at Urbino.

Both in paste and workmanship Medici porcelain was defective. Wares were translucent, the body exhibiting a yellowish tone and covered with a heavy glutinous glaze apt to develop bubbles or cracks in firing. Few surviving examples of Medici porcelain are truly symmetrical due to the clay tending to sag in the kiln during firing.

Oriental designs, floral motifs and painted decoration inspired by maiolica wares were principally favoured in the embellishment of Medici porcelain. Patterns derived from Chinese porcelain made an early appearance on Medici productions. Polychrome painted decoration on Turkish wares was also copied, but in blue-and-white instead of the full range of bright colours.

An authority, Arthur Lane, has written of the 'faintly magical quality' of Medici porcelain, arising from its unique character, its scarcity (only about sixty examples are known to survive), and the somewhat romantic aspect of its origin. That it is beautiful and of unique character cannot be denied. We find expressed in this first European ware produced in emulation of the great ceramic art of China both profound admiration and a passionate desire to continue the pursuit of its elusive secrets. Craftsmen in the Medici workshops were no doubt only too acutely aware of technical defects that marred their porcelain productions. Opportunity of improving techniques were unfortunately curtailed by the death of Francesco I in 1587. A century was to pass before further experiments in porcelain production were initiated in Europe.

Not quite the first, but certainly the most important concern to manufacture porcelain in Italy was the celebrated factory established at Doccia in 1737 by the Marquis Carlo Ginori. By curious chance, the factory at Doccia was situated only a few miles from Florence where the Medici workshop was set up.

It is believed that the Marquis became interested in the production of porcelain at the beginning of the third decade of the eighteenth century, and that in or about 1735 he commenced experimenting with Italian clays. His opportunity came during a visit to Vienna in 1737 when he met and took into his service a number of experienced ceramic modellers, artists and workmen. Most eminent among these was Johann Carl Wendelin Anreiter von Zirnfeld, a talented porcelain decorator thought to have worked briefly in Vienna for du Paquier. Both Johann Anreiter and his son Anton worked as decorators at Doccia. The father was experienced in porcelain-making techniques though he appears to have been responsible for little besides painting while at Doccia.

Carlo Ginori himself, ably assisted by Giovanni Targioni-Tozzetti and Jean Baillou, conducted the early experiments to produce a satisfactory paste. He was granted porcelain production rights in Tuscany without delay but does not appear to have produced sufficient wares for marketing until about 1746. Meantime, the firm's chief modellers were the sculptor Gaspare Bruschi and his son Giuseppe. The latter entered the Ginori factory shortly before 1778 when his father died. Both Anreiters left Ginori employ in 1746 and returned to Vienna where, after his father's death in 1747, Anton took up employment in the imperial porcelain factory. The Ginori factory did not become commercially successful until Lorenzo Ginori succeeded his father in 1757, by which time the famous *masso bastardo* paste was in general use at Doccia. *Masso bastardo*, of which the basic ingredient consisted of clay from Lucchesia, though quite satisfactory to work with, was not used after the early years of the nineteenth century when the formula was lost. The early *masso bastardo* hard-paste body was greyish in colour and the somewhat dull glaze was sticky-looking and yellowish in tone. The finest late eighteenth-century Doccia wares were composed of a translucent white body over which a cold white glaze incorporating tin oxide was applied. From a technical viewpoint, the Doccia paste may have seemed better suited to modelling than to production of tablewares.

Underglaze blue decoration was much favoured at Doccia under Carlo Ginori. Bowls, cups, coffee-pots and teapots, among other useful wares, were produced in baroque style, painted a greyish-blue under the glaze in designs that show Chinese influence. The Anreiters worked in an elaborate manner whether depicting landscapes or flowers and foliage. Their successors at the factory carried on an established

34 *(left and right)* PAIR OF DECORATED ITALIAN FAIENCE INKSTANDS AND COVERS
FORMED AS SEATED PAGODA FIGURES. *H 8in;* *(centre)* A VENICE (COZZI) DECORATED
PAGODA FIGURE. Seated holding a flower and a disc bearing the letter V. *H 5¼in.*
Seated in a contemporary silver pavilion with foliage in silver wirework enriched
with seed-pearl grapes: with Turin silversmith's mark RVP, c1765

tradition as the century passed, though following the prevailing rococo style with
the admirable restraint characteristic of Doccia. The technique of scratching painted
surfaces in order to create details in white on a coloured ground was much used in
the period 1780–1800. Sèvres blue ground and arrangement of designs were emulated, usually very successfully. Doccia artists were highly competent, almost
invariably selecting their subjects and colours carefully with due regard to ultimate
effect, a procedure unfortunately not followed by all painters of porcelain elsewhere
at the period. Some interesting work was executed by Giovanni Battista Fanciullacci,
a 'miniaturist' who often signed his pieces.

Undoubtedly, the outstanding productions of the Doccia factory include the
delightful varied series of figurines made since the early years when porcelain
figures from Meissen and Vienna were being enthusiastically copied by every factory
in Europe. Many Ginori figures have been erroneously attributed to Capodimonte,
but certain distinctive characteristics simplify identification. On the whole, Doccia
porcelain figurines are less sensitively and skilfully modelled than Capodimonte
productions. Small heads and large hands are characteristic of Doccia figures.
Moreover, Doccia bright colouring, the frequent presence of firecracks and a
rather sticky-looking glaze are absent from Capodimonte porcelain figures.

107

The earliest series of Doccia figurines included characters from the Italian Comedy, frequently standing on shell-encrusted bases. There is considerable speculation as to which factory deserves credit for their invention, but unquestionably Italian Comedy figures made at Doccia are much more attractive than similar models produced in the imperial factory at Vienna. Doccia modellers were very successful with their animals. During the early period dwarfs were represented in brilliant colours, also sea-monsters and Oriental characters in a style similar to that favoured at Meissen and Capodimonte. Fine groups of the four seasons were mounted on plain or rococo scrolled bases. Peasant figures, grouped against trees, standing on elaborately moulded and relief-decorated bases, were produced in quantity from the late eighteenth century until well into the following century. The Doccia factory proceeded to reproduce many of its earlier models during the nineteenth century, working with a different paste but using the original moulds.

Interest in Venice in the potential of porcelain manufacture existed from an early period when, according to tradition, an alchemist named Master Antonio discovered a secret process and produced simple porcelain vessels in his workshop.

The first Venetian porcelain factory was established in 1720 by Francesco Vezzi, a goldsmith by calling who was also an enterprising man of business. After his ennoblement in 1716 he travelled extensively abroad and probably while in Vienna first met Christoph Konrad Hunger, a goldsmith, the partner of Claude Innocentius du Paquier, the ceramist granted a patent to manufacture porcelain in Austria.

There is little doubt that Vezzi learned the secrets of porcelain manufacture from Hunger who showed no scruples in revealing the formula which had been filched from the royal porcelain factory at Meissen. Hunger was a competent painter of porcelain besides being a goldsmith. During his brief association with each man in turn he took advantage of opportunities to obtain vital technical information concerning the making of porcelain from Böttger, reputed European discoverer of the secret process, and later from Stölzel who deserted the Meissen factory at Hunger's persuasion and joined him in Vienna. Hunger began his association with du Paquier in 1717. The latter was at that period engaged in experiments which did not yield hoped-for results until 1719, at the time that Samuel Stölzel defected from Meissen. The three men, du Paquier, Hunger, and Stölzel, continued their uneasy association for only a brief period. After quarrels and accusations Stölzel returned to Meissen, while du Paquier struggled on alone after despicable conduct by Hunger brought about the termination of his connection with the imperial factory.

In 1720 Vezzi formed a syndicate in Venice for the manufacture of porcelain. Hunger was invited to Venice to join Vezzi in his experiments to compose a satisfactory paste. Documentary evidence survives proving that not long after the establishment of the concern Vezzi transferred control to his son Giovanni who ran into financial difficulties in 1727 and brought about the dismantling of the kilns.

35 (*left*) GROUP OF THREE CHILDREN. Around a sundial. After a Sèvres biscuit model. Green, yellow and puce colouring. Doccia, Italian. *H 5¾in*; (*right*) FIGURE OF ISABELLA'S MAID. From Italian Comedy, modelled by Simon Feiner. Höchst, German. *H 8¾in*

Giovanni later fled into exile. China clay for making porcelain had to be obtained from Aue in Saxony. Owing to export licence difficulties Vezzi smuggled the material into Italy by pretending it was blue starch. The use of this clay, which was also used by the royal factories at Meissen and Vienna, accounts for the similarity of the pastes produced at the three factories. Following his flight to Meissen when the financial crisis brought operations to an end at Venice, true to character, Hunger notified the authorities that the Vezzi factory secretly obtained its most essential material from Aue, which resulted in a complete ban on its export and the end of production in Venice.

Owing to the short life of the factory Vezzi wares, especially figurines, are extremely rare. Indeed, some authorities maintain that none exist. It appears improbable that Vezzi produced more than a few free-standing figures. The colour of the translucent paste is greyish, cream or cold white, while the glaze has a wet

36 GINORI ARMORIAL
PLATE. From the Isola-
Marana service. Centre
painted crowned
coats-of-arms within a
purple baroque scroll
cartouche. Borders with
formal foliage and
trellis-work in green and
iron-red, and reeded
hexafoil rim. Arms of
Marchese Francesco
Marana and his wife
Laura Isola to whom it
was delivered before
30 October 1750. Italian.
D 9¼in

appearance and is brownish where thickly applied. In almost every aspect Vezzi porcelain exhibits the characteristics of German porcelain. In early productions the surface of the cold white porcelain has an uneven appearance, the bases are not completely covered with glaze and the shapes tend to be slightly unsymmetrical. Early wares were frequently painted in underglaze blue or black, the designs often rather sketchy, with touches of enamel colours and occasionally rich gold outlines on the edges of figures and flowers. Oriental motifs were also favoured in imitation of Meissen porcelain. Little information has come to light concerning the artists and modellers employed in Vezzi's factory. Hunger, of course, possessed technical knowledge and was a competent designer and decorator, otherwise we have no documentary sources from which to obtain information as to who besides Hunger and a painter named Ludovico Ortolani executed the decoration on some of the charming wares produced over a period of seven years.

Geminiano Cozzi founded one of the most successful Venetian porcelain factories in 1764. The concern flourished until 1790 when financial difficulties caused a serious set-back in production. Disaster was averted and the factory continued producing earthenwares and porcelain until 1812 when the end of Venetian independence brought its closure.

Between 1764 and 1790 the output of the Cozzi factory was enormous. Productions included figurines and groups of widely varying quality and character. It is not easy to identify Cozzi figures with certainty as they were rarely marked and the paste closely resembles that of other Venetian factories, Le Nove in particular. Sometimes the hard grey Cozzi paste is mistaken for that of Doccia, but it is considerably paler in tone than the Doccia paste. Moreover, the shiny Cozzi glaze bears no resemblance to any used at Doccia. Compared with the productions of other rival Venetian factories, some Cozzi figures are considered to lack vitality principally due to poor modelling. Early Cozzi figures and groups are mounted on rococo scroll bases. Circular pedestals are characteristic of later models. Cozzi specialised in modelling Italian Comedy characters, Chinamen and dwarfs. Colours in general use included purple, brownish-red and a distinctive, rather repellent, yellowish-green.

It is known that Cozzi acquired much of his expertise from his earlier association with Pietro Lorenzi. The Venetian Senate readily granted Cozzi permission to erect a kiln at Canareggio. Undoubtedly, Cozzi was fortunate in procuring supplies of clay from the Tretto quarries near Vicenza for his first experiments. Although Cozzi's hard-paste was once referred to as 'hybrid soft-paste' by no less an authority than Alexandre Brongniart, distinguished director of Sèvres, it is, by all recognised characteristics and standards, hard-paste. As Arthur Lane has pointed out, both Doccia and Cozzi pastes were undoubtedly of the hard variety, different, for example, from Capodimonte paste. The greyish Cozzi paste was not free of defects, but any inferiority of the paste was compensated for in the quality of design and decoration.

Cozzi employed technical experts as well as the best artists he could find. Arduini, the geologist, was one of his principal advisers. The modeller Sebastiano Lazzari, who also worked at Le Nove, was only one of many talented craftsmen whose excellent work contributed to the success of the Cozzi factory.

Decoration on Cozzi tablewares was very diverse in form and in most instances of high artistic merit. Flowers were a favourite subject for painted designs on coffee-pots, cups and services. Oriental as well as European flowers were depicted by artists, in garlands, sprays, and twining above crowned monograms. On excellently modelled Cozzi figures the colouring was nearly always pleasing, applied with commendable restraint except when an artist over-indulged in the use of the distasteful yellowish-green already referred to. Perhaps Cozzi figures of Venetian youth, garbed in brilliantly coloured, rich attire, are the most charming objects made in a factory which over a period of nearly half a century consistently produced fine wares.

Le Nove di Bassano, a village situated on the mainland not far from Venice, had long been a traditional centre for pottery manufacture when Pasquale Antonibon, a successful maker of maiolica, opened his new porcelain factory in 1762. Experiments in porcelain production had been conducted at Le Nove for ten years preceding the opening of the factory. Antonibon was assisted in his experiments by Johann Sigismund Fischer, a native of Dresden, formerly employed as an artist

37 PAIR OF VASES. Porcelain. Stippled by Giovanni Caselli, one with scenes of Flora offered flowers and fruit by cupids and putti, the other with Diana and Actaean. Borders with gilt bands. Capodimonte (Carlo III), Italian. *H 14in*

at the imperial porcelain factory in Vienna and who subsequently worked as a painter at the Capodimonte factory. In his later experiments to produce porcelain Antonibon was assisted by the geologist Arduini and Pietro Lorenzi, a former associate of Geminiano Cozzi.

Antonibon unfortunately fell ill soon after being granted a concession to manufacture porcelain and was absent from his factory until 1765. Many of his craftsmen left his employ to work for Cozzi, although as time passed after Antonibon's resumption of work a number returned to Le Nove. Employment of the same craftsmen by Cozzi and Antonibon resulted in a close similarity of their wares. Antonibon continued production of porcelain until 1773 when, after his ennoblement, he gave up business and entered political life. The porcelain factory apparently remained inoperative until 1781. Antonibon leased his maiolica factory to Giovan Maria Baccin who ran a successful concern for some thirty years. In 1781 Antonibon leased the porcelain works to Francesco Parolin who built up a thriving concern over the following twenty years after which, from 1802 until 1825, the factory was controlled by Giovanni Baroni.

The Le Nove paste scarcely differs from that of Cozzi, and there is little variation in colours used in either factory for the simple reason that many craftsmen worked in both factories. In later years, however, under Parolin, artists at Le Nove worked with a more extensive palette that included an attractive rose-pink and a beautiful green never seen on Cozzi wares. Le Nove decoration of the Parolin period was altogether finer and more interesting than that on wares produced under Antonibon, especially richly ornate painted designs on services. Domenico Bosello and Giovanni Marcon were outstanding members of Parolin's staff. Bosello modelled a range of delightful animated figures, peasants, mythological deities, putti, musicians, children at play, dancers and rustic characters, all executed in a highly individualistic manner with great sensitivity and realism. Groups usually stood on rococo-style bases, but frequently with supports in neo-classical taste. Giovanni Marcon was a somewhat eccentric but brilliant artist with an exceptional talent for decorating porcelain. He signed much of his work, but even when unsigned it is not difficult to recognise his painting on Le Nove porcelain.

Jean-Pierre Varion, a Frenchman, worked as a modeller for Antonibon in early years at the Le Nove factory. Varion later moved to Este where he worked with Brunello and later collaborated with another eminent modeller, Gerolamo Franchini, trained as a goldsmith, in the creation of a magnificent porcelain pyramidal centrepiece called *Parnassus*. Varion's compositions were delicately executed, always animated and true to life.

Le Nove figurines and groups often resemble Cozzi models, with the difference that they are usually of finer quality and are distinguished by their ornate bases representing rock work pierced with holes into which greenery and flowers are inserted. A series of pairs of figures representing fashionably attired eighteenth-century men and women, standing on circular pedestals, were produced at Le Nove. Although the original Le Nove porcelain factory closed in 1825 ceramic production has continued in the locality. White and cream-coloured earthenware has become a modern Le Nove speciality and many figurines in eighteenth-century style, emulating porcelain prototypes, are made by craftsmen following old techniques and traditions.

Charles of Bourbon, King of Naples and the Two Sicilies, built the palace of Capodimonte outside Naples in 1734. His wife, Maria Amalia Christina of Saxony, was the grand-daughter of Augustus the Strong, founder of the renowned Meissen porcelain factory. Charles came to share his grandfather-in-law's passion for porcelain and in 1743 he erected a factory in his palace grounds. Production continued for only a relatively brief period of sixteen years, until 1759, when Charles succeeded to the Spanish throne. Before he departed for Spain the king persuaded most of his staff to leave Italy in order to continue working for him in the new porcelain factory he established adjacent to the palace of Buen Retiro at Madrid.

Translucent, usually pure white, beautiful soft-paste Capodimonte porcelain is deservedly admired. Without exception, it is the finest porcelain produced in Italy during the eighteenth century. In the initial stages of the enterprise Livio Ottavio Schepers of Naples was made responsible for the all-important composition of a satisfactory paste, but when he proved unreliable after only a few months in the factory, his son Gaetano Schepers was put in charge of experiments and succeeded in developing a superb paste that served the needs of the factory throughout its existence. The chief painter until 1752 when he died was Giovanni Caselli who was succeeded by Johann Sigismund Fischer, an artist formerly employed at Le Nove. In his turn, Fischer was succeeded upon his accidental death in 1758 by Luigi Restile.

Giuseppe della Torre, an outstanding painter, specialised in the decoration of tablewares, principally tea-services. Della Torre's work is notable for interesting landscapes, marine and battle scenes and figure subjects. In his early years at Capodimonte, della Torre usually painted in monochrome, black, red, violet or blue. He later worked in polychrome with an extensive palette. Giovanni Caselli's niece Maria also showed herself to be a capable porcelain decorator in both monochrome and polychrome. Her best work consisted of floral subjects of such high standard that her compositions rivalled, and cannot always easily be distinguished from, her uncle's flower painting.

Occasionally Capodimonte porcelain is found with a slightly greenish-yellow or pinkish tinge, but pure whiteness is characteristic. The glaze is not 'wet'-looking nor glossy, as found on wares of some other Italian factories, but is lustrous, closely fused to the body, and frequently has a fired matt surface advantageous to painters in the execution of complex designs. Gilding for the most part was carefully applied, intended to enhance a design by setting off colours rather than as decoration in itself. Gilding was undoubtedly applied too thickly on some wares which have survived with their painted decoration unimpaired but with the gilding worn away.

Early Capodimonte figures and groups modelled by the celebrated Gricci are among the most exquisite objects of their kind ever produced in Europe and certainly by far the finest created in Italy. Gricci was principal modeller at Capodimonte throughout the factory's existence. All Capodimonte figures attributed to Gricci are brilliantly modelled, not always with the closest attention to detail, but invariably beautifully decorated. Jesters, lovers, characters from the Italian Comedy, are realistically depicted with vitality and captivating grace. Gricci's power as a modeller was unsurpassed. From the Neapolitan State Archives, which contain much information concerning operations at the Capodimonte factory, it is known that, besides subsequently specialising in figure-modelling, Gricci made moulds for other types of wares, including snuff-boxes. In this branch of production Gricci was assisted by, or worked in collaboration with, his brother Stefano and Gaetano Fumo, a specialist in flower modelling. Ambrogio di Giorgio, by trade a gem-cutter, also made moulds of flowers and fruit for attachment to sweetmeat-baskets and moulds for portrait-medallions.

From details given in the Neapolitan State Archives concerning Capodimonte porcelain it is possible to gain a clear idea of Gricci's wide range in figure production. Although the paste was considered difficult to work, Gricci manipulated it with extraordinary skill and the self-assurance of a master. Perhaps the charm of his

38 TERRACOTTA MODELS FOR CAPODIMONTE FIGURES AND GROUPS: (*left*) a
spaghetti eater modelled by Giuseppe Gricci. *H 10½in*; (*centre*) a model for a
group of Neapolitan peasants. *H 8in*; (*right*) Pantaloon from Italian Comedy
modelled by Giuseppe Gricci. *H 8¼in*. All Italian

figures and groups owes more to graceful poses and their gay animation than
attention to detail and exactitude, indeed fine detail in figures by Gricci is not
characteristic. He concerned himself much more with attractive poses. Small heads
are typical of Gricci figures.

The magnificent 'Porcelain-Room', a masterpiece in Capodimonte porcelain,
made in the period 1757–9 for the royal villa at Portici, now stands in the palace of
Capodimonte bereft of its famous great chandelier, shattered during World War II.
The room, measuring approximately 18 by 14 feet, is made entirely of porcelain
and is decorated in rococo taste with gay *chinoiserie* ornamentation. Superb
craftsmanship bears witness to the accomplishment of Giuseppe and Stefano
Gricci, who modelled it, and Fischer and Restile who executed the fine decoration
on the pure white walls in brilliant enamel colours enhanced by gilding. The master
craftsmen of Capodimonte could have no more striking and fitting memorial than
this unique room made for the queen who was initially responsible for Charles of
Bourbon's consuming passion for porcelain.

Ferdinand IV, King of Naples and Sicily, who succeeded his father, Charles of
Bourbon, in 1759 at the age of eight, grew up to become a porcelain enthusiast. He

founded the royal factory at Naples in 1771 which flourished until 1800 when the kingdom became involved in the Napoleonic struggle. Royal Naples porcelain is composed of a highly translucent soft-paste with a distinctive glassy appearance. The factory began production in rooms which Ferdinand built on to the royal villa at Portici. Production can be divided into three periods, at Portici in 1772, under the second director Tomas Perez, 1772–9, and under directorship of Domenico Venuti, 1779–1806.

The Marquis Ricci, ably served by his modellers Francesco Chiari and Francesco Celebrano, produced excellent wares until his sudden death only a few months after the commencement of activities at Portici. Under his successor, the Spaniard Tomas Perez, the factory staff was increased. Among the painters newly engaged was Saverio Maria Grue a member of the noted family of maiolica makers at Castelli in the Abruzzi.

As the materials used were basically the same, early Naples porcelain naturally bears close affinity with later productions of Capodimonte. The Naples paste was prepared by a former member of the Capodimonte staff, Gaetano Tucci. For some years all the productions of Naples were executed in rather feeble rococo style. Unfortunately, wares were often impaired by flaws resulting from miscalculated or badly controlled firing. Busts of Roman emperors, biscuit ware, figures of women in elaborate costume and groups of mythological gods and goddesses became specialities of the factory.

With the appointment of Domenico Venuti as director in 1779, production was expanded and the style of wares underwent rapid change. Neo-classicism had meanwhile superseded rococo in Western Europe. Venuti, who proved an able and enterprising director, was quick to perceive that growing interest in the classical antiquities being excavated at Herculaneum would promote a complete change in taste. As a result, a number of painters and modellers employed at the factory who either refused to or could not change their style were sacked. The celebrated sculptor Filipo Taglioni was appointed chief modeller in Celebrano's place. Antonio Cioffi and Giacomo Milani became the leading painters specialising in the embellishment of magnificent services, including a famous one made to the order of the king for presentation to his father at Madrid.

During Venuti's directorship the character of the Naples glaze underwent transformation due to adoption of an opaque tin glaze which caused the body to lose translucency but at the same time imparted extraordinary brilliance to painted decoration. Wares took on a striking maiolica effect.

Taglioni was an unusually vigorous modeller particularly interested in the production of biscuit figures. He often worked in collaboration with the modellers Giosué d'Antonio and Giovanni Pecorella. A massive biscuit group depicting Jupiter and the Titans executed by Taglioni survives at Capodimonte. The group, which is about five feet high, may not appeal to modern taste but leaves no doubt concerning Taglioni's ability as a modeller.

Following the French occupation of Sicily in 1806 the factory passed into the control of Jean Poulard Prad. With his advent the entire concept of porcelain production at Naples changed.

Traditional techniques and standards of good craftsmanship in ceramic production endured in Italy through the nineteenth century and have continued to prevail until the present time. New factories were established when conditions became more settled and a number of master potters produced excellent wares. After the unification of Italy ceramic design and ornamentation followed the general European trend towards flamboyance. Use of garish colours and fanciful shapes were indicative of universal decadence during the last quarter of the nineteenth century. Since the mid-twentieth century, however, Italian studio potters have taken the lead in a significant return to good design and form that augurs well for the future.

GERMANY AND AUSTRIA

Germany has an ancient tradition in pottery production reaching far back into the past. Earthenware and stoneware made by the German potters through the centuries are comparable in interest and quality with the best wares of similar type produced elsewhere in Europe. The most important achievement of German experimentalists in the sphere of ceramics was the development and production of porcelain following the initial discovery at Meissen, near Dresden, in Saxony.

For the practical purpose of this book, attention is here focused upon the techniques, productions and careers of master potters, modellers, designers and decorators associated with the first two European hard-paste porcelain factories established at Meissen and Vienna. Consideration is also given to the work of a brilliant Nymphenburg *modellmeister*, regarded by some as the most accomplished modeller of porcelain figures to have worked in Europe.

At most other important German factories, including Frankenthal, Höchst, Berlin, Fulda, Ansbach, Ludwigsburg, Fürstenberg and the Thuringian factories, excellent wares were produced. In general, craftsmen in other German factories endeavoured to emulate the styles and techniques of Meissen. Until the rise of Sèvres later in the eighteenth century, it was to Meissen that designers, modellers and artists constantly looked for inspiration.

It will not be considered necessary, it is hoped, to give an account here of the sequence of events leading to the founding of the royal porcelain factory at Meissen by Augustus the Strong, except to briefly relate the circumstances of an association between two men closely concerned with the project. That Augustus was a passionate admirer of porcelain who started his own factory in 1710 in order to make the first European hard-paste porcelain is widely known, but precisely how Meissen porcelain evolved may be less a matter of common knowledge.

Although Johann Friedrich Böttger is usually regarded as the first man to produce hard-paste porcelain in Europe there can be little doubt that its development was initially due to the prolonged experiments of the Graf von Tschirnhausen. The earliest porcellanous body produced in the Meissen factory was in any case not true porcelain due to the use of alabaster in the composition. It was not until much later that feldspathic rock was used as a fusible stone and the Meissen body thereby became true porcelain.

Von Tschirnhausen, a Bohemian nobleman attached to the Saxony court, became interested in discovering the secret of porcelain manufacture in the last quarter of the seventeenth century when he began an extended series of experiments. After research into the uses and potential of fusible substances, including

39 (*left*) COLUMBINE WITH A DOVE. Porcelain figure, modelled by J. F. Eberlein.
In a gold trimmed hat, white bodice, yellow apron and turquoise skirt. *H 4¾in*;
(*centre*) COFFEE POT WITH COVER. Stoneware, by J. Böttger. Spout with gilt
metal terminal. Sides decorated with prunus sprays and incised baroque cartouches, and with stepped square cover and engroiled angels. *H 6in*; (*right*)
PANTALOON. From a series of porcelain Italian Comedy figures modelled for the
Duke of Weissenfels by J. J. Kändler and P. Reinicke (inspired by Joullain's
illustrations for Riccoboni's *Histoire du Theatre Italien*, Paris 1727). Meissen,
German. *H 5¼in*

his efforts to fuse *kaolin* by means of radiant heat, generated with the aid of an iron
reflecting mirror, by the last decade of the century von Tschirnhausen had acquired
extensive technical knowledge of ceramics. He made important research into the
nature of clays and chemical reaction.

All von Tschirnhausen's experiments were conducted without the aid of a kiln.
No kilns had yet been constructed in Europe capable of attaining the great heat
required in firing hard-paste porcelain. Von Tschirnhausen was therefore obliged
to work principally with adjustable reflecting mirrors. There is slight evidence that
von Tschirnhausen did in fact produce a body closely resembling Chinese porcelain
at some time prior to the awakening of Augustus's interest in his experiments. It
was probably at the instigation of Augustus that von Tschirnhausen visited Delft
in 1701 to study kilns used by Dutch potters which were known to be capable of
reaching high temperatures. In the same year von Tschirnhausen travelled to
Paris and was permitted to observe production methods in the soft-paste porcelain
factory at St Cloud.

40   SOUP TUREEN, COVER AND STAND. Porcelain. Decorated Kakiemon style. Finial
modelled by J. F. Eberlein in 1741. Meissen, German. *W 15in*

It is practically certain that by the time Böttger appeared on the scene von
Tschirnhausen, encouraged by Augustus, was on the threshold of attaining his
objective. Little good can be stated concerning Böttger's early career. He was born
in Thuringia in 1682. After gaining some knowledge of chemistry in his youth he
became apprenticed to a Berlin apothecary who was more interested in alchemy
than in soundly training his apprentice in chemistry. In 1700 Böttger fled from
Berlin where he had convinced King Frederick I of Prussia that he would ulti-

mately transmute base metal into gold. After a spell in Wittenberg Böttger contrived to ingratiate himself with Augustus the Strong on whose behalf he undertook to conduct metal transmutation experiments at Dresden. Böttger failing to produce the promised gold, the king placed him under the surveillance of von Tschirnhausen who possibly pleaded for Böttger's life when he was imprisoned in the Albrechtsburg Fortress. No doubt von Tschirnhausen saw in him an able assistant. The king agreed to the two men continuing to work together in efforts to make porcelain and in 1707 even provided a new laboratory.

As an 'arcanist', namely a man professing to know the secret processes of porcelain manufacture, Böttger did in fact make practical contribution to the eventual success of the workshop experiments instituted by von Tschirnhausen. Böttger's knowledge of production methods was far less extensive than he claimed, however. Within a year of the setting up of the new laboratory the two men were able to show Augustus wares they had made and plans were formulated for the erection of a factory at Dresden-Neustadt where it was proposed to produce faience. A decision was subsequently taken to make red stoneware, an early speciality of the Meissen factory particularly associated with Böttger who managed the workshops while von Tschirnhausen continued with experiments.

According to a number of German authorities, some time before he died in 1708 von Tschirnhausen may have succeeded in making true porcelain incorporating feldspathic rock as an ingredient. If this is so, he appears to have withheld the discovery from Böttger, who used alabaster as a fusible stone in his early wares which were thus not true porcelain.

Von Tschirnhausen's sudden death in 1708, followed by Böttger's assuming complete control of experiments in progress and his announcement of the discovery of the porcelain manufacturing secret in March 1709 have given rise to considerable uncertainty as to who made the final technical break-through. The debatable question as to who actually invented the paste and glaze, and devised the method of colouring and production processes generally, remains unanswerable. Presumably Böttger brought experiments to a successful conclusion in the few months that elapsed from the time of von Tschirnhausen's death to Böttger's dramatic and sensational announcement. If, as is highly probable, the unveiling of the porcelain secret was the culmination of von Tschirnhausen's lengthy research and experiments, then the credit of discovery was justly his. The king, however, cared little about rights and wrongs. All that mattered to Augustus was that success had come at last and the prospect of unlimited quantities of porcelain being produced in his factory excited and dazzled him.

At that early stage, although the Albrechtsburg soon housed a new porcelain factory, Böttger was far from confident concerning the quality of the wares he proposed to manufacture. He felt anxious about technical problems for which he had not yet found a solution. Uncertainty was created by the unpredictability in firing of the white Colditz clay used during the first months of manufacture. A search was subsequently made to locate a more suitable material and at the end of 1710 a satisfactory and reliable clay was discovered at Aue which led to a much-needed improvement in Böttger's paste.

The secret porcelain production techniques developed at Meissen did not remain secret for long. For a time only two directors of the factory shared the secret, one the composition of the body and the other the composition of the glaze. Secrecy ended when three men who defected from the factory between 1717 and 1719 carried away with them vital technical information put to good use elsewhere. Christoph Konrad Hunger joined du Paquier in Vienna in 1717. Samuel Kempe established his own red stoneware factory and Samuel Stölzel defected to the Vienna factory in 1719.

Böttger's first commercially successful productions made at Meissen were stonewares, principally red stoneware although other varieties were made. For a considerable time after 1708 Böttger was bedevilled by technical problems, but his worries did not prevent him from turning out a diverse array of wares made from an extremely hard red body. There followed white and blackish-grey stonewares,

41 (left) EARLY MEISSEN CHINOISERIE BEAKER and odd saucer. By J. G. Höroldt. Figures within cartouche in iron-red lustre and gold; (centre) COFFEE POT AND COVER. Pear-shaped. Scroll handle and gilt spout painted in manner of C. F. Höroldt with river landscape scene and finely coloured *indianische blumen*, puce and gold *laub-und-bandewerk* cartouche. *H 8in*; (right) EARLY MEISSEN CHINOISERIE BEAKER AND SAUCER. Painted by J. G. Höroldt. Decorated with figures in gold lustre in *laub-und-bandelwerk* cartouches. All three porcelain.
Meissen, German

also a black-glazed type in a somewhat softer paste. These wares varied considerably in quality.

Red stoneware was produced in greatest quantity. Although the body of all stonewares produced in Böttger's time at Meissen was basically of the same composition, variation in surface colouring was probably obtained by firing control. It has been suggested that Böttger's black-glazed stoneware was developed from kiln-wasters. The ware was coated with an attractive glaze composed of a mixture of cobalt and manganese. Occasionally heavy gilding was applied, possibly to conceal surface faults.

Böttger's stonewares were frequently elaborately decorated. Incised decoration was applied by using a glass-engraver's wheel, a leaf-and-strap-work design of the *laub-und-bandelwerk* type being the most common. A technique of producing patterns by means of the glass-engraver's wheel used in grinding and cutting the hard surface of stoneware was followed by Bohemian glass-engravers employed at Meissen for the purpose. Böttger's stonewares were occasionally mounted in gold and silver, or even set with semi-precious stones, the work usually being entrusted to Augsburg and Munich craftsmen.

Moulded decoration was also applied to stonewares, usually in the form of naturalistic representation of acanthus and ivy leaves and flowers, the plastic work generally being of high order. Red stoneware was usually highly polished, the craftsmen following the same technique as used in polishing glass. Gilding was normally applied after firing. Enamel colours and lacquer pigments were only infrequently applied. Most surviving examples of Böttger's stonewares have moulded or incised decoration; colour, if used, has worn away.

At the commencement Böttger's wares were inspired by the works of German goldsmiths and Chinese ceramic wares. Undoubtedly Johann Jakob Irminger, goldsmith to the Saxony court, was responsible for a number of designs. That inspiration was derived from metalwares is evident from the frequent use of modes of ornament more suited to metal objects.

Böttger's earliest figures in stoneware were produced from moulds. Moulds were used in production of a variety of decorative objects. The stoneware body was also considered a suitable medium for making large vases and tablewares. In course of time all technical difficulties were overcome and the material then presented few problems in plasticity and firing in the making of an extensive range of ornamental and useful wares. Stonewares continued to be produced at Meissen until the 1730s, but after Böttger's death in 1719 the scale of production gradually diminished.

Böttger's experiments in glazed and unglazed white porcelain progressed far enough to enable him to exhibit examples at court. The body, containing alabaster, was considered satisfactory when manufacture commenced in 1713. Meissen porcelain did not lose its yellowish tinge until the advent of J. G. Höroldt, who perfected a pure white porcelain body. White clay obtained from Aue greatly improved the body in early years but as Böttger continued to use alabaster – though it seems improbable that he could have been totally ignorant of the superiority of feldspathic rock in paste composition – Meissen porcelain continued to lack the whiteness achieved later when feldspathic rock replaced alabaster. The presence of tiny bubbles in the glaze may have been due to firing into biscuit before application.

Böttger was never altogether successful in use of enamels. The development of Meissen enamel decoration in a range of brilliant colours that could be satisfactorily fired was not brought about until J. G. Höroldt, a trained enameller, arrived from Vienna with Stölzel. Böttger's enamel colours comprised a frequently used rose-pink, violet, yellow, green, blue and iron-red. In about 1715 Böttger introduced a purplish-coloured lustre, perhaps accidentally developed during experiments. If rarity of surviving examples is any indication, Böttger seldom applied the colouring to his wares. Possibly in preference to lustre, Böttger made frequent use of gold and silver, which could be satisfactorily fused on the glaze. Gold was used in a number of ways, often to excess, to enhance colours or as a ground. Silver ultimately ceased to be used in decoration because it invariably oxidised to black.

Despite difficulties experienced, Böttger made extensive use of enamel colours in the decoration of white porcelain wares, but the standard was never high compared with the exquisitely painted enamel decoration executed by painters in later

42 SET OF FIGURES OF SOLDIERS. Porcelain. In the Electoral Saxony uniform of lime-green and iron-red; on white bases. Meissen, German. H 4½in

periods. Floral designs were carried out in enamels in formal baroque style. Patterns of flowers in rose-pink enamel were popular. In later years a limited amount of monochrome decoration appeared, but under Böttger's direction Meissen artists displayed little enthusiasm for monochrome painting. The use of iron-red in depicting landscapes and buildings on porcelain may indicate Böttger's aim to vary the decoration on wares, but the standard of such work was generally far from high.

When he commenced porcelain manufacture Böttger seems to have felt hesitant about introducing new shapes and modes of decoration. Much of his early porcelain imitated the conventional forms of his red stoneware. Formal baroque moulded decoration applied in designs of flowers and leaves had already appeared on stonewares. Only occasionally were Böttger's early porcelain wares decorated in lighter vein, the formal moulding replaced by pleasing naturalistic flowers and foliage executed in relief. Böttger endeavoured to devise a satisfactory underglaze blue using cobalt as a medium, but judging from surviving examples of his porcelain thus decorated in a faulty manner it is evident that his attempts met with only moderate success. A serious technical problem was presented by the tendency of cobalt blue to blacken unless fired at precisely the right temperature. Colour chemists at Meissen did not succeed in developing a satisfactory cobalt blue for use in underglaze decoration until 1720. At best there was always a risk that the decoration would develop defects during firing. As a result, underglaze blue decoration was never applied to early Meissen wares to any large extent.

Among the few Böttger porcelain figures extant probably the most striking are figures of dwarfs, considered by some authorities to have been modelled by Georg Fritzsche and which were undoubtedly inspired by the engravings of Jacques Callot, later a source of inspiration for modellers in other European factories. A mould production technique used by Böttger in making Chinese-type porcelain figures entailed producing moulds directly from Chinese prototypes in the royal collection.

Samuel Stölzel remained at Vienna until 1720 when, according to early accounts, as an outcome of not receiving his promised salary from du Paquier, he returned to Meissen. Apparently as a gesture of reconciliation, he persuaded one of his colleagues at Vienna, the young enameller Johann Gregor Höroldt (alternatively spelt Herold), to accompany him home to Saxony.

It was Höroldt's destiny to assume an important role in affairs at Meissen almost from the time of his entering the factory. His influence and authority remained strong until 1735. Little is known of Höroldt's antecedents except that he was born in Jena in 1696 and is believed to have trained as a painter in enamels on ceramics at Vienna under C. K. Hunger. Höroldt subsequently added new enamel colours to the Meissen palette. It has been suggested that Höroldt acquired his knowledge of secret colouring processes from Hunger and passed off new techniques as his own inventions. Höroldt took his place in the forefront of Meissen painters from the time he arrived at the factory with Stölzel, and within the space of two years, due to Höroldt's brilliant work, Augustus appointed him court painter.

Höroldt's arrival at Meissen initiated or perhaps merely coincided with the commencement of what is referred to as the 'painter's period' at the factory, which lasted until 1735 when the 'modeller's period' began, during which the production of figurines became of major importance. Figure production then took precedence over all other activities until about 1763.

As chief painter, Höroldt assumed complete control of painters employed in the factory. He decided what designs should appear on wares and supervised all decorative work. Groups of artists were made responsible for certain types of decoration, specialising in subjects according to their individual talents.

Höroldt prospered and became increasingly influential after his appointment as factory manager in 1731. He usually had matters his own way and encountered little opposition concerning the design and decoration of wares until the advent of Johann Joachim Kändler, a young gifted modeller. Kändler was the protégé of a forceful director at the factory, the Graf von Brühl. It became apparent from the start that friction between Höroldt and Kändler would lead to serious trouble. Kändler's influence, promoted by von Brühl, grew stronger with passing years, particularly when figure production took precedence over the manufacture of other wares. With Kändler's increasing importance in affairs, Höroldt's position at the factory grew more untenable. Despite frequent quarrels, however, the two men continued in their respective capacities until 1756, which saw the opening of the Seven Years War that ultimately brought disaster to the factory. Höroldt fled to Frankfurt and did not return to Meissen until 1763 where he worked for another two years before retiring. He died in 1776.

Soon after Böttger's death in 1719 a decision was taken to attempt to improve the Meissen paste by the substitution of feldspathic rock for alabaster. It is not known who was responsible for making the change, which proved successful. The body improved in quality, gained in tractability and a denser whiteness was obtained. Among a number of problems that confronted the factory management following the death of Böttger the most serious was connected with enamel colours. Böttger never divulged all his secret knowledge concerning the techniques of preparing enamels and their application. A crisis in the factory was averted by the timely appearance of Höroldt who was much more accomplished in the use of enamel colours than anyone previously connected with Meissen. His knowledge of enamel techniques was certainly far in advance of Böttger's. As a result of Höroldt being given a free hand in development of an extensive new palette of brilliant enamel colours, Meissen became celebrated for painted decoration on wares, particularly magnificent decoration applied over coloured grounds. Höroldt increased the range of colours, introducing a vivid purple, new shades of green, an intense red and a rich turquoise; he also imparted greater purity to the colours and firing became less a matter of hazard. A number of technical problems were not

43   PAIR OF MEISSEN PORCELAIN AND LOUIS XV ORMOLU FIGURES OF A COCK AND
HEN. Modelled by J. J. Kändler. First modelled in 1741. German. *H 10in*

overcome by Höroldt for several years. Blue continued to give trouble. An enamel
blue was introduced in about 1728 but was little used.

Höroldt did not originate the use of *chinoiserie* decoration on porcelain. *Chinoiseries* were painted in enamel on Meissen wares in Böttger's time, but in a different
style. Höroldt took great interest in the art of *chinoiserie*, as is borne out by an
engraving depicting *chinoiserie* subjects published in 1726 which bears his name.
Engravings were the principal source of inspiration in *chinoiserie* decoration at
Meissen but Höroldt, it appears, only permitted artists to draw on his own works.
Chinoiseries were either painted directly upon the white porcelain or, less frequently, executed on coloured grounds. Designs were usually carried out in brilliant
polychrome. Gold was sometimes used to enhance colours. Often when *chinoiseries*
appeared on the plain white surface of wares they were in 'picture' form, extending
round an object and connected with trailing flowers or framed within elaborate
gilt scrolls. Variation in the style of *chinoiserie* embellishment consisted of painted
scenes or single figures executed in reserve panels bordered in gold. On Böttger's
wares decorated with *chinoiserie* touches of lustre pigment were occasionally used,
but after his death the lustre pigment was seldom used and not at all after 1730.

In the period of Höroldt's greatest influence at Meissen less use was made of
mould techniques and the finest wares were thrown on the wheel. For a time the

44 *Vase and cover.*
Chinoiserie. Augustus
Rex, Meissen porcelain.
Rare yellow ground,
painted with two large
panels depicting
Chinamen. German.
H 14in

use of moulds practically discontinued and craftsmen were encouraged to develop their skill with the wheel.

Höroldt introduced a series of striking ground colours in the late 1720s. Chinese forms and modes of decoration were in favour at the time, but the colours used, though inspired by ancient Chinese colouring, were considerably different in tone. In or about 1726 Höroldt invented a beautiful yellow ground that particularly delighted Augustus. Höroldt subsequently succeeded in producing the colour in tones varying from palest ochre to an intense yellow. The colour was used most effectively as a ground for *chinoiseries* and floral patterns.

Johann Joachim Kändler succeeded J. G. Kirchner as *modellmeister* at Meissen in 1733. Kändler was the most accomplished and celebrated of the Meissen modellers. Whether he was a more brilliant *modellmeister* than the famous Bustelli of the Nymphenburg factory is a matter of opinion.

Kändler was born at Fischbach, near Dresden, in 1706. In 1723 he was apprenticed to the court sculptor Benjamin Thomae. As a young sculptor Kändler displayed such exceptional talent that the king appointed him court sculptor in 1730. Von Brühl, a director of the porcelain factory, supported Kändler in his continuous opposition to the master modeller Kirchner and Höroldt. Kändler frequently voiced his disapproval of the ideas and methods of the other two men. In a very short time he proved himself a much more competent modeller than Kirchner. In 1733 Kirchner resigned and Kändler took his place, continuing as chief modeller at Meissen until 1775.

As with Höroldt in his capacity as chief painter, as chief modeller at Meissen Kändler controlled the large group of modellers employed in the factory. For the greater part of time artists followed his instruction in design and techniques but were occasionally left to work out ideas of their own. It is perhaps hardly necessary to note that the predominant influence of Kändler is evident in all Meissen models of his time. It is estimated that Kändler created, either entirely unaided or in collaboration with one of his two principal assistants J. F. Eberlein and P. Reinicke, upwards of one thousand different models. His highly original figures were not only copied by modellers who followed after him at Meissen, but also inspired modellers working during his lifetime and long after in the principal European porcelain factories.

As Kändler's fame rests upon his achievements as a figure modeller, it may be of some interest and value to outline the techniques of porcelain figure production followed in most German factories during the eighteenth century.

For the most part, German porcelain figures were produced from moulds cast from an original master-model usually made of clay or wax. Wooden master-models were also used, but seldom. Use of moulds facilitated unlimited reproduction. Due to shrinkage of the clay figure in firing it was important for the modeller to make allowance in size. In order to allow vapour to escape from the hollow figure during firing a small vent-hole was made in the back or base which, as the various factories placed the hole in different positions, helps in determining the provenance and authenticity of figures. Where a considerable amount of undercutting was necessary figures were usually made in sections in separate moulds. The parts of elaborate groups and single figures were joined together by a skilled assembler, known as a 'repairer', who was specially trained in the vital technique of joining up the moulded sections with slip before they hardened. A repairer normally worked from a master-model. Although he assembled figures from sections cast in the same mould variation often occurred in their finished appearance owing to slight differences in the position of limbs or heads, intentionally or accidentally effected during assembling.

Whether modelling an Italian Comedy character, an animal, a monkey-band, street vendors, dancers, gallants or peasants, Kändler's unsurpassed mastery of techniques, novel invention and sense of humour gave his models a unique character. Kändler's finest creations appeared during the period when the baroque style reached its zenith, preceding the exuberant exaggerations of rococo. As was practicable, indeed essential, in their design, the majority of Kändler's male figures stand supported by pedestals or tree stumps. Ample crinoline skirts provide sufficient support for female figures. An admirer and exponent of the baroque style, caring little for the exuberance of rococo, Kändler demonstrated his unfavourable reaction to neo-classical trends in fashion during his declining years by his somewhat apathetic attitude to the style, as is evident in his last works.

As a craftsman from whom only the finest work could be expected, Kändler retained his reputation throughout his career. His least satisfactory creations, from his own viewpoint, were the porcelain animals he made alone, or assisted Kirchner to make, for Augustus the Strong's Japanese Palace at Dresden. The animals were designed to be as near life-size as the material allowed. Firing difficulties proved almost insurmountable. It was found that many animals would not withstand even a single firing, which made the use of enamel colours in decoration impracticable. Lacquer colouring was tried but proved unsatisfactory. In consequence, many figures were left white.

Kändler preferred to model from nature, particularly when creating animal figures. Even the life-sized animals he modelled for the Japanese Palace were in most cases made after studying living animals in Augustus's menagerie. Kändler also had opportunity to observe the shape and movement of birds in the royal aviary. His talent for realism and his keen perception of form and character enabled him to infuse life into his models. Although the point remains controversial, it is not unreasonable to opine that even Bustelli failed to impart greater animation to his figures. For the most part Kändler gave his animals extraordinary life-like expressions, while their natural postures are indicative of his training as a sculptor and knowledge of anatomy.

Porcelain figurines were first conceived at Meissen as table ornaments. Some of the earliest figures made were attached to sweetmeat dishes. Kändler's originality and versatility as a modeller gave a new dimension to the porcelain figure. Examples which issued in growing number from Meissen, mostly of Kändler's invention and entirely his work or completed by highly competent modellers and repairers under his supervision, set a new fashion in Europe.

Before 1735 Kändler was principally occupied in designing moulded decoration for services, of which the first notable production was a superbly designed and executed service made for Count Sulkowski. In production of the magnificent so-called Swan Service Kändler was aided by his talented assistant J. F. Eberlein. After 1735 Kändler devoted much more time to modelling figures, beginning with a series of Italian Comedy characters.

Kändler's earlier figures were painted in richer enamel colours and stood on less elaborately shaped bases than his later lightly coloured creations mounted on decorated scrolled bases in rococo taste. Baroque heaviness was earlier expressed in use of brilliant colour and contrasting black. As the years passed, with rococo superseding baroque, Kändler gave his figures bases of elaborate character, often richly gilded.

As already noted, Kändler evinced little admiration for the rococo style, but he found it expedient to follow fashion. His later work in a style he disliked did not detract from the charm and quality of his productions. As an example of his skill and versatility he designed a splendid mirror and console table for Augustus III to present to Louis XV of France. The royal gift was taken to Paris by Kändler himself in 1750.

Much of Kändler's work in figure production during the 1740s and 1750s was executed in collaboration with his two brilliantly accomplished assistants Johann Friedrich Eberlein and Peter Reinicke, but undoubtedly Kändler's finest and most original models of the period were entirely his own in conception and production. His mythological figures, created to meet the popular taste of the day, were superb, as were a series of figures which appeared in 1745 inspired by the *Cris de Paris* engravings of the Comte de Caylus after Bouchardon's drawings. Satirical and humorous themes often inspired Kändler in his modelling. His interest in classical mythology and other popular subjects of the period, such as the seasons, love and courtship, matrimony and all manner of allegories, offered wide scope for his talents. His hunting figures, depicting men, women and animals involved in the chase, were brilliantly conceived in realistic poses and amazing variety. Realism was perhaps the most striking characteristic of Kändler's figure modelling.

Some writers on the subject contend that Kändler's Italian Comedy figures fall short of the technical perfection, realism and vitality of Bustelli's similar figures produced at Nymphenburg. Whether such an assertion expresses a majority opinion or not, it is indisputable that Kändler revealed the full extent of his creative power with his captivating theatrical figures. He was always fascinated by the character of Harlequin whom he modelled in many different poses beginning with an early series.

Possibly as an outcome of his collaboration with Kirchner in the production of massive animal figures for the Japanese Palace, Kändler always displayed interest in large-scale production. His failure to complete the *Reiterdenkmal*, a huge equestrian statue of Augustus III, was one of the major disappointments of his life. The work was conceived with great enthusiasm. Preparations began in 1751. The *Reiterdenkmal* was to be created by means of a series of plaster moulds and a building was erected in the Albrechtsburg in order to carry out the project. When, by reason of insurmountable technical difficulties stemming from the great size of the porcelain monument, the project had finally to be abandoned, Kändler experienced bitter disappointment that affected him for many subsequent years. Nearly all the partially completed monument was destroyed. All that remained was a bust of Augustus.

Christian Friedrich Höroldt (or Herold), born in 1700 and probably a kinsman of J. G. Höroldt, was one of the most brilliant ceramic artists employed at Meissen during the eighteenth century. It is believed that he trained as an enameller in the workshop of Alex Fromery in Berlin. Most of Höroldt's working life was spent at Meissen where he remained from 1725 until 1777. Through a period extending over more than half a century Höroldt, like his more eminent kinsman, executed painted decoration comparable with the finest work on German porcelain. His work in *chinoiseries* executed during the late 1720s and into the 1730s was unsurpassed in mastery of style and brilliant composition. It is probable that C. F. Höroldt was responsible for the introduction at Meissen of a *chinoiserie* style, featured with notable success, that consisted of replacing the conventional scroll-work bases of *chinoiseries* with grass and rock ornamentation. Höroldt was also a talented landscape painter and worked skilfully in miniature.

Apart from his undoubted success in factory management, as chief painter at Meissen the work of Johann Gregor Höroldt was of first importance. From his earliest years in the factory he exercised strong influence on Meissen painting styles. In addition to his knowledge and skill in the use of enamel colours, his flair for devising arresting colour combinations and complex designs gave him artistic superiority over all other Meissen artists of his day and placed him in the forefront of ceramic artists at work in Europe. He was particularly successful in designing the decoration of services. Under his instruction and influence Meissen painters executed some of the finest painted decoration ever seen on tablewares.

Flower painting at Meissen, which principally comprised two distinctive types, was also invariably brilliantly executed. Flowers depicted, divided into two categories, comprised *indianische Blumen* or Indian flowers and *deutsche Blumen* or German flowers. Indian flowers included Oriental-inspired varieties, principally of Chinese and Japanese derivation. German flowers – first introduced at Vienna and featured extensively at Meissen from the mid-1730s – included European flowers in varying form and style.

Until late in the 1730s floral decoration by Meissen artists continued very formal with no attempt at innovation. By the end of the decade, however, painters were executing attractive naturalistic floral decoration in the form of colourful sprays and bouquets on a white ground. Johann Gottfried Klinger became one of Meissen's most notable flower painters. He was apprenticed in the factory and remained there until 1746 when he left to work at Vienna where he died in 1781. Klinger had a dislike of heavy gilding and was responsible for its eventual discontinuance at Vienna.

45   CAPTAIN OF THE GUARD. Porcelain figure modelled by Franz Anton Bustelli, c1755. Nymphenburg, German. *H 7¼in*

Franz Anton Bustelli stands in the same degree of importance and influence as *modellmeister* at Nymphenburg as Kändler at Meissen. Who was the greater master in *kleinplastic* will always remain a matter of personal opinion and taste. It suffices to observe, perhaps, that no other master modellers conceived such a diverse array of charming porcelain figures that by any criterion deserve to be adjudged works of art.

The Nymphenburg factory in Bavaria produced excellent tablewares and became renowned for the quality of its porcelain, but its reputation rested largely upon Bustelli's brilliant work as a modeller.

The Graf Sigismund von Haimhausen was director of the factory under the patronage of the Elector Maximilian III Joseph in the year 1754 when Bustelli first appeared at Nymphenburg though it is not known if he owed his appointment and advancement to von Haimhausen. Little is known of Bustelli's earlier life. He was born in Locarno in 1723. Perhaps due to his Italian origin, it is sometimes suggested that Bustelli may have worked at Doccia and acquired his knowledge of porcelain and figure modelling there, but there is no evidence to support the theory. Even the notion that Bustelli worked at Ludwigsburg for a brief period is not borne out by known facts. All that is known for certain is that he must have developed his remarkable talent as a ceramic modeller in young manhood prior to his arrival at Nymphenburg and that he owed his style to the influence of Franz Ignaz Günther, a Munich sculptor.

At first, Bustelli employed his talents in designing and modelling tablewares and services for the Bavarian court. He specialised in moulded decoration on dishes and tureens, executing flowers, fruit and leaves in rococo style. All signs of immaturity were entirely absent from Bustelli's work produced at Nymphenburg. Consistently, from start to finish, through some ten years spent in the factory, his productions were obviously the works of a man of exceptional skill executed at the peak of his creative power. In the opinion of some critics Bustelli's early figures do not exhibit quite the same powerful mastery of techniques, nor the characteristic realism of later productions, but the point is debatable. All Bustelli's models, of consummate elegance and charm, spontaneously conceived and executed with unsurpassed skill, are a joy to the eye.

To a greater extent even than Kändler, Bustelli gave his figures and groups theatrical poses and expressive gestures that seem curiously appropriate to their character. The open-mouthed Bustelli figure is characteristic, but if parted lips is to be adjudged a fault, the master turned it to advantage, so that a head moving in conversation or a smile loses nothing in attraction.

Like other modellers at work in Germany in his day, Bustelli drew inspiration from engravings, including the works of J. E. Nilson and Jacques Callot. Bustelli's celebrated series of sixteen figures from the Italian Comedy attest to his remarkable versatility. Bustelli's figures are endowed with a unique quality. Whatever his subject, street vendor, gallants and their ladies, or Harlequin, they display a spontaneity and animation combined with elegance and graceful pose that no other modeller of porcelain figures has surpassed. Early Bustelli figures on flat, undecorated bases and later productions on bases elaborately ornamented with rococo scrollwork exhibit the same high standard of material and craftsmanship found in all Bustelli figures made at Nymphenburg. Bustelli subsequently preferred his figures to be left white or only lightly touched with colour. Examples found painted in strong colours usually date from his first years at the factory.

Europe's second hard-paste porcelain factory began production on a commercial scale in 1717. For some time previous unsuccessful experiments to produce a satisfactory body and glaze had been conducted under the supervision of Claudius Innocentius du Paquier. In 1717 the Graf von Virmont, an Austrian nobleman posted to the court of Saxony, persuaded C. K. Hunger to leave the Meissen factory and join du Paquier at Vienna. According to Hunger, he learned the secret of making porcelain from his friend Böttger while the latter was intoxicated.

Hunger probably at first only possessed limited knowledge of the techniques of porcelain production. On his arrival at Vienna he commenced making porcelain using Passau clay but failed to produce a fine quality body. Whether or not the poor quality of Hunger's virtually experimental Vienna porcelain was really due to the use of Passau clay in the paste remains obscure. Certainly in his subsequent period at Vienna, working with Vezzi and using secretly imported Aue clay, the quality of Hunger's porcelain was relatively high. The fact that Hunger and du Paquier urged Stölzel, Böttger's kiln-master at Meissen, to join them at Vienna in 1719 suggests that Hunger lacked extensive knowledge of vital firing techniques in addition to his apparent inability to compose a good paste. Two significant changes coincided with Stölzel's arrival. Aue clay replaced Passau material in composition and the quality of Vienna porcelain immediately improved.

Stölzel undoubtedly saved the day at the Vienna factory by instructing workmen in firing processes. A further serious crisis in the running of the factory occurred when, as a result of a dispute with du Paquier concerning salary, Stölzel decided to return to Meissen, taking with him the Vienna factory's most competent enameller, the young J. G. Höroldt. The departure of the two men marked the beginning of a chain of troubles at du Paquier's factory which continued until the Empress Maria Theresa assumed control in 1744.

Vienna designers and decorators at first sought to achieve nothing more than emulation of Meissen wares. The early Vienna porcelain body has some affinity with that of Meissen except that it is rather less translucent and the glaze is generally free from the tiny bubbles present in Böttger's glaze. Vienna soon developed a distinctive style that owed nothing to Meissen influence. In the early period Vienna designers favoured moulded wares. The high standard of decoration on Vienna porcelain, especially painting, soon rivalled that of Meissen. Decoration known as *laub-und-bandelwerk*, a type of leaf-and-strap-work ornament long favoured at both Meissen and Vienna, was meticulously executed on white porcelain by Vienna

46   TEA BOWL AND SAUCER. Porcelain. Decorated in black and gold, with battle
scenes. Du Paquier period c1740, Vienna, Austrian

painters. Other German porcelain factories used this form of decoration and helped
to popularise it. At Vienna patterns were executed with exquisite delicacy and
artistry. *Laub-und-bandelwerk* ornamentation on Meissen wares usually encircled
painted scenes and *chinoiseries*. Vienna leaf-and-strap-work decoration was featured
in all-over designs on wares, with charming results.

Figure production commenced at Vienna during the early du Paquier period.
For the most part the first figures made at Vienna were used as ornamental mounts
on wares. Few free standing figures appeared, and of these, examples that survive
usually exhibit mediocre modelling and decoration. Under J. J. Niedermeyer,
appointed *modellmeister* in 1747, figure modelling at Vienna considerably improved
and production of porcelain figures became important. Niedermeyer was undoubtedly
a competent modeller who could be relied upon to produce pleasing figures, largely
inspired by the creations of other famous master modellers. On the whole, Niedermeyer's figures lacked originality and in consequence were generally uninspiring.
His techniques and style, developed through a conventional training in plastic
art, apparently excluded innovation, with the result that all his figures exhibit a
certain dull sameness and lack of spirit. During Sorgenthal's control of the Vienna
factory in the period 1784–1805, a series of charming biscuit porcelain figures were
produced in emulation of Sèvres productions, but though excellent in quality and
workmanship the Vienna figures were inferior to the French prototypes.

Vivid, lavishly applied decoration in enamel colours imparted richness to Vienna porcelain made in the last quarter of the eighteenth century. Designs were original, often extremely complex and invariably competently executed by the first-class painters who earned for the Vienna factory its reputation for exquisitely painted porcelain. Although decoration occasionally erred on the side of over-brilliance and artists did not invariably exercise restraint, painting on Vienna porcelain was consistently of the highest quality. One of the Vienna factory's most accomplished artists in the late eighteenth century, Philipp Ernst Schlinder, trained at Meissen, was unrivalled in the high standard of his work at Vienna both as a painter and arcanist. He was appointed chief painter in 1770.

Schlinder's collaboration with Josef Leithner in technical experiments proved invaluable. Leithner's knowledge of colour chemistry, supported by Schindler's practical experience in the field, led to their successful partnership in developing new colours. An attractive blue – Leithner blue – introduced in 1792 was enthusiastically received by the factory painters and used with notable success. In addition to introducing a number of other colours Leithner also invented a fine biscuit body.

In the latter decades of the eighteenth century, due to anxiety arising from the growing prosperity of the Sèvres manufactory following discovery of the hard-paste secret, the Vienna factory endeavoured to emulate decoration on the French wares. Sèvres porcelain had become superb in whiteness and texture, and its magnificent painted decoration in unique colours captivated all Europe. Colour chemists at Vienna made protracted experiments in efforts to discover the secret of the celebrated Sèvres *bleu-de-roi* and *rose Pompadour* but only limited success was achieved due, in part, to vital basic differences in the composition of the Vienna and Sèvres glazes.

FRANCE

Bernard Palissy, French Huguenot writer, sculptor and physicist, is undoubtedly the most notable figure in the history of the development of French 'rustic' faience. Born at Agen, Lot-et-Garonne, in 1510 (or, according to D'Aubigne, in 1499), Palissy first became interested in pottery during his travels in the Ardennes and the south while serving as a government surveyor. He had previously learned the techniques of painting on glass. Palissy settled in Saintes, near La Rochelle, in 1539, and began a long series of experiments in enamels. He knew virtually nothing of the potter's craft when he began interesting himself in the decoration of faience and was at first hampered by lack of knowledge and practical training. Palissy left a moving account of frustration, disappointment and disasters experienced through the sixteen years he laboured fruitlessly in his workshop. Years spent in unsuccessful experiments attest to the fervour of his dedication. As evidence of his determination to succeed, he recorded how, driven to desperation to keep his kiln going, he burned his furniture. Moreover, in his *De l'art de la terre* Palissy described how he conducted his experiments in constant dread of arrest due to his religious beliefs. He ultimately succeeded in producing an improved ware of maiolica type with a pure white enamel surface that presented a perfect ground for plastic decoration in the style known as *rustiques figurines*.

His technique perfected, Palissy proceeded to manufacture a range of wares chiefly comprising circular and oval dishes, sauceboats and ewers, exquisitely decorated with consummate skill. The ware was developed through four phases, the decoration principally consisting of nature subjects, mythological subjects such as Water, Fertility, etc, allegorical subjects in low relief and, in later years, imitations of metalwork. Plates were for the most part ornately embellished with designs of leaves, flowers, birds, fish and reptiles, the latter including lizards, frogs, salamanders, eels and snakes.

It does not appear that Palissy ever used a wheel. He seems to have preferred the mould process, finishing objects by hand, modelling and applying relief ornament. To recognise Palissy's individual work is not easy. He had many imitators and followers and the abundant productions of the Palissy school closely resemble prototypes made by the master. Furthermore, few of Palissy's pupils, including his sons, attained his degree of technical skill in the application of coloured glazes to the white enamelled body. Colours were rich, purple, yellow, blue, applied in harmonious arrangement on wares, contrasting with a greyish-white enamel that Palissy often used with brilliant effect. Palissy ware resembles faience, with a firm, non-porous body. In addition to his splendid productions in the *style rustique*

Palissy invented a ware known as *terres jaspées*, with moulded designs enriched with glaze in the manner of French medieval green-glazed ware from which it was derived.

As his beautiful enamel-decorated pottery became known and admired by wealthy patrons who acquired it for the adornment of their homes, Palissy attracted the attention of powerful personages who did not always prove to be his friends. His patron and protector the Duke de Montmorency probably saved his life on at least one occasion when he was seized and imprisoned as a Huguenot. The title of *inventeur des rustiques figurines de roi* was conferred on Palissy in about 1565 when, in order to save him from persecution, the duke persuaded the queen mother, Catherine de Medici, to take him into her service. A colourful pottery grotto was erected for the queen in the grounds of the Tuileries in Paris, where Palissy was also allowed to set up a kiln to work assisted by his sons. His last period of imprisonment on religious grounds began in the Conciergerie in Paris in 1588. He was

47　OVAL DISH. Bernard Palissy. Moulded in relief and naturally decorated in colours with an eel, a lobster, a snake and fish, frogs, and other reptiles among scattered shells on a blue ground, the reverse splashed in blue-green and manganese. French. *D 19in*

subsequently transferred to the Bastille dungeons where he died either in the same or the following year.

Italian maiolica inspired many potters at work in France during the sixteenth century. A leading Rouen potter, Masseot Abuquesne, produced pottery tiles and drug jars in the Faventine style, also favoured by Antoine Syjalon at Nimes in production of an impressive varied range of albarellos and dishes. Cornelius II Floris, working at Lyons, specialised in the production of wares inspired by the Urbino school. Pierre Esteve, at work at Montpellier later in the century, also adhered to the Faventine style. While the majority of French potters engaged in making faience at the period were inspired by Italian wares, in the St Porchaise pottery from about 1525 to 1560 an original style, indubitably French, prevailed. St Porchaise potters remained free of Italian influence until later years when the Urbino style was closely imitated. St Porchaise techniques were in several ways remarkable, particularly in the production of hard-bodied wares with incised and filled-in decoration in geometrical patterns. The technique probably derived from the engraver's art. Oriental porcelains and contemporary metal wares inspired early St Porchaise productions. In a later period, when the influence of Urbino became strong, the finest St Porchaise wares were skilfully decorated in relief in an Italianate manner.

48   OVAL TUREEN COVER AND STAND. Porcelain. Four-lobed. Painted Kakiemon style with Oriental flowers and insects. Chantilly, c1740, French

From the early seventeenth century to the mid-eighteenth century when maiolica, or faience as it is called in France, became very popular and was made in great quantity, Nevers was one of the chief production centres. In the most prosperous period, extending over nearly a century-and-a-half, the more important potteries expanded and numerous small potteries sprang up. A predominant Nevers decorative style of Near Eastern character embodying white and yellow birds and flowers on a deep blue ground was superseded in the eighteenth century by decoration in Chinese taste.

Rouen had long been a pottery manufacturing centre when, beginning in the late seventeenth century and continuing through the following century, a growing number of progressive, successful potteries were established. Of these, by far the most important was the concern owned by the faiencier Edme Poterat (d 1687). By the time that Edme's more famous son Louis began working in the factory Edme had become a potter of note. His son Louis's talent and ingenuity ultimately proved greater than his own.

To Louis Poterat (d 1696) is usually credited the introduction of *lambrequins*, a form of lace-like decoration with scallops that became extremely popular on both faience and porcelain. *Lambrequins* incorporate pendant lace-work, drapes and scrollwork as derived from the ornamental stamped patterns on leather book-bindings and patterns in lace. Floral and fruit swags were also sometimes embodied in design. Originally, *lambrequins* were looped and tasselled bed-valances. So far as is known, Louis Poterat was the first to feature designs based on *lambrequins* on ceramic wares.

The *style rayonnant*, a radial variant of *lambrequin* decoration, became a characteristic mode of decoration on Rouen faience at the end of the seventeenth century. While the introduction of the aforementioned new decorative styles and the production of porcelain are generally credited to Louis Poterat, there is little doubt that the enterprising potters of Rouen included other men of invention and knowledge who contributed in no small measure to the development of Rouen faience in the late seventeenth century. Louis Poterat specialised in wares decorated in the *style rayonnant*, producing hard-bodied maiolica that varied from red to grey in firing. The glaze used on this type of ware, on Poterat's originals and the productions of his imitators, was at first blue on white followed by the addition of ochre, red and green.

Louis Poterat was granted a privilege in 1673 to manufacture porcelain. Doubtless he had acquired a working knowledge of the techniques of porcelain manufacture, but for reasons unknown he produced very little. Technical difficulties experienced in attempting to manufacture on a commercial scale may have proved too formidable for Poterat to consider the project worthwhile. His claim that he knew all the vital secrets of porcelain production was supported by his assertion that the small amount of porcelain made in his factory was created by his hand alone for fear that workmen who might have assisted him would discover the techniques. Soft-paste porcelain attributed to Louis Poterat is characteristically covered with a brilliant greenish- or bluish-tinted glaze embellished with ink-blue lineal decoration When he died in 1696 Poterat's secret formula was lost.

A new technique in the decoration of faience reached France from Germany in the mid-eighteenth century. During the 1740s the Höchst factory in Germany developed a technique for applying enamel colours in *petit feu*. The method was introduced at Hannong's Strasbourg factory by the German ceramic artist Adam Friedrich von Löwenfinck. French potters adopted the new technique with enthusiasm. As a result, high-fired enamel decoration on wares was discontinued. Tin-glazed wares enamelled in *petit feu* colours to resemble porcelain, including the variant known in France as *faience-porcelaine*, were manufactured in numerous French pottery centres. The manner of decoration varied considerably. Late eighteenth-century faience produced at Strasbourg, Moustiers, Niderviller and Marseilles show affinity both in colours employed and decorative style. At Sceaux the noted faiencier Jacques Chapelle imitated the styles of Marseilles and Strasbourg faience with his finely decorated statuettes and tablewares.

The earliest French experimentalists who vainly endeavoured to discover the basic ingredients and learn the true nature of Chinese porcelain believed that glass was incorporated in the paste. As elsewhere in Europe, the French potters traditionally used a form of glass rendered opaque by the addition of tin oxide to glaze their wares.

When eventually the French potters devised a mixture of clay and ground glass the refractory character of the clay proved a stumbling block, since the melting point of clay is only attained in intense heat greatly in excess of that required to melt glass. However, by trial and error a workable clay and glass mixture was obtained and objects exposed to the heat of the kiln on the whole kept their shape but as heat could not be satisfactorily controlled and owing to the unpredictable nature of the body, a large proportion of wares collapsed in the kiln and were known as 'wasters'. A substitute or 'artificial' porcelain was invented when it was eventually realised that clay (sometimes with the addition of soap, as at Sèvres) gave the essential plasticity while melting glass produced vitrification. It was essential to balance ingredients carefully in correct proportion in order to obtain a workable mixture and avoid expensive kiln wastage. A white-burning clay and lime were included in the ingredients of French soft-paste porcelain.

Naturally, French experimentalist potters hoped to discover the secret of hard paste or true porcelain, as appeared imperative if their wares were to compete with Meissen productions. Several Frenchmen claimed to have discovered the process in the course of the eighteenth century and it is probable that the secret was in fact known in France long before the first objects made in hard-paste porcelain issued from the Sèvres factory. Jean-Etienne Guettard, a chemist associated

49 SEAU A BOUTEILLE.
Porcelain. Decorated in
chinoiserie, the shell and
foliage scroll handles
enriched with gilding,
and painted *en camieu
rose*. Vincennes, c1753,
French. *D 10¼in*

with the Duke of Orléans in experiments at the abbey of St Geneviève, announced
in 1751 that he had made hard-paste porcelain. It is not certain if the rare surviving
examples attributed to Brancas-Lauraguais can be accepted as proof that he also
made hard porcelain from a paste incorporating Alençon clay. Brancas-Lauraguais
porcelain, if such it is, is greyish in colour and of poor quality. Sèvres produced the
first true porcelain of quality made in France in 1769 after the factory's representa-
tives, Millot and Macquer, located *kaolin* deposits at St Yrieix near Limoges. In a
short time a number of other French factories began producing fine hard-paste
porcelain comparable in quality to Sèvres wares which they assiduously copied.

For the most part, French porcelain factories specialised in services and tablewares, and in ornamental objects, particularly vases. Figures and groups, except at
Sèvres where productions in biscuit porcelain assumed great importance, were not
produced on a large scale. French porcelain was usually decorated in enamel
colours, painted over glaze. It eventually became customary to apply underglaze
decoration only on inferior wares supplied to the lower classes. In early years, as
at St Cloud, painted relief decoration in Chinese style was popular, featuring prunus
blossom, inspired by the *blanc-de-chine* porcelain of Tê Hua. Painting on porcelain
was invariably the work of well-trained artists since decoration on wares so costly
to produce had accordingly to be of high standard. Unlike the situation experienced
at Meissen and other German factories, where cobalt blue underglaze decoration on hard porcelain was only achieved with difficulty, and at Meissen never
proved altogether satisfactory, French painters working on a soft-paste surface,
painting in cobalt blue, over which glaze was applied, were confronted with no
such problems.

50 EVENTAIL JARDINIÈRE (Vase Hollandaise). Porcelain. Painters mark of
Vieillard. Vincennes, c1754, French. W 10in

Soft porcelain lent itself admirably to the application of enamel colours. A
'muffle' (low temperature) kiln was used in firing which sometimes had to be repeated several times according to the colours used. The nature of soft porcelain
being as it was, sensitive to heat, during the firing of enamels the surfaces of wares
were prone to melt, thus absorbing the deeply fused colours.

Coloured grounds were used at most French factories. It was a mode of decoration at which Sèvres artists excelled and became pre-eminent. Reserved white
panels, outlined in gilt to conceal uneven edges, upon areas of colour, were decorated with an extraordinary variety of motifs. Ground colours were applied by different
methods, blown on as a powder or sponged on, which frequently resulted in uneven
distribution and depth of tone.

Among French porcelain factories which became celebrated for the quality and
beauty of their productions, the three earliest, those at St Cloud, Chantilly
and Vincennes-Sèvres, warrant special attention when considering the technical and
artistic development of French porcelain.

It has not been conclusively established that soft-paste porcelain was made at St Cloud prior to 1678 when the widow and family of Pierre Chicaneau, who died in the same year, were granted a privilege to manufacture. Letters patent to manufacture porcelain had in fact been granted in 1664 to Claude and François Réverénd who established a factory at St Cloud, near Paris, where they specialised in the production of tiles, quantities of which were used in the embellishment of the palace of Versailles. François Réverénd was subsequently assisted by his factory manager, François de Morin, apparently an arcanist of considerable practical experience and knowledge, but precisely what type of porcelain was produced is not known. From contemporary accounts it appears that a factory was operating at St Cloud in the last decade of the seventeenth century under the direction of a M. Morin.

By the close of the seventeenth century François Réverénd and M. Morin had both disappeared from the scene, at least in so far as may be concluded by lack of surviving evidence of their continued activity at St Cloud. It is not clear what became of their factory. It is relevant to mention again at this point, that besides the Réverénd and the Chicaneau family, as already noted, Louis Poterat of Rouen was also granted a privilege to manufacture porcelain in 1673.

The first authenticated soft-paste porcelain produced in quantity was made by the Chicaneau family under an important second privilege granted in 1702 by Louis XIV to the widow of Pierre Chicaneau and her children. The family had been engaged in porcelain manufacture since 1678, greatly improving on Pierre Chicaneau's original techniques and wares. By the end of the century the family claimed to make porcelain 'as perfect as the Chinese'. Production at St Cloud was under the patronage of the Duke of Orléans, the king's brother. Under control of successive members of the Chicaneau family porcelain continued to be made until 1766 when the concern went into liquidation.

St Cloud porcelain is distinctive in quality and appearance. The body is seldom pure white but has an attractive ivory or yellowish tone which is much admired. Potting is often somewhat heavy and firecracks are present. Due to the glassy nature of the body, the surfaces of wares are firm and smooth-textured. The glaze, resembling that of Mennecy wares, is brilliant and hard, with a firmly pitted surface. Undoubtedly, early St Cloud porcelain derived both its shapes and manner of decoration from Rouen faience. At Rouen, *lambrequins*, the *style rayonnant* and arabesques remained in fashion until well into the eighteenth century. A large proportion of St Cloud wares were inspired by contemporary silverwares, although at St Cloud designers displayed considerable versatility in adapting designs. Reeding, gadrooning, moulded and applied relief designs were executed, skilfully avoiding a heavy effect. St Cloud decorators shared a predilection for depicting Chinese prunus blossom, especially in relief decoration applied to the beautiful *jardinières* for which the factory became noted. Distinctive moulded scale patterns that appear on earlier *jardinières* were discontinued after about 1720.

Painted decoration in blue in *Louis Quartorze* style, derived from faience decoration originated at Rouen, informal arrangement of *lambrequins* and scrolls, is characteristic of St Cloud porcelain. Japanese enamel decoration was imitated, principally Kakiemon designs and colour arrangements. Some of the most exquisite painted decoration by St Cloud artists appears on charming porcelain snuff-boxes in the shape of animals, all beautifully modelled, many examples bearing dates covering the period 1730–50.

Blanc-de-chine figures, copies of Chinese originals, were made in limited quantity at St Cloud during the early period, but few examples surviving can be ascribed to an earlier date than 1730. As only a relatively small number of figures of various kinds were produced at St Cloud specimens have become very rare.

Chantilly, the most famous French porcelain factory after Sèvres, owed its establishment to Louis-Henri de Bourbon, Prince de Condé. The prince passionately admired Oriental porcelain and assembled a large collection of Japanese wares – chiefly Kakiemon decorated wares – in his chateau at Chantilly. In common with other wealthy European princes of the time, the prince desired to establish his own porcelain factory. An opportunity came in 1725 when he met Ciquaire Cirou, thought to have been formerly employed at the St Cloud branch factory in the rue Ville l'Eveque in Paris. As Cirou was apparently experienced in porcelain manufacture the prince lost no time in appointing him director of the new Chantilly factory. Cirou remained in control at Chantilly until his death in 1751, after which the factory passed through various hands and was finally owned by an Englishman, Christopher Potter, who became involved in disastrous speculation in about 1800 and was forced to close down. The beautiful soft-paste porcelain wares for which Chantilly justly became famous were not produced after about 1780.

Although it was possibly more tractable, the Chantilly body closely resembles that of St Cloud. Luzarches clay and la butte d'Aumont white sand were basic ingredients, with potash as a flux. During Cirou's period the porcelain produced at Chantilly was of extremely fine quality, covered with a distinctive glaze resembling that used on faience and rendered white by the use of tin-ash. The Chantilly factory was unique in this technique of using an opaque white tin enamel faience glaze over a porcelain body. Held against the light the original Chantilly body has a pale yellowish-green tone. Occasionally, air bubbles or 'moons' that occur much more rarely in English than French soft-paste porcelains are present in the Chantilly body. Practically no change was made in the paste and glaze until about the time of Cirou's death in 1751. At a period when increasing competition from rival factories was causing concern the Chantilly management decided to produce less costly wares. Possibly small quantities of tin-glazed wares may have been made from time to time thereafter, but from 1751 the factory specialised in the production of underglaze blue-decorated wares and ordinary transparent glaze was used. It is improbable that the early tin-glazed Chantilly porcelain, unrivalled in its pure whiteness and smooth texture, ceased to be made as early as 1735, as has been asserted.

51 (*left*) GROUP OF A RETRIEVER, ETC. After Oudry. Porcelain. Tournai. *H 7in*;
(*centre*) CLOCK CASE. White porcelain. Depicting Zephyrus discovering the sleeping
Flora. Vincennes. *H 11in*; (*right*) POT-POURRI VASE. Porcelain. Tournai. *H 6¾in*.
All three French

It should also be pointed out that, notwithstanding that from about 1750 a slight
alteration was made in the paste, imparting a creamy or yellowish tone to the body,
and ordinary lead glaze superseded the faience glaze, Chantilly porcelain retained
its quality and beauty.

Little is known concerning the identities of modellers and decorators employed
at Chantilly. Judging from surviving wares, only well-trained workmen of high
artistic and technical ability were engaged in production. Gilles and Robert Dubois,
the latter said to have been trained at St Cloud, and Louis Fournier, believed to be
the Vincennes modeller of the same name, are among individuals employed at
Chantilly known to us. The brothers Dubois deserted Chantilly for Vincennes
where they gave unsatisfactory service and were ultimately discharged. Fournier
arrived at Chantilly in 1752, having left Vincennes. He is thought to have principally modelled figures at Chantilly until 1756. A Chantilly kiln-master, Humbert
Gerin, who accompanied the Dubois brothers to Vincennes, erected the first kilns
used there. François Gravant, a former Chantilly grocer who developed skill and
knowledge in the preparation of pastes and potting generally, followed his friends
to Vincennes. Gravant's son, Louis-François, succeeded his father at Sèvres in
charge of paste-mixing. The younger Gravant took over the old Chantilly factory
in 1776. He was succeeded by his wife when he died three years later.

The restless, and in some respects unfortunate, German ceramic artist Adam Friedrich von Löwenfinck spent some time working at Chantilly after fleeing to France from Bayreuth in about 1736. Von Löwenfinck, accompanied by his artist brother Carl Heinrich, remained in France until 1740, but it is not known precisely how long he worked at Chantilly. Mention of Löwenfinck at Strasbourg has already been made. At Meissen he is thought to have introduced a variant of *chinoiserie* decoration which enjoyed a brief vogue. At Chantilly he was employed in flower painting, but among conventional floral designs executed on Chantilly porcelain of the period no work has been attributed with certainty to Löwenfinck.

Japanese wares from Arita provided the principal source of inspiration for early Chantilly designers and painters. Artists at the factory were eminently successful in the decoration of Oriental-inspired figures of which only a small number were made judging from present rarity. As a rule, the robes of figures, usually decorated in Japanese style, were embellished with floral designs composed of Indian flowers derived from Vincennes and Meissen. These very rare Chantilly figures were probably produced for a short period between 1740 and 1750 and in the absence of marks may usually be identified by the tin glaze covering the body.

Kakiemon porcelains from Arita in the Prince de Condé's collection were freely copied at Chantilly in the early period. Later, when the factory began producing original forms, the style of decoration was still strongly Japanese. As it was first believed that Kakiemon wares came from Korea, the Japanese-French style of Chantilly ware came to be known in France by the misnomer *à décors Coréens*. It does not appear that Kakiemon-style decoration continued in favour at Chantilly after the prince's death in 1740. Certain patterns became well known and variants appeared on wares made at other French factories as well as in England, at Bow, Chelsea and Worcester. The much imitated, so-called Prince Henri pattern, executed in red and gilt and based on a red dragon pattern popular at Meissen, was derived from Arita decoration. Chantilly painters also developed the popular squirrel and 'banded hedge' designs (*écureuil* and *haie fleurie*), the wheatsheaf (*gerbe*), quail or partridge (*caille* or *perdrix*), stork (*cigogne*) and others.

Meissen wares decorated in Oriental taste inspired Chantilly painters. From whatever sources Chantilly artists derived inspiration, their work was usually distinctive and finely executed. The soft, yet bright colours applied to the white tin-glazed surface, the patterns sometimes finely outlined in black, were invariably applied with charming effect. Rich red, bluish-green, pale yellow and serene blue fused deeply into the glaze in the manner peculiar to Chantilly porcelain.

In imitating Kakiemon decoration Chantilly artists worked with a palette constituted to allow almost exact copying. The palette comprised red, blue, brown,

52 (*Facing page*) PSYCHE. Statuette in biscuit porcelain on a base of *bleu du roi* porcelain painted with flowers. After Etienne Falconet. Base of statuette inscribed T 1762 and on base appears MDCCLXIV (1764). Sèvres, French.
H figure 9¼in, H stand 4⅝in

yellow, green, black and sometimes gilt. All colours were in tones as near to the original Kakiemon colours as could be achieved by the very efficient Chantilly colour-mixers.

When it became necessary to produce less elaborately decorated, cheaper wares after 1750, the resulting productions, decorated in a much simpler style, were nevertheless considered attractive and became popular. German flowers in under-glaze blue appeared on plates and dishes, the floral patterns combined with rococo scroll patterns. The Chantilly 'sprig', small sprays of flowers, was widely copied in France and abroad. Sometimes festoon borders in blue or other monochrome colours were printed round the edges of plates. The use of monochrome at Chantilly and elsewhere in France became imperative after 1752 when, in order to give the Vincennes factory in which he had a financial interest an advantage, the king issued an edict forbidding the manufacture of porcelain or the painting in colour of white pottery for a period of twelve years. Needless to add, supported by a royal mono-poly, Vincennes took precedence over all other porcelain manufactories in France.

Differing accounts have been given of the founding and early development of the Vincennes-Sèvres porcelain factory. It is generally accepted that the factory was established in 1738 by workmen from Chantilly, namely the Dubois brothers, the enameller and kiln-master Humbert Gerin and François Gravant, with the financial support and patronage of Orry de Fulvy, brother of the Minister of Finance. Per-mission was granted to set up a workshop in part of the disused royal Chateau of Vincennes.

For a considerable time soft-paste porcelain wares produced at Vincennes were unsatisfactory. The proportion of kiln-wasters was disastrously high owing to a lack of technical knowledge on the part of Gilles and Robert Dubois who became addicted to heavy drinking. They were dismissed by Fulvy in 1741 and replaced by Gravant whose skill and knowledge had increased as a result of studying and im-proving on the methods of the Dubois brothers and obtaining technical information from the St Cloud and Chantilly factories. Preparation of the paste remained Gravant's responsibility until he died in 1765.

A new company formed in 1745 with the obvious advantage of the king's interest engaged the services of the court goldsmith Duplessis, who took charge of modelling, and the enameller Mathieu, who supervised decoration. A well-known chemist, Jean Hellot, took charge of the laboratory, while Millot became kiln-master. In 1747 Jean-Baptiste de Machault, Controller of Finances, who assumed responsi-bility for the financial affairs of the Vincennes factory, issued an order prohibiting the manufacture of porcelain elsewhere in France and imposing a ban on the employment by other factories of workmen from Vincennes.

François Gravant justified Fulvy's confidence in the successful outcome of his experiments. Gravant continued in charge of all experiments made to improve body and glaze. At his death in 1765 his son Louis-François took charge of the production of paste and glaze until his removal to Chantilly to take over the old factory there. In his efforts to perfect the beautiful soft-paste body, which for long remained excessively unstable in the kiln, the elder Gravant devoted many hours to experiment. The principal ingredients of the paste as finally adopted at Vincennes comprised soda of Alicante, alabaster, salt and saltpetre and Fontainebleau sand. Soap mixed with clay was added to ensure plasticity. Gravant's near-perfect soft-paste body was pure white.

Decoration on Vincennes porcelain became characteristically French after the early years when Meissen styles were imitated, principally consisting of floral designs and painted figures. The influence of Meissen is evident in designs embodying formal scrolls and elaborate borders, the use of green and crimson monochrome and occasional bold use of black. Gilding employed without colour in embellishment of wares was a Vincennes innovation. A method of gilding devised by a Benedictine monk, Brother Hippolyte, was purchased for a considerable sum. Gilding was subsequently used with notable success superimposed on a series of beautiful ground colours which began with the introduction of the celebrated *gros-bleu*. Probably the painter Vieillard was the first to paint landscapes with human figures and birds on a blue ground in a free, graceful style both novel and charming that quickly became extremely popular. Vieillard was the chief exponent of a style successfully followed by other artists of the factory, including Xhrouet, Ledoux, Aloncle, Gomery and Evans. A team of able assistants helped Hellot to extend the palette of enamel colours. Bailly, in charge of the colour department from 1751, was a clever colour-chemist who played an important part in the development of the unique Sèvres palette.

Following the death of Orry de Fulvy in 1753, yet another new company was formed in which the king substantially invested. Fear of Meissen rivalry and competition from other French factories prompted issue of the royal interdict prohibiting the production of porcelain anywhere else on French soil. The factory was transferred to Sèvres in 1756 and in 1759 the king was persuaded to purchase the concern outright.

Hellot set his heart upon the ultimate production of hard-paste porcelain at Sèvres. When the new company was formed in 1753 he endeavoured to obtain the formula from Paul-Antoine Hannong, whose factory at Strasbourg was disastrously affected by the royal interdict. Hellot was prevented from parting with the Sèvres company's funds in order to obtain Hannong's secret formula. The porcelain kilns at Strasbourg were dismantled and Hannong departed to the Palatinate in Germany where he founded the Frankenthal factory. It was believed that failure to find *kaolin* deposits in France caused the financial director Boileau to oppose the purchase of the hard-paste porcelain formula from Hannong as urged by Hellot.

From the beginning the Vincennes-Sèvres management adhered to their intention to emulate Meissen in figure production. According to Bachelier, appointed art director in 1751, coloured figures only were produced until 1749 and all models were originals by a group of accomplished modellers, including, among others, Laurent, Goubet, Fournier, Blondeau, Deperrieux and Patouillet. In addition to coloured figures, a series of glazed white figures was made. Groups were the specialised work of Sèvres modellers whose individual compositions cannot now be identified. Exceptionally fine figures and groups were expressly modelled for Madame de Pompadour, notably the well-known series of eight white-glazed *Enfants d'après Boucher* modelled by Blondeau. The same series was repeated in biscuit porcelain at a later date to the order of Madame de Pompadour.

At some time between 1749 and 1753 Bachelier introduced his excellent biscuit porcelain used in production of figures and groups that greatly enhanced the reputation of the Sèvres factory. Sèvres fine biscuit ware became the envy of rival European factories and inevitable imitation was extensive. For some forty years biscuit porcelain figures and groups ranked among the principal productions of Sèvres and an immense variety of models appeared. Boucher's works were the principal source of inspiration. Children were favourite subjects. White-glazed and coloured figures were largely superseded, although production did not cease entirely, as is evident in the work of Louis-Felix de la Rue, who created a popular series of figures of children.

Figure-modelling at Sèvres was under the direction of Etienne-Maurice Falconet

53 TWO-HANDLED BOWL, COVER AND PLATE. In *rose Du Barry*. Painted by Aloncle with birds in landscape in rocaille style. Louis XV style, date letter 1759. Sèvres, French. *H bowl 4⅝in, D plate 7⅞in*

from 1757 until his departure to Russia in 1766. Falconet's original works, finely executed in biscuit porcelain, enhanced his own and the factory's reputation. The modellers Fernex and Suzanne created superb works at about the same period, but undoubtedly Falconet was the most accomplished modeller in the factory during the nine years he remained director of sculpture at Sèvres. His outstanding accomplishment in modelling is evident, for example, in one of his brilliantly conceived and executed compositions *Leda and the Swan*, which rates among the greatest masterpieces in biscuit porcelain made at Sèvres.

Louis-Simon Boizot was appointed chief modeller in 1774. With Boizot's advent the factory began turning out figures in hard-paste porcelain. Boizot was a skilled modeller capable of producing excellent work in different styles, but he was not a modeller of genius.

Flower-painting on Sèvres wares reached a high peak in the brilliant work of specialist floral painters among whom the most notable were Noël, Tandart, Cornaille, Taillandier, Meraud *aîné*, Thevénet, Buteux *aîné* and Levé *père*. Flowers were painted with great delicacy and skill during the early period, usually in soft colours and often in a stylistic manner. In time, as the *Louis Seize* style became predominant, the character of floral decoration changed, becoming more naturalistic, with graceful arrangements of festoons and swags. Exotic birds, sometimes portrayed against backgrounds of flowers and foliage, were most frequently depicted in the early period. Towards the end of the eighteenth century birds appeared in more naturalistic representation.

The Sèvres factory became noted for the quality of gilding applied on wares, especially on soft porcelain. Gold was almost invariably applied thickly, the burnishing and engraving executed by highly skilled craftsmen. A technique used at Sèvres with marked success entailed grinding gold with honey and applying the mixture by brushing on thickly and lightly firing. A rich, dull appearance was obtained, eliminating 'brassiness'. Etienne-Henri Le Guay was foremost among outstanding early Sèvres gilders. Gilding continued in favour at Sèvres until·the end of the century and returned to favour during the imperial epoch in the early nineteenth century. The fine gilding on early Sèvres wares was altogether superior to later work which became opulent to the point of vulgarity.

Potters in other French factories produced an impressive variety of wares when the secret of hard-paste porcelain became generally known. The work of potters at Lunéville, Niderviller and Mennecy may be considered the most important.

At Lunéville, in Eastern France, pleasing soft biscuit earthenware figures and groups were produced in the early period prior to the manufacture of hard porcelain wares for which the factory became noted. Paul-Louis Cyfflé, working *c* 1755, is credited with the finest Lunéville figures. Cyfflé established his own hard-paste porcelain factory at Lunéville in 1766. He continued to specialise in the production of figures and groups in much the same style as his earlier works. When Cyfflé closed his factory in 1780 the Niderviller management acquired a number of his moulds which were later used for reproductions.

The Niderviller factory, where hard porcelain manufacture commenced in 1765 and has continued until the present day, made excellent wares, including figures in both faience and porcelain. Charles Sauvage modelled many of the best Niderviller figures in hard porcelain, also a number left in biscuit state after the fashion set by Sèvres. Baron Jean-Louis Beyerle established the Niderviller factory and for a time prospered, but increasing competition from the royal factory at Sèvres ultimately proved too strong. In 1770 Beyerle was forced to relinquish the concern to Count Adam Philibert de Custine, a court favourite and General of the Royal Arms. The count, who was guillotined during the Revolution, continued production of both faience and porcelain wares. Beyerle and de Custine shared a taste for rococo, in consequence their wares were somewhat extravagant in style, contrasting un-favourably with the less exuberant, more elegant Sèvres productions.

François Barbin founded a factory in 1734 in Paris which was transferred to Mennecy in 1748 and from there to Bourg-la-Reine in 1773. The Mennecy factory, as it is generally known, first flourished under the patronage of Louis-François de Neufville, Duke of Villeroy. The later milky-white Mennecy soft-paste porcelain with its distinctive 'wet'-looking glaze resembles that of Bow. Sometimes the wares of the two factories are erroneously attributed for this reason.

In conclusion, a brief note concerning the factory at Tournai in Belgium, terri-tory once successively ruled by Austria and France. Both faience and porcelain were made at the factory founded by François Carpentier but brought into pro-minence by François Peterinck who was granted a privilege to manufacture por-celain in 1752 by the Empress Maria Theresa of Austria. The factory became noted for its excellent wares produced in the French tradition. There were interesting and not unimportant links between the factories at Tournai and Chelsea during the eighteenth century.

ENGLAND

The English slip period, as it may be termed, besides bringing rapid increase in the production and use of fired clay vessels and ornaments, also brought the appearance of skilled craftsmen regarded as the first master potters in the country. In the period extending from the second decade of the seventeenth century to the end of the eighteenth century, when slipwares of a common type were made in most parts of England, Wrotham in Kent, North Staffordshire and Derbyshire became important pottery-making centres.

The use of clay slip by potters through the ages has been referred to in preceding sections of this work. Slip is ordinary clay reduced to the consistency of cream by mixing with water. English potters became adept in a trailed decoration technique achieved by use of a spouted vessel through which liquid slip was dotted or trailed over wares before firing. Slip was sometimes applied decoratively to objects by the use of a brush. A pointed cutting instrument was employed to produce lines and incisions in the surface in the *sgraffiato* technique derived from the Italians who developed it in the fifteenth century. The process will be found explained in the section concerning Italian ceramic wares. In *sgraffiato* decoration on pottery, as practised in England, an applied ground or engobe of slip in a colour contrasting with that of the body was cut through in patterns to expose the colour beneath.

White clay slip was coloured by the addition of various oxides. Green, blue and red were supplemented by manganese which was frequently used to obtain a colour varying from black to purple-brown. Slip-decorated wares were usually coated with a fine lead glaze produced from galena – sulphite of lead – mined in Derbyshire. Galena was pulverised and dusted over wares before firing. Exposure to the kiln's heat caused the formation of a silicate in its reaction to the silicate of the body. Wares were generally fired at an oven temperature of around 1250 °C.

The name Toft is that of an old Staffordshire family of potters whose connection with the industry has extended from the beginnings of pottery manufacture in the region to Charles Toft, a well-known potter at work in the closing decades of the nineteenth century, and others bearing the name beyond his time into the twentieth century. Thomas and Ralph Toft, possibly brothers or father and son, makers of slip-decorated wares, were far from being exclusive makers of the type of wares now somewhat misleadingly referred to as 'Toftware'. Dishes and plates, 'chargers', their centres decorated with primitive portraits of royalty, cavaliers and ladies, floral devices and heraldic beasts, and borders embellished with trellis patterns executed in white slip were characteristic productions of other Staffordshire potters besides the Tofts. Names inscribed in broad raised slip lettering on wares are

54   PRINCE RUPERT OF
THE RHINE. Stoneware
bust by John Dwight.
English, c1680. H 24in

thought to be those of the makers. Owing to the frequent recurrence of the name Toft on English seventeenth-century slip-decorated wares, it is now generally applied to the type.

Simeon Shaw referred to Thomas Toft as the first English potter to use aluminous shale or fire clay. From weathered fire clay the early Staffordshire potters obtained a yellow-burning slip which was eventually widely used. Throughout the greater part of the seventeenth century the North Staffordshire potters used only local clays which fired to shades of red, brown, buff and drab. The clay was left to weather, but little time was spent in preparation, consequently the body produced was coarse. In most respects, ordinary clay wares made in Staffordshire during the first half of the seventeenth century were little less primitive in character than similar wares produced long before in Europe and Asia. English potters made their first attempt at improving their wares when they began giving more care to the preparation of materials. Local clays, without addition of foreign substances, continued in use, but potters endeavoured to refine the paste. When they became aware of the attraction of light-burning clays, making possible the production of a whitish or light-yellow body, the potters perceived how they might also be used

156

decoratively in contrast with ordinary red clay. Light-coloured clays were employed in the creation of twisted rolls, lozenge and banded slip decoration applied to dark-bodied wares. The use of slip as decoration evolved with a technique of applying semi-liquid, light-coloured clay over a common red-clay body.

English peasant pottery acquired distinctive character for the first time in the first half of the seventeenth century when slip decoration became popular. Potters used slip decoratively in a variety of ways, in spots, blobs, bands, or trailed over the surface of wares. By the end of the seventeenth century skilled potters became adept in a technique of using various coloured clays in trailed decoration. A popular decorative style entailed 'combing' the surface of objects before they hardened, using a wire, horn or leather comb. Potters developed considerable skill in the combing technique and were able to decorate both round and flat.wares in this manner.

Slip decoration, as developed by the English potters, is traditional and has never become obsolete. Pottery decorated with slip continues to be produced in England at the present time. Artist potters of repute working in England during the past century have made admirable use of slip in the ornamentation of their wares.

John Dwight, experimenting in his Fulham workshop in the late seventeenth century, became one of the most enterprising, resourceful and successful English potters in his own or any age. In considering the important nature of his experiments and discoveries, together with the superb quality of his productions, their charm and, for the period, novel character, it may appear strange that Dwight apparently did not exercise strong influence on the development of English ceramic sculpture. While it is true that the extent of Dwight's influence cannot readily be assessed or defined, it was nevertheless in all probability more far-reaching and vital than is generally realised. In his own time few potters in England possessed Dwight's practical knowledge and skill in ceramics. Moreover, there are grounds for assuming that Dwight designed and modelled many of his figures and busts which, if true, adds the attribute of remarkable artistry to his outstanding technical accomplishment.

Dwight was of good birth and education. At the outset of his career, coinciding with the Restoration, he is believed to have held the post of private secretary to three successive Bishops of Chester. How or why Dwight became interested in and acquired his knowledge of ceramics, or when and where the dramatic new turn in his career occurred, is not known for certain. It appears probable that he began delving into the mysteries of ceramic production before his period of episcopal service terminated.

At this point it is relevant to reconsider the nature of stoneware and give some account of the English salt-glazing process, these being of vital interest to John Dwight when he established his pottery. Stoneware is a composition of plastic clay and sand, fired to render it hard and durable by semi-vitrification. During the sixteenth century, arising from experiments directed towards perfecting the glazing process, German potters developed an advanced technique in the production of finer quality stoneware than previously made in Europe. Some modern authorities contend that the salt-glazing process, as applied to their stoneware, was invented by twelfth-century German potters. Even if this be true, the process was not generally adopted until much later and was certainly not practised in England until the seventeenth century at the earliest. The salt-glaze technique involved the use of sodium chloride – common salt – shovelled into the kiln during firing at maximum heat. Men naked to the waist, kept cool by being swathed in wet cloths, performed the task of casting salt into ovens. Intense heat caused the salt to volatilise, while the reaction of sodium chloride vapour and water vapour, forming hydrochloric acid, produced a silicate of soda covering the objects placed on saggers in the kiln with a coating of soda-glass pitted with fine granulations.

Dwight applied for his first patent in 1671, claiming that he had discovered 'the mixture of transparent earthenware commonly known by the names of porcelaine or China and Persian ware, as alsoe the Misterie of the stoneware vulgarly called Cologne ware; and that he designed to introduce a manufacture of the said wares into our Kingdome of England where they have not hitherto been wrought or made'. The last words would seem to imply that stonewares had not previously been made in England despite the fact that for a century past patents to manufacture had been granted to successive applicants claiming to have discovered the secrets of stoneware production. Dwight was probably no exception in making bold claims. Statements made by defendants at the time of Dwight's lawsuit claiming infringement of his patent rights indicate that others were already making stonewares in England when production commenced at Fulham.

Dwight was unsuccessful in his efforts to make true porcelain, but his brilliant achievement in developing a stoneware far superior to the German and Flemish varieties brought him fame and fortune. His wares attracted great attention immediately they appeared. In 1684, when Dwight was granted renewal of his patent, he stated that he was engaged in the production of 'White Gorges, Marbled Porcelaine Vessels, Statues, and figures, and Fine Stone Gorges and vessels never before made in England or elsewhere'.

Design and techniques employed in the production of his figures are proof of Dwight's unrivalled ability and versatility. Notwithstanding his initial success as a potter, he never ceased experimenting, always with the object of improving his paste and glazes. Experiments were probably carried out in stages. On the whole, in surviving examples of his work, the body shows less variation in composition than the glazes and the manner in which they were used. Figures such as the well-known *Flora* and the *Sportsman* have a pure white vitreous, moderately translucent body and are very thinly glazed, whereas a figure of James II is quite thickly coated with glaze. Figures of mythological gods have a thin layer of ferruginous clay, applied in order to achieve a resemblance to bronze, and a thin coat of salt glaze.

In 1869 Charles and Lady Charlotte Schreiber visited the old Fulham factory and

55 THROWN SLIPWARE DISH. Inscribed 'Ralph Toft 1677'. Decorated with stylised tulip pattern. Staffordshire, English. D 17½in

discovered two notebooks containing entries in Dwight's handwriting made between 1689 and 1698. Dwight's notes included formulae for various pastes and observations concerning techniques. In accordance with the usage of the time, Dwight referred to pottery as porcelain whenever it differed from common earthenware. Some of the pastes to which Dwight referred in his notebooks were never used, as far as has been ascertained, in the productions of his figures. Thus Dwight's 'opacous red porcelain or China clay', probably an unglazed red stoneware, was used in the production of tea-wares. This particular body became the subject of dispute in Dwight's lawsuit against the Elers brothers and other potters. Dwight's red stoneware closely resembled, if it was not identical in composition to, the celebrated Elers redware and no doubt he felt justified in protesting against infringement of his patent rights.

Stoneware figures identified with certainty as being Dwight's productions present a combination of imaginative composition and technical virtuosity that is little short of astonishing. Sensitive handling of the material and superb modelling place Dwight's figures in the forefront of English ceramic sculpture. It should be noted, however, that even a potter of Dwight's calibre now and then fell short of his own high standards of craftsmanship. Not all of Dwight's productions are of equal merit. Possibly not one of his statuettes displays such mastery of technique as is discernible in his splendid portrait bust of Prince Rupert. Yet even those figures which are considered to be among the least attractive are worthy of a master.

56 TWO MUSICIANS.
Earthenware figures of a
bagpiper (H 6¼in), and a
singer (H 5in). Astbury-
Whieldon c1745.
Staffordshire, English

Dwight's figures were white, grey or bronze-coloured, all being original models
which were never repeated.

Dwight's productions were of such vital, unique character as to arouse speculation concerning the identity of the modeller. Some authorities have found it difficult
to accept that in some instances at least John Dwight was his own modeller,
despite the fact that at the period he worked at Fulham it was normal practice for
an English potter to undertake his own modelling. By all accounts, Dwight was
a craftsman with artistic talent as well as great technical ability. It is therefore not
unfeasible that he was also a proficient modeller. Solon believed this to be true, as
he implied in his *Art of the Old English Potter*, referring to the well-known recum-
bent effigy of Lydia Dwight dated 1673: 'in this beautiful and touching memorial
of a beloved child we trace the loving care of the bereaved father, in the reproduction of the features and the minute perfection with which the accessories,
such as flowers and lace, are treated'.

Others are inclined to give credence to a theory that Grinling Gibbons may have
had some association with Dwight and executed work at Fulham for the potter.
If this is at all credible the fact cannot be disregarded that Gibbons was not born

160

until 1648 and would therefore have been quite young at the period when Dwight may have commissioned him to model figures. Attribution of certain Dwight figures to Grinling Gibbons may appear absurd until careful consideration is given to certain facts and reasons put forward.

The theory that the young Grinling Gibbons modelled a number of Dwight's stoneware figures is based upon exercise of the carver's technique thought to be discernible in certain examples. Apart from the figures, the superb portrait bust of Prince Rupert in the British Museum is remarkable for its incisive detail, indicating the possible execution of the model by a skilled woodcarver. Reginald Haggar drew attention to the floral bouquets featured in the *Flora* statuette and the effigy of Lydia Dwight, mindful of the fact that Grinling Gibbons became celebrated for his woodcarvings of flowers and fruits. Even so, after considering the flimsy 'evidence', making close study of Dwight's figures and comparing their style with authenticated examples of Gibbons's work, to conclude that all or any originated from the hand of the latter artist does not seem tenable.

Perhaps the *Sportsman* and *Flora*, both of which are without a doubt creations of the same modeller, were modelled by the Restoration sculptor Cibber (1630–1700). It is difficult to accept that a factory modeller without extraordinary talent could have been responsible for models of such superb character. It appears less likely that an ordinary factory modeller or even contemporary sculptors had a hand in the modelling of Dwight's figures than that he was sufficiently talented and trained to execute them himself. Until his death in 1703 Dwight remained the most successful and renowned master potter in England.

At no period in any other country of the world were salt-glazed wares of such fine quality and attraction produced comparable with salt-glazed stonewares made in England during the first half of the eighteenth century. The development of salt-glazing in Staffordshire owed much to the Elers brothers. Other enterprising potters who became interested in the expansion of the industry after the departure of the Elers from North Staffordshire succeeded in imparting a unique character to their white salt-glazed stonewares. Simeon Shaw, in *A History of the Staffordshire Potteries*, published in 1829, stated that the development of the fine white body was achieved in stages, using successive formulae in the following order: can marl and fine sand; grey coal measures, clay and fine sand; grey clay and ground flint. The introduction of ground flint in about 1720 is usually credited to John Astbury.

It is almost certain that John Dwight was conversant with the use of ground flint as a means of whitening the stoneware body, as is indicated in a formula entered into his notebook in 1690. Dwight noted that 'Calcin'd beaten and sifted flint will doe instead of white sand . . .'. One of the first patents for an engine for grinding flint was taken out by Thomas Benson in 1726, but the introduction of iron into the ground flint caused discoloration. In 1732 the machine was reconstructed, using hard stone only, and proved a useful aid to potters. The first flint mill was erected in the grounds of Ivy House, Hanley.

Thomas Astbury, son of the more celebrated elder Astbury, most probably initiated the use of South of England clays and calcined flint to achieve whiteness in stoneware. It is also sometimes asserted that Thomas Astbury, being the first potter to mix white Devon clay and calcined flint in production of a lighter-coloured body, was accordingly the inventor of English cream-coloured ware, but the available evidence is inconclusive. However, it will scarcely be disputed that John Astbury was closely associated with constant endeavour on the part of Staffordshire potters to improve the whiteness of earthenware and stoneware.

John Astbury was a talented, imaginative potter whose reputation as a maker of figures has endured through more than two centuries. He was an indefatigable experimentalist. Astbury was probably the first Staffordshire potter to seriously devote his talents to the production of small ceramic figures. Astbury's son Thomas apparently inherited much of his father's skill, so much so in fact that it is difficult and frequently impossible to distinguish the work of father and son.

Salt-glazed stoneware figures made in Staffordshire during the approximate period 1730–50 are now regarded as being among the most beautiful and interesting productions of the English master potters. White salt-glazed stoneware figures made in Staffordshire have become so rare that few are seen outside museums. All that survive are competently modelled and usually have an exceptionally fine surface texture. Early examples were undoubtedly inspired by Chinese porcelain figures. It should be borne in mind that during the whole of the early period, which was largely experimental, Staffordshire potters did not relinquish hope of ultimately developing a body as beautiful, durable and translucent as Chinese porcelain. Salt-glazed stoneware figures made in emulation of Chinese porcelain originals were unquestionably of high standard in design and workmanship, but as the body lacked translucency and was really quite inferior, Staffordshire imitations of Chinese porcelain figures fell considerably short of the quality and attraction the English potters desired to achieve.

Early attempts to apply decoration on white figures led to the use of brown clay in representation of eyes, hair, mouth and details of clothing such as buttons. Coloured clays were used later in ornamentation, while later still cobalt was used as a stain. In the final phase of decorative development brilliant on-glaze enamels were used. Figures of a type now known as agate ware were produced by blending coloured clays.

Techniques employed in the production of salt-glazed figures commenced with the making of master models which were never duplicated. Alabaster or metal moulds were used at a later period. Increased output was achieved by the introduction of plaster of Paris moulds. Josiah Wedgwood believed that alabaster moulds were introduced into Staffordshire by the Elers brothers, but there is no definite proof. Moulds made of clay, metal and alabaster were all in general use during the early period. Alabaster, which was easily carved into the required shapes, was obtained from Staffordshire and Derbyshire mines. According to Simeon Shaw, in about 1745 Ralph Daniel, a potter of Colbridge near Burslem, visited France and returned to Staffordshire with the first mould made from plaster

57 BEAR. Tortoiseshell glazed earthenware figure. Probably Whieldon, c1750.
Staffordshire, English. H 5½in, L 8¼in

of Paris seen in the Potteries. Other potters were impressed with the advantages of
working with plaster of Paris moulds with the result that clay, metal and alabaster
moulds gradually became obsolete. Plaster of Paris moulds were made more easily
and quickly, and casts were turned out with greater speed, the only serious draw-
back being rapid loss of sharpness in repeated casting. Figures produced from
plaster of Paris moulds invariably lacked the crispness of those taken from
alabaster moulds.

An original or master mould was made from clay, metal or alabaster, or after
1745 from plaster of Paris. Plaster copies of the master mould were made for use
as working moulds. The method of casting was simple. In the production of all
stonewares, including figures, parts produced from separate moulds were joined
up in the assembling workshop. Slip clay mixed with water was poured into a
mould and left to stand for a short time. A thin lining of hardening clay gradually
covered the walls of the mould. Superfluous slip was then drained off leaving the
firm clay within the mould ready to be removed when quite dry. As it dried the
clay shrank. Usually, in the process of simple casting, the contents of the mould
were removed by turning upside-down. Occasionally, in more complicated work,
a mould had to be taken apart in order to remove the cast.

The question of the extent to which metal moulds were used by early eighteenth-
century English potters has given rise to considerable speculation. In point of fact,

58 ST GEORGE AND THE
DRAGON. Earthenware
figure by Ralph Wood,
c1770. Decorated with
coloured glazes.
Staffordshire, English.
H 11¾in, L 7in

metal moulds were unsuitable for use in pottery casting as the mould needed to be porous. Metal moulds were principally used in pressing and stamping. Delicate pieces of salt-glazed stoneware made in imitation of porcelain were produced by pressing clay between two metal moulds carrying a pattern, the shape and ornamentation of an object being accomplished in a single operation. Objects such as spoons, small dishes and trays, of astonishing thinness, comparable with eggshell porcelain, were produced by this method, but figures obviously could not be made by the same process.

Mould makers were known as block-cutters. Aaron Wood, a member of the celebrated Wood family of Burslem, became the best known and was probably the most skilled of the early eighteenth-century block-cutters. Wood was apprenticed to Dr Thomas Wedgwood in 1731. The brothers Aaron and Ralph Wood modelled some of the finest early Staffordshire pottery figures, possibly including examples of the fascinating so-called pew groups.

Pew groups, now so rare that only a few examples are known to exist, are perhaps too readily ascribed to John Astbury with whom they are particularly associated. There is reason for believing that Aaron Wood executed pew groups although no surviving examples of his work can be identified with certainty. The finest pew group extant is undoubtedly in the British Museum collection and is almost certainly the work of Astbury, executed in his characteristic style. Pew groups, never two alike, are usually composed of two or three figures seated on a high-backed chair or bench decorated with leaf forms, also pierced relief ornament. The figures are depicted in attitudes and situations expressing rustic sentiment or quaint humour. Nearly all pew groups have details of features and clothing accentuated by touches of black colouring.

Towards the middle of the eighteenth century Staffordshire salt-glazed figures began to lose their spontaneity and varied character, tending to become stereotyped and heavy in appearance. Design became conventionalised. Workmanship, however, remained of high standard. At this juncture enamel colours were introduced for the decoration of figures.

Enamel colours were used extensively in decoration of salt-glazed wares after 1750. Examples of enamel-decorated salt-glazed stoneware figures are now rare. Colouring of stoneware figures was introduced with practise of the technique known as 'scratch-blue' which consisted of making incisions and rubbing in a cobalt-stained clay. Enamel colours applied to English salt-glazed wares were fixed by refining in a muffle kiln.

William Littler of Longton Hall in Staffordshire is reputed to have produced a small number of salt-glazed figures in Oriental style based upon Meissen prototypes. Modern research has given rise to speculation concerning Littler's productions. It now appears that some, if not all, of these figures were really the productions of a certain 'Dr' Mills associated with Littler at Longton Hall. According to Simeon Shaw, while acting as Littler's principal assistant Dr Mills was 'not only a good practical potter, but a valuable modeller'. William Littler introduced a distinctive cobalt stain sometimes referred to as 'Littler blue', much admired by modern collectors.

While in production of ornamental and tableware the English master potters made important progress during the second half of the eighteenth century, in preceding decades it was in the sphere of figure-making that they most excelled. Today we find it convenient to place various types of eighteenth-century English pottery figures in well-defined categories such as Astbury, Astbury–Whieldon, Whieldon and Wood. It cannot be doubted, however, that a considerable proportion of the stoneware and earthenware figures thus classified were in fact made by potters whose names are not recorded. The term 'image-maker' was often applied to a potter, from the earliest period, but the term 'chimney ornament', indicating small figures and ornamental pottery for cottage mantelshelves, was not heard until late in the eighteenth century and was not in general use until the early nineteenth century. Simeon Shaw, writing in 1829, referred to Thomas Whieldon as 'a maker of image toys and chimney ornaments' but the latter appellative would have somewhat mystified Whieldon. The 'image man', a pedlar who carried diminutive clay figures in his pack and travelled from village to village selling his wares, appeared in the Victorian era.

Although he became the most distinguished potter in Staffordshire in his time and amassed a fortune, retiring, according to his one-time partner Josiah Wedgwood, when the mechanisation of the English pottery industry threatened his business, Thomas Whieldon's career was not an overnight success story. To quote Simeon Shaw, 'In 1740 Mr Thomas Whieldon's manufactory at Little Fenton consisted of a small range of low buildings, all thatched.' Shaw went on to state, 'He also made toys and chimney ornaments, coloured in either the clay state or bisquet, by zaffre, manganese, copper &c. and glazed with black, red or white lead.'

Tortoiseshell wares were a Whieldon speciality that other potters of his time endeavoured to imitate. Whieldon did not invent the technique, as is sometimes believed. Staffordshire potters at work in the late seventeenth century produced earthenware decorated with a type of coloured glaze obtained by blending lead ore with manganese. Subsequently, oxide of iron, copper and cobalt in the form of

59 OVAL PLATE. Creamware. Decorated with a view of Kenilworth Castle. From Josiah Wedgwood's Frog Service, c1774. Staffordshire. English. L 14⅛in, W 10⅞in

zaffres were used in development of the tortoiseshell and mottled glazes that up to about 1760 Whieldon skilfully used to embellish his cream-bodied wares.

Whieldon's enchanting image toys may appear to lack the quality and refinement of his other wares. 'Toys' generally do not exhibit the high technical excellence of figures by Ralph Wood or Josiah Wedgwood for example, but for richness of colouring and the quality of the glazes they are unrivalled. The embellishment of figures and other wares by application of varicoloured glazes is an art in which no other English potter surpassed Whieldon, as may be discerned from his wares, including examples of charming equestrian figures, animals and birds, graceful figures derived from Chinese porcelain originals and figures of classical subjects.

Whieldon was first and foremost a craftsman. He preferred to adhere to traditional techniques and stubbornly resisted the industrialisation of his trade. Whieldon's rigid conservatism proved a source of irritation to Josiah Wedgwood during their brief period of partnership and was the underlying cause of their separation. For fully a decade before Whieldon retired from the pottery industry, appalled by what was taking place, the Staffordshire potters began moving into a new era of industrialisation brought about by the invention of mechanical processes which served to advance mass-production. By about 1775 more progressive potters began enlarging their factories in order to cope with the steadily increasing demand for their wares.

The most forward-looking potter active in North Staffordshire during this period of expansion and change was Josiah Wedgwood. If, as has been written, Thomas Whieldon was the last of the English peasant potters, Josiah Wedgwood was the first English potter to perceive the vast potential of the industry and to envisage production on a modern commercial scale. By his astuteness, energy and drive Wedgwood not only placed himself in the forefront of English potters but instigated revolutionary changes within the industry. It was chiefly due to Wedgwood's continuous efforts to increase his output while improving the quality of his wares, achieved by adopting new techniques in his factory, that other Staffordshire potters who emulated him followed suit and transformed their humble workshops into well-equipped factories.

The story of Josiah Wedgwood's life and career needs no recounting here. He was one of the most enterprising potters of his day, an accomplished, practical craftsman descended from a line of potters, with a keen eye constantly trained upon fashion, a cultivated taste and sense of artistry combined with high standards and a passionate admiration for classical art. It was characteristic of Wedgwood, being aware of his own artistic and technical limitations, that he engaged some of the most talented designers, modellers and decorators of the day to work in his factory.

Wedgwood began his training as a potter in 1739 when he was nine years old, working in his brother's workshop. After a brief partnership with Whieldon, beginning in 1754 and ending in 1759, he set up independently at the Ivy House Works, Burslem. In 1762 he became potter to Queen Charlotte and from that time rapidly progressed to become the most successful potter in England.

Creamware, for which his factory became renowned, was greatly improved by Wedgwood in both body and glaze. The ware had developed considerably in quality and colour since Thomas Astbury's early experiments. Referring to cream-ware, Enoch Wood wrote: 'Before flint was introduced they used a certain pro-portion of slip for the body in the glaze to prevent crazing, and to make it bear a stronger fire in the glaze oven.' Wedgwood developed the fine glaze applied to his creamware by the introduction of growan or Cornwall stone. In a short time, by virtue of its pleasant colour and greater durability, creamware superseded salt-glazed ware and became a principal product of the Staffordshire potters.

In 1768 Wedgwood perfected an attractive black stoneware which he called black porcelain but afterwards designated black basalt. The first plaques and figures to be made in the black body appeared in 1769. So-called 'Egyptian black' is reputed to have been the invention of the Elers brothers. Wedgwood's black basalt was of much finer texture than the early ware. The body, which was black all through, was composed of local clay mixed with ground ironstone, with added proportions of ochre and oxide of manganese. Black basalt wares were given a final polish on a lapidary's wheel in order to bring out the lustrous beauty of the surface. Wedgwood principally used black basalt for medallions and vases, but a number of excellent figures were produced, among the most successful and best known being a remark-able figure of Voltaire regarded as a masterpiece considering that the black body was difficult to work even by a first-class modeller. Black figures were made up to two feet high. Statuettes of Rousseau and Linnaeus, and some others, were perhaps less competently modelled than the Voltaire figure. Nearly all Wedgwood figures in black basalt were neo-classical in concept.

Jasper, the ware for which Wedgwood became renowned, was entirely his own invention. Sulphate of barytes constituted the largest proportion of the ingredients in the crystalline body. The jasper paste was coloured by adding oxides. Cobalt was used for colouring the extremely popular blue jasperware. Solid jasper, as it is known, with the body coloured all through, first appeared in about 1775. Later, a more economical process was devised known as jasper dip by which surface colouring could be applied instead of mixing colours into the paste. Jasper colours included blue, olive and sage green, pink, yellow, lilac and black, with a white jasper body used principally in production of cameos.

Wedgwood's modellers were extremely competent, either working according to his concepts or with complete freedom to follow their own creative bent. Wedg-wood was an exacting, if generous employer and modelling for him required the artist to give of his or her best. Theodore Parker modelled the *Sleeping Boy* in 1769, also *Cupid Reposing* and *Boy on a Couch*. Mrs Landres modelled for Wedg-wood at various periods between 1769 and 1774. Her best work included sea nymphs and naiads, a set of figures representing Faith, Hope and Charity and a number of religious figures. John Bacon worked for Wedgwood as a modeller in 1770. During the year 1769, when an unusually large number of figures issued from the Wedg-

60 OTHELLO TEAPOT. Modelled by John Voyez. Reputed to be by Ralph Wood,
c1775. Earthenware. Staffordshire, English. *H 8in*

wood factory, John Coward was appointed principal modeller. His finest work was a large, superbly modelled figure in black basalt, called *Somnus* or *Sleeping Boy*, copied from an antique original. Coward also modelled the fine black basalt figure of Voltaire.

In later years two Italian modellers executed brilliant compositions for Wedgwood. Dalmazzoni was a talented modeller, besides being an artist of repute, who worked for Wedgwood from about 1787 assisted in his Roman studio by Angelini, his pupil, who also supplied Wedgwood with a number of attractive figures. In mentioning some of Wedgwood's better known modellers, John Voyez, probably the most gifted of them all, cannot be overlooked. Wedgwood had a brief association with the erratic French modeller which, to say the least, was ill-starred. A more fruitful partnership was subsequently formed between Voyez and Ralph Wood.

It is generally conceded that the finest English porcelain was produced in a relatively short period of approximately thirty years, between about 1745 and 1775. Artificial or soft porcelain and hard porcelain were manufactured. The former resembled the glassy soft porcelain of France and there can be little doubt that the formula first used in England was obtained from a French source. The latter, closely resembling Chinese hard-paste porcelain, was the invention of an Englishman, the Plymouth Quaker chemist William Cookworthy, who studied Chinese

169

methods of manufacture. In briefly considering here the productions of four famous English porcelain factories operating in the eighteenth century, it must suffice to indicate, and indeed emphasise, the unique qualities and characteristics of early English porcelain. For grace and charm of figures and the elegance and beauty of table and ornamental wares the early English porcelain factories became renowned.

In the light of present-day research it appears probable that the Chelsea factory produced the first porcelain manufactured in England. Certainly Chelsea is of foremost importance in the history of the development of English porcelain. Charles Gouyn first owned the factory which began turning out wares from about 1745. Nicholas Sprimont, a brilliant silversmith of Flemish extraction, took over management of the factory in about 1750. To Sprimont's remarkable artistic and technical accomplishment the Chelsea factory undoubtedly owed its fame and success.

The history and productions of the Chelsea porcelain factory are usually divided into four periods, as follows: the triangle period, 1745–9; the raised anchor period, 1750–3; the red anchor period, 1753–8; and the gold anchor period, 1758–77. These names indicate the marks used throughout successive periods.

The early Chelsea paste, with its high percentage of glassy ingredients, is outstanding for its translucence and is the whitest of English porcelains. A beautiful soft milky-white glaze covers the smooth body, significantly different to the paste and glaze used in later periods. Painted decoration was usually copied from Meissen porcelain and principally comprised Japanese flowers and motifs. Insects and floral sprays frequently seen on early Chelsea porcelain were often applied to conceal blemishes on the surface of wares.

Soon after 1750, at the commencement of the raised anchor period, when Nicholas Sprimont managed the factory, the composition of the paste was changed, with the result that the body became more coldly white, covered with a somewhat waxy glaze. It has been suggested that the reason for making this change in the paste was to increase stability of the wares during firing. Among the more notable Chelsea productions of the period are tablewares decorated by the so-called 'fable painter'. Illustrations derived from Aesop's *Fables* were composed in a very original style by an unidentified painter with rare talent. It now appears probable that more than one artist working at Chelsea at the time specialised in fable subjects, imitating the style of the originator. Usually, decoration applied to Chelsea wares in the three years or so of the raised anchor period was of high standard. Furthermore, it is obvious that sensitive artists delighted in the material they handled. Appreciation of the beautiful white porcelain is evident from the manner in which designs were carefully arranged to set off rather than conceal the ground.

Raised anchor Chelsea figures are rare and consequently coveted by collectors. They include some pleasing well-modelled Italian Comedy figures in the Meissen manner. Far and away the most important, interesting and attractive productions of the period were singularly beautiful figures of birds, some of which are believed to have been decorated by William Duesbury, the Longport enameller destined ultimately to purchase and close down the Chelsea factory. These fine bird figures

61 VOLTAIRE. Black
basalt figure by Josiah
Wedgwood. Modeller
John Coward, c1775.
Staffordshire, English.
H 12in

are found variously decorated, some painted in natural colours, while others
display brilliantly colourful plumage foreign to their species.

The Chelsea red anchor period of approximately 1753–8 marks the supreme
achievement in English porcelain. No other English factory made such near-
perfect porcelain, the culmination of combined effort over a lengthy period by the
competent Chelsea workpeople and management to produce the finest objects of
their kind ever made in England. The quality of paste and glaze remained consistently high despite further changes in the composition. Most importantly, the

62 QUEEN VICTORIA.
Parian portrait bust,
c1890. Minton or
Copeland, Staffordshire.
English. *H 18in*

body retained its remarkable translucency. Characteristic of both raised and red anchor Chelsea porcelain is the presence of 'moons', as found in early French soft porcelains and already commented upon. Some authorities are of the opinion that 'moons' observed in the soft-paste body when held to light indicate the use of coarse frit in the composition in order to counteract instability of wares during firing.

Many people regard Chelsea figures of the red anchor period as the factory's highest achievement in ceramic art. Few will dispute that they are the finest English porcelain figures created and are rightly included among the ceramic masterpieces of the world. Chelsea modellers of the time attained the utmost degree of technical prowess and artistry ever reached in England. Figures of captivating grace and beauty were invariably essentially English, to whatever extent they owed their inspiration to foreign sources. These vigorously modelled, animated Chelsea creations have a quality and appeal unique in English ceramic sculpture.

Decoration on Chelsea red anchor figures and other wares shows the influence of Meissen, especially in Oriental designs. Enamels were applied with restraint, particularly in the execution of floral designs. Sprays of flowers, bouquets and single blooms were delicately painted, the enamels sinking into the soft paste as in early French porcelain.

When Sprimont took complete control of the factory in about 1758 he instigated a further important change in the composition of the paste by adding bone-ash. With the commencement of the gold anchor period other important changes were effected in Chelsea wares, not only in the paste and glaze, the latter becoming more glassy and thickly applied, but also in style and decoration techniques. In the years 1758–70 Sprimont guided the factory through its most commercially successful period. Although magnificent wares were produced, these, on the whole, were made with less feeling for the beauty and unique qualities of the material.

During the gold anchor period the influence of Sèvres upon Chelsea style became strong. English decorators endeavoured to emulate French painters in the use of exquisite ground colours and gilding. Chelsea chemists did not succeed in imitating the immensely popular Sèvres *rose Pompadour* but instead introduced their sumptuous claret ground which every other English factory tried to copy. Likewise, Chelsea also failed to successfully imitate the fine *gros-bleu* of the French factory but contrived to introduce the rich dark-blue ground colour called 'mazarin'. The extremely glassy glaze used at Chelsea during the gold anchor period served to enhance the beauty of rich ground colours and many superb objects became truly magnificent when embellished with the fine gilding that became fashionable in the 1760s. Lavish colouring and profusion of gilding are characteristics of later gold anchor Chelsea wares. While decoration became more elaborate the productions of the factory fortunately retained their elegant shapes. Massive figures standing against flowering shrubs – 'bocage' – and mounted on gilded rococo scroll bases perhaps lack the charming grace of earlier models but are invariably of the finest workmanship and cannot be regarded as less than masterpieces.

The Bow factory was established at some time after 1744 when Thomas Frye, an Irish painter and engraver, and Edward Heylin, a merchant, entered into partnership. A second patent was taken out by Frye in 1748 after he had apparently developed a new method of producing bone-ash which, when combined with calcined flint or sand and water, formed a paste that required to be rolled into balls and fired. The paste balls were then ground and mixed with a third part of pipe clay to produce a porcelain paste. Owing to the inclusion of a high proportion of bone-ash in the paste subsequently introduced by Frye, Bow porcelain produced after 1748 shows a high phosphorus content.

Frye, an artist of considerable talent and excellent taste, continued to manage the factory after 1750 when Weatherly and Crowther, both merchants, became the owners. After the retirement of Frye in 1759 the quality of Bow wares markedly declined. William Duesbury acquired the factory in 1776 when it closed down and the models, moulds and equipment were removed to Derby.

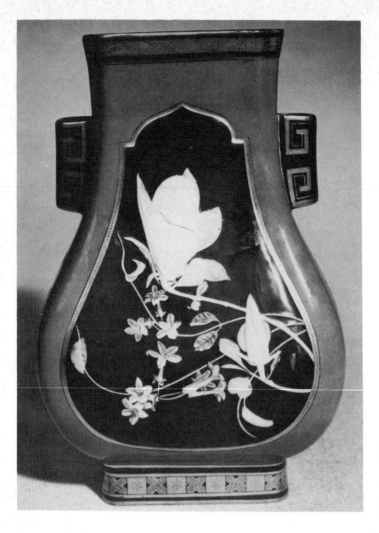

63 VASE. Decorated in *pâte-sur-pâte* by Marc-Louis Solon, c1890. Minton, Staffordshire, English. *H 10in*

A probable, though somewhat mysterious and brief association between Frye and Heylin and the American potter Andrew Duché began with the latter's visit to England in 1744. The Bow factory's possible American connections have been the subject of considerable speculation. Duché's experiments, the reasons for his voyage to England and some account of his relations with English potters will be found included in the section concerning ceramic production in colonial North America.

Early Bow soft-paste porcelain is extremely beautiful whether left in the creamy-white and ornamented with applied prunus blossom after the manner of Chinese *blanc-de-chine* or exquisitely decorated with enamels. Colours are clear and usually delicately applied. Bow figures, largely derived from Meissen prototypes, are nonetheless distinctively English in appearance and always competently modelled.

After Thomas Frye's departure, when Bow wares lost much of their aesthetic quality, the beautiful creamy-white paste was superseded by another somewhat greyish in colour. In modelling, style and finish Bow wares were of consistently excellent standard, but decoration grew coarser in the last years. With a continuously expanding palette Bow painters drew on a wide choice of colours which, however, sometimes resulted in unpleasing colour combinations.

There is reason to believe that the potter André Planche made soft-paste porcelain at his Cockpit Hill factory in Derby as early as 1751. By 1756, in association with others, including William Duesbury, Planche was actively engaged in porcelain manufacture in a new factory in Nottingham Road, Derby.

Cream-jugs and tablewares appear to have been the principal productions of the Derby factory in the early period. Some attractive figures were also made. These were well modelled, often in imitation of Chinese porcelain figures, and usually left white, although a few coloured examples are believed to have been decorated by Duesbury. Judging from the similar technique employed in modelling, these charming early Derby figures were in all probability the work of a single modeller.

A somewhat abrupt change in style occurred in Derby wares when the manage-

64. GROTESQUE FACE JUG. By the Martin brothers. Earthenware, c1895. Southall, English. *H 7in*

ment aimed at colour emulation of Meissen productions, more particularly in respect of figures. As the Derby modellers endeavoured to comply with their employer's requirements their productions became less attractive. Light-coloured figures of the period were superficially pleasing, but the inferiority of Derby modelling is apparent in most examples. Brilliant colouring lent attraction to the figures, but even lavish decoration could not adequately compensate for poor modelling.

It is conjectured that the several dark patches to be observed on the bases of Derby figures made throughout the existence of the factory were caused by clay pads upon which the figures were supported during firing. The same technique was occasionally used elsewhere but was not employed over such a long period or to such extent as at Derby.

Floral decoration on early Derby porcelain is of high standard, executed with great sensitivity by artists who followed the Meissen style in depicting sprays of flowers. An unidentified painter responsible for fine floral decoration on Derby porcelain, notably for delicately drawn flower stalks, is referred to as the 'cotton stalk painter'. His work is occasionally seen on figures. The unidentified Derby artist who added one or two moths to his painted decoration in a variety of subjects is known as the 'moth painter'.

Derby, like other English factories at the period, turned envious eyes on the magnificent productions of the royal factory at Sèvres. The Derby modellers were the first in England to emulate Sèvres biscuit figures in neo-classical style. Although usually of good quality and in most respects pleasing, Derby biscuit figures bear no comparison with Sèvres productions.

William Cookworthy of Plymouth searched long for materials and made exhaustive experiments in his efforts to produce hard porcelain. It is believed that his interest was awakened by study of the letters of Père d'Entrecolles, the French Jesuit priest who lived in China at Ching-tê-chên between 1712 and 1722 and reported details of the formulae and manufacturing techniques used by Chinese potters.

It appears that Cookworthy also made the acquaintance of Andrew Duché, the American potter. Cookworthy presumably met Duché early in 1745.

When Cookworthy at last discovered china-clay deposits near St Austell in Cornwall in 1768 he applied for a patent. A porcelain factory was established at Coxside, Plymouth, financed by a partnership of twelve men, including Richard Champion, subsequent sole owner. After two years the factory was transferred to Bristol. Champion assumed control of the concern in 1773 after purchasing Cookworthy's patent rights. The patent expired in 1775 and was renewed in a modified form. In 1781 when Champion became involved in financial difficulties he sold his patent rights to a company at New Hall, Shelton, Staffordshire, where the formula was used in the manufacture of hard porcelain wares.

Great difficulty in firing was experienced by potters at Plymouth and Bristol. Hard-paste porcelain required to be fired at very high temperatures which needed to be controlled if the wares were to be taken from the kiln free of flaws and

65 TILE ('John Dory')
by Bernard Leach,
c1930. St Ives, English.
9in square

warping. The technique of firing hard, or true, porcelain for long presented potters
with harassing problems. Mastery of the kiln, as the ancient Chinese knew, always
remained the most vital factor in porcelain production. Firing difficulties were no
doubt responsible for a great deal of Plymouth porcelain being smoke-stained.

While Cookworthy's porcelain is of paramount interest as being the first hard
porcelain made in England, most wares produced at Plymouth and Bristol have
relatively little aesthetic appeal. Decoration was generally poor, whether in underglaze blue that developed a greyish tone, but was not unpleasing, or in enamel
colours used in imitative Oriental designs and sprays of flowers that lacked life
and were somewhat crudely executed. The best painted decoration, chiefly depicting birds in landscapes, is attributed to 'Monsieur Soqui', described as a
decorator trained at Sèvres. A somewhat mysterious repairer, Mr Tebo, who worked
later at Worcester, was employed by Cookworthy and Champion. At Bristol he
specialised in shell dishes and vases. Extant examples bear his signature 'To'.
Under Champion's direction the factory also issued a series of plaques in biscuit
ware ornamented with finely executed applied flowers. The craftsmanship of these
plaques is of high order but as they were designed in poor taste they are practically
devoid of artistic merit.

Students and collectors are sometimes surprised to discover that a number of
Cookworthy's figures and others made at Longton Hall in Staffordshire are identical.
The most acceptable explanation is simple. When the Longton Hall stock was
sold at Salisbury in 1760 Cookworthy had become deeply involved in his experi-

ments to produce hard porcelain. In all probability he availed himself of the opportunity offered to acquire moulds cheaply at the Longton Hall stock sale. It is probable, of course, that a modeller in Cookworthy's employ may have created models that were exact imitations of Longton Hall figures but it is generally accepted that Cookworthy used original Longton Hall moulds procured at the Salisbury sale.

New wares introduced by English potters during the nineteenth century included parian, the name being derived from that of Paros, the Greek island from whence ancient sculptors obtained the beautiful creamy or ivory-tinted marble which parian resembled. The first parian ware, referred to as statuary porcelain, issued from Copeland and Garrett's factory in 1842. Accounts of the invention vary, though it appears most likely that the ware was developed by chance at a period when Thomas Battam, working at the Copeland factory, made costly experiments to rediscover the Derby biscuit porcelain process. The first object Copeland's produced in statuary parian was a reproduction in miniature of John Gibson's *Narcissus*. A counter claim to be the inventor of parian was made by John Mountford of Minton's who was experimenting in the field at the same time. Mountford later became a successful manufacturer of parian wares.

Two kinds of parian were eventually produced: first, statuary parian used in the making of figures and reproductions of sculpture, and secondly, 'standard' parian, probably introduced by Charles Meigh of Hanley, principally used in the manufacture of hollow-wares. Statuary parian, containing a glassy frit, is classified as soft porcelain. Standard parian, with a larger proportion of feldspar in the composition and no frit, is hard porcelain. The ivory tint of early parian statuary was due to the presence of iron in the feldspar used. A search for feldspar of greater purity, free from iron silicate content, ended when deposits were located in Sweden and later in Ireland.

Parian statuary became immensely popular and gave the Victorians opportunity to fill their gardens and houses with figures and busts of every type and size. The ware was manufactured in large quantity by many nineteenth-century English and American potters who obtained knowledge of the Copeland and Garrett formula or worked out their own. Only highly skilled master potters were successful in producing fine parian statuary. The mould process was used, in principal following the technique used in the production of other porcelain figures, the parts being produced separately in moulds and joined up by a repairer using slip. As statuary parian was apt to warp or even collapse in the kiln during firing, assembled figures had to be supported by props made of the same material and dusted with powdered calcined flint to prevent adhesion. As the ware contracted in great heat, allowance for shrinkage was necessary, the majority of figures being reduced in the firing process by approximately one third.

Prior to firing, statuary parian figures were left to stand for a few days in order to dry out completely. Firing to the biscuit was carried out in a low-temperature oven

66 CHINAMAN. Porcelain figure. In red and black conical hat and a long flowered coat trimmed black and gold. Chelsea. Raised anchor period, c1750. English. *H 4in*

and might extend over two or three days. Low firing was essential to avoid cracking. After the first firing was completed and the figures had cooled and were removed from the kiln they were cleared of props and examined for flaws that might have developed during firing. A second firing in intense heat was necessary to obtain high vitrification. At this stage the object to be fired was placed in a protective sagger filled with sand.

Techniques used in production of standard parian wares were somewhat different, mainly because standard porcelain, unlike statuary porcelain, did not develop a 'natural' glaze during firing. Standard parian therefore required to be glazed. Ordinary lead glaze was unsuitable as it concealed relief ornament. The problem was eliminated by the use of the smear-glazing technique. In preparation for firing

179

the object was placed in a sealed sagger together with a small container holding the glaze. Alternatively, the glaze might be spread over the interior of the sagger. In the rising temperature of the oven the glaze melted and finely coated the ware.

Statuary parian techniques were already known to a number of successful potters by the time of the Great Exhibition in 1851 when a great variety of parian reproduction sculpture and original figures ranging from the diminutive to the massive were exhibited. In their individual composition of parian paste, and in other stages of manufacture, potters followed techniques best suited to their purpose. Production of fine statuary parian depended upon the greatest technical skill, however, and techniques employed were generally only slightly varied.

Original wares of many kinds were devised by inventive Victorian potters. The firm of Minton, under the progressive direction of Herbert Minton, an astute master potter with a shrewd eye for business, introduced a number of attractive new wares during the Victorian era, including the immensely popular colourful ware called majolica after Italian maiolica which it superficially resembled. Without a doubt, among the most important sumptuous Minton wares are the creations of Marc-Louis Solon decorated by the process known as *pâte-sur-pâte* or paste-upon-paste. Both modelling and painting techniques are involved in *pâte-sur-pâte* decoration by which stained parian ware is embellished with reliefs in translucent

67 PLATE. Octagonal. Porcelain. Painted with poppies. Chelsea. Red anchor period, c1755. English

white or tinted slip, one colour laid upon another, culminating in an effect of incredible beauty.

According to his own story, Solon was inspired by a celadon vase ornamented with embossed flowers that he admired in the museum at Sèvres where he worked. After a period of failure, painting slip on biscuit porcelain which peeled when dry, he achieved success when he applied the layers of slip upon a damp surface. Solon introduced his technique at Minton's where he worked from 1870 until 1904. In a short time Minton *pâte-sur-pâte* became the most coveted, albeit the most costly, ceramic ware produced in England at the period.

As Solon wrote, '*Pâte-sur-pâte* may be executed upon any semi-vitrifiable body, but the material used for the applied parts must always be of the same nature as the mass of which the piece itself is formed. The hard porcelain, is for density and fineness of substance, superior to any other: it is the one employed in France and Germany. But, as few metallic oxides can stand the high degree of heat to which it has to be submitted, the scale of available colours is very limited. With the body in use at Mintons, on the contrary, a great variety of colours can be obtained. It is a sort of parian, the elements entering into its composition are the same as those used for hard porcelain, but mixed in different proportion.' Few English craftsmen who ventured to emulate Solon's work achieved similar complete mastery of the technique, excepting his most brilliant pupil, Alboin Birks, whose work was of practically the same superb quality.

English artist potters of the late nineteenth century and their modern successors engaged in the production of what is now referred to as studio pottery have made important contributions to the development of modern English pottery forms and decoration. Perhaps, in the opinion of many, twentieth-century English artist potters have too often sought inspiration from Oriental sources. Far Eastern influence has somewhat diminished during post-war years, however, and over the past two decades there has been a significant increasing tendency among English studio potters to produce works that owe their inspiration to sources other than ancient Far Eastern ceramic wares.

The first potters successfully to engage in the creation of individualistic art pottery in England were the Martin brothers. They made a great deal of pottery of less bizarre character in brown and blue-grey salt glazes, but the grotesques in which they specialised, while being their less successful wares commercially and artistically, brought them fame. Success did not come quickly or easily to the four brothers. Using the large kiln they constructed at Southall in 1877-8 – it could hold some 600 pieces for firing at one time – they worked long and arduously in the production of high quality salt-glazed wares. Of the brothers, only the eldest, Wallace, trained as a modeller in a Barnstaple, Devon, pottery, acquired an all-round practical knowledge of techniques. Walter Martin developed remarkable ability in throwing and used the wheel to produce unusual wares notable for their surprising light weight. Both Wallace and Walter Martin were skilled in mixing clays. The latter made exhaustive study of clays and took charge of mixing in addition to acting as kiln-master. Edwin Martin developed great skill in the execution of engraved, raised and inlaid decoration on pottery. Charles Martin acted as business manager and salesman.

Several of the schools of arts and crafts founded in London and elsewhere in England towards the end of the nineteenth century provided excellent training centres for aspiring potters. Of these, the Camberwell School of Arts and Crafts in London took the greatest interest in offering training in pottery techniques. Among leading English studio potters of later years William Staite Murray, Roger Fry and Charles Vyse, the last a sculptor who became interested in Chinese glazes and assisted by his wife, a chemist, produced striking wares inspired by Chinese pottery, received early instruction at Camberwell.

The sculptor Reginald Wells studied pottery techniques at Camberwell School of Art and later established a studio pottery at Coldrum in Kent where he specialised in the production of brownish-glazed earthenware decorated with white slip in the style of seventeenth-century wares produced at Wrotham in Kent. Wells was the first modern artist potter to follow the English tradition. He subsequently changed his style after first removing to Chelsea then to Storrington in Sussex where he concentrated on the production of stoneware pots in the ancient Chinese tradition decorated with crackle, greyish-white and matt blue glazes.

With the exception of Bernard Leach, who had the good fortune to be able to study Oriental pottery techniques while living in Japan in his youth, William Staite Murray became the most vital and influential figure associated with the development of modern English art pottery techniques and styles. After training as a painter he began making pottery in 1912, mainly producing brush-decorated low-fired wares in a gas-fired kiln. When World War I ended Murray set up as a potter at Rotherhithe making pots of somewhat primitive character, variously decorated with streaked or splashed glaze effects or left undecorated. At the period Murray was interested in the advancement of production techniques and the development of equipment to aid the studio potter in his work. Improved kiln processes occupied much of his attention and at Brockley in Kent he designed, constructed and subsequently patented a crude oil-burning kiln for firing wares at high temperature, the first of its kind operated in England.

Murray's wares produced in the 1920s exhibit a significant change in style. Bodies coarsened and, being of sandy texture, wares usually fired to light red ochre. He made use of glaze as decoration, but not always glazing the entire pot, often applying scratched or brush decoration. The style of his later wares was bolder and the modelling vigorous. At times productions verged on the bizarre, but in the course of development his changing techniques rendered his work extremely individualistic. All Murray's wares were ornamental, since he regarded pottery purely as an art form. In the mid-1930s he was influenced by the English medieval style and his work took on an entirely new character. Brush decoration on his productions of the late 1930s suffered from a certain dullness but there was no diminution in the beauty and interest of his glazes, although, as a rule, Murray exercised restraint in the use of colour.

In 1925 Murray became principal of the Pottery School in the Royal College of Art, London. Many of his pupils developed great skill and achieved distinction as potters in later years. Thomas Samuel Haile (1909–48), who studied ceramics under Murray for three years, did not specialise but was highly accomplished in slipware and stoneware techniques. Haile's finest work was produced in the United States where, accompanied by his wife Marianne de Trey, herself a potter of considerable ability, he became established a few years after leaving the Royal College of Art. Haile studied and was consequently influenced by pre-Columbian sculpture and ancient Indian pottery. 'Sam' Haile studied and taught at New York State College of Ceramics at Alfred and was subsequently appointed instructor in pottery at the

68   MUG. Porcelain.
Painted underglaze blue.
Plymouth, c1770.
English. H 6⅝in, D rim
4¼in

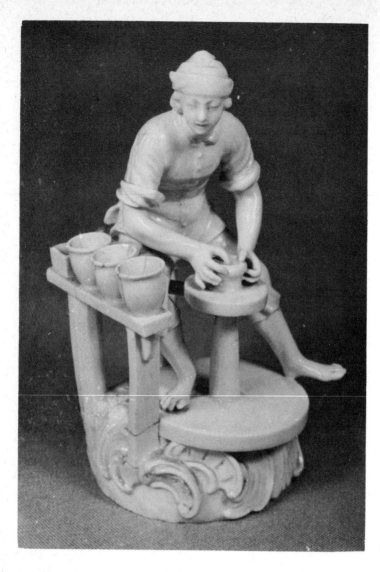

69 THE DERBY POTTER
(from a Meissen
original). Porcelain.
Derby, c1770. English.
H 7¾in

College of Architecture of the University of Michigan at Ann Arbor. Following the end of World War II, returning to England, he worked at the Shinner's Bridge Pottery near Dartington Hall, Devon, established by Bernard Leach. A brilliant career ended with Haile's accidental death in 1948.

No one interested in the development of modern pottery and the techniques employed by innumerable artist potters at work today in their workshops in Europe and America should miss reading Bernard Leach's invaluable *A Potter's Book*. The work is a treatise on traditional techniques in pottery production handed down by the great potters of the past and explains how those traditions may be followed by potters today.

Leach, a remarkably individualistic master potter of the highest artistic and technical ability, has exerted enormous influence on contemporary potters, not only in England, where the Leach Pottery at St Ives, Cornwall, has become the most widely known and successful of its kind, but also on the Continent and in the United States where Leach's work is much admired. In America Leach has a large following among potters who unashamedly emulate his techniques and styles. We are informed in the preface of his book that the work was the outcome of thirty-three years' experience of making pots in the Far East and in England. Twelve of those years were spent resident in Japan where Leach studied the techniques of early Japanese potters. As he reveals, he became aware of the urgent need of potters to relate the spirit and methods of the ancient Oriental potters to the Western birthright of traditional craft. Through his own pottery and boundless enthusiasm he largely inspired the revival of the English tradition in pottery.

To attempt to generalise upon or adequately describe within the space of a few pages the many varied techniques and styles of the supremely talented potter Bernard Leach, developed over many years, would be futile. Love of pottery-making and pottery motivated him from his early manhood. In all his brilliant works we perceive the self-confidence and creative power of a master in the exercise of superior skill, and love for his art expressed in dexterous manipulation of common clay.

3
AMERICA

ANCIENT CULTURES

It becomes apparent after study of examples that ancient American pottery owes little or nothing to European and Asiatic influences. Here and there one may come across specimens of pottery from one of the more advanced ancient American cultures which exhibit characteristics of Old World pottery, but such resemblances must be regarded with caution as coincidental or accidental. Pre-Columbian American pottery, much of it of excellent quality, was made by potters working at great distances from each other, and who, moreover, knew nothing of Old World techniques. Even the wheel was unknown.

The production of clay vessels was pursued among ancient American peoples from a remote period. Glaze was used decoratively but never to seal porous wares. Porcelain was entirely unknown. Primitive potters followed the mould technique as early as the first millennium BC and made domestic pots by building up from clay rings. Vessels are believed to have been produced by the latter method during the second millennium BC. Due to the non-existence of the wheel, potters carried out all modelling and finishing processes by hand. Clay naturally varied in different localities. Materials might include calcite, sand and sometimes powdered mica added to increase ductility. The presence of mica in the paste, which imparted a glistening effect to wares, gave rise to a belief among Europeans that ancient American potters mixed gold with other materials. Firing techniques were essentially simple, the results not always being predictable owing to difficulty in controlling temperatures. An oxidising flame was used for firing brown, red and orange wares, while black and white wares were fired in reduction. A great deal has yet to be learned and understood concerning the techniques of ancient American potters.

Pottery of sorts was extensively made in pre-Columbian America, but the most brilliantly conceived objects made at the zenith of technical and artistic development were created in areas of the south-west United States, Mexico, Central America, Peru and Bolivia. To describe in detail all the varied pottery produced in these regions up to the time of the Spanish Conquest is not possible here. Therefore, the productions of a few of the most highly developed cultures will be considered, beginning with the fine pottery made in an area of the United States covered by Arizona, New Mexico and parts of Colorado and Utah.

Pueblo Indians living on the plateau are descendants of the Anasazi who inhabited that corner of the south-west at least as early as the commencement of the Christian era. At first, the Anasazi only made fine baskets, but in course of time they learned

70 SEATED MAN. Large
figure with body
coloured orange.
Nayarit, Western
Mexico, AD 400. Mexican.
H 20in

the techniques of making crude pottery. By about the eighth century AD an upsurge
in Pueblo artistic development led to great improvement in the quality of their
wares. Anasazi pottery decorated black over white slip became characteristic and
was made in a variety of strikingly decorated shapes until about AD 1300 when a
further remarkable advance in technical and artistic skill took place.

The potters of the region, for no reason that is yet known, began producing polychrome wares that rapidly superseded the conventional black-on-white wares the
Anasazi had specialised in making for several centuries. The new colourful wares
were quite different in form and ornament to any previously produced in the region.

Stylised life forms, particularly animals and birds, geometrical designs and masked human figures became popular. Red and yellow backgrounds, which predominate in south-western pottery of the period, resulted from the use of local iron-bearing clays and the effect of an oxidising atmosphere during firing.

As has already been pointed out, ancient American potters did not use glaze as a waterproofing agent although it was used extensively as decoration. From at least the beginning of the fourteenth century glazes containing copper or lead were used in the ornamentation of wares, first applied over a red ground and subsequently on a white ground, combined with red painted decoration. Polychrome decoration, which developed later, was at first finely executed, but as time passed ornament was carelessly applied and grew more decadent. In the final stages glaze returned to favour, but as the artistic and technical skill of the potters had entered upon decline wares thus decorated were considerably less attractive and of poorer quality than early examples.

The Hohokam, who became established in Arizona at about the beginning of the Christian era, and remained settled in the region for about 1,400 years, had some affinity in culture with Mexican peoples. They made excellent pottery, specialising in the production of figurines, chiefly representing nude women, which are believed to have had some religious significance. The most common Hohokam ware is buff-coloured with painted red decoration, a type with a greyish background being much rarer. Hohokam pottery followed the ancient technique of building up wares with coils or bands of clay, finishing by thinning and shaping the walls of a pot by beating the clay with a heavy spatula or paddle. An extensive variety of wares was made. After about AD 800 decoration grew more elaborate, with bird and animal motifs repeated over the surface or applied in broad patterned bands. Geometrical designs did not appear until the so-called Sedentary Period, AD 900–1200, when plaited and woven effects were introduced. During the ensuing two centuries both the fabric and decoration of Hohokam ware gradually declined, probably due to strife which brought the ultimate extinction of their culture.

The Mogollon area of the south-west, occupied by the third century of the Christian era, produced only mediocre pottery until about AD 1000 when the unique attractive black-on-white wares in a style known as Mimbres, possibly inspired by black-on-white Anasazi wares, first appeared. Mimbres pottery chiefly consists of bowls with complex designs painted inside. It is believed that Mimbres bowls were concerned with burial rites as the majority extant have been taken from graves. An interesting feature, the subject of considerable speculation, is the hole pierced through the middle, obviously an act of religious significance performed during the burial ceremony, as the portion of the bowl removed by punching has frequently been found lying in the grave.

Occasionally dark brown replaced black on Mimbres wares. Decoration principally comprised narrow bands encircling the top of vessels, embellished below with stylised yet animated representations of people or animals, or alternatively with scenes of men and animals fighting. Painted geometrical designs were fairly common, as a rule executed with care, applied in broad bands in a circular arrangement. Mimbres black-on-white wares were apparently produced over a relatively brief period of approximately two centuries, after which, during the thirteenth century, migration took place, when it is believed that many craftsmen found their way into the Chihuahua state in Mexico.

Pottery-making was one of the crafts raised to the level of fine art in Mexico over a period extending roughly from the middle of the second millennium BC to the Spanish Conquest. The original pottery of Mexico, infinitely varied and beautiful in form and decoration, was largely produced by following techniques unknown in the Old World. These wares attest to the skill and artistry of early Mexican and Central American potters. The first shapes to evolve in the valley of Mexico appear to have been vases supported on tripod bases. Later, in the area of the Gulf coast, where enterprising potters evidently experimented in design, numerous entirely new pottery forms evolved.

While the ancient Mexican potters were principally concerned with producing utilitarian vessels, their artistic bent found expression in the creation of clay figurines modelled by hand in much the same tradition as evolved in many parts of the Old World at a remote period. Details of features were usually incised or punched. Undoubtedly, these figurines served as votive offerings. In later centuries the art of ceramic sculpture was developed to a remarkable degree by Mexican craftsmen. Representations of human beings, animals and birds were fashioned to serve as vessels, particularly splendid large vases used in ceremonial.

Mexican potters rarely refrained from ornamentation of their wares. Only vases used for storage were left devoid of ornament. Monochrome painted slip decoration in brown, red, black or white was favoured, usually finished by burnishing. Incised geometrical patterns were delicately executed, these superseding earlier curvilinear designs. The potters of ancient Mexico displayed notable skill in what is known as the 'negative-painting' technique which involved painting designs in hot wax on wares, followed by painting over the wax which was then removed leaving the design in the original body colour. Early Mexican potters also excelled in another decorative technique in which slip was scraped from the body of wares thereby exposing the original surface in a different coloured pattern.

The Maya culture attained unprecedented heights in artistic development, not least of which was superior skill and artistry in pottery. During what is generally referred to as the Classic period, approximately AD 300–980, as far as pottery is concerned the most important developments occurred in later centuries. Monochrome wares of the earlier period were unremarkable. First of several new techniques developed was that now known as 'fresco' or *cloisonné poterie* in which the entire surface of wares was thinly coated with coloured plaster which was subsequently cut away to leave narrow partitions between surface areas decorated in other colours. The pastel shades employed, pink, green, blue and white, imparted a delicate beauty to the ware. Due to its extreme fragility scarcely any intact examples have been recovered from excavated sites. The later 'champleve' technique entailed covering wares with brown or black slip which was then cut away to leave a design in low relief, the background being filled in by painting with cinnabar.

Development in Maya pottery of the early Classic period began with the introduction of polychrome decoration in either conventionalised or geometrical designs. Wavy lines were frequently used to divide broad or narrow red or black bands and panels enclosing stylised serpents and geometrical patterns. Wares were painted inside and outside. Animal forms were favoured in painted decoration, particularly that of the jaguar. Among the most striking wares were vases with painted decora-

71 STIRRUP POT. Chimu blackware. Twelfth century AD. South American. *H 9in*

tion portraying aspects of Maya religious ceremonies. Vases on tripod feet were produced in variation of form and decoration.

Colourful polychrome-decorated vessels and a type of monochrome were embellished with low relief carving that rendered simple decoration in grey or red slip dull by comparison. Relief carving was hieroglyphical in character, but the symbols became so conventionalised as to be virtually unreadable. Hieroglyphics were apparently not intended to be read but to serve simply as ornament. This form of decoration was used extensively at one period and was usually extremely well executed.

Other cultures isolated from spheres of influence existing in the valley and highlands of Mexico included skilled potters in remote regions such as Michoacan who were responsible for much highly original work. Perhaps the best known, the Colima culture of far Western Mexico, adhered to artistic traditions different in many respects from those followed elsewhere. It may be reasonably concluded that Colima potters took a less serious view of life and the pursuit of their craft than prevailed in other Mexican cultures as their productions have a lightness of form and ornament rarely seen in other wares made in Mexico and Central America. Colima potters evidently spent much time producing figures, sensitively modelled and usually painted red or white. Early figures were quite small but larger effigies of people and animals were eventually made in quantity. It is worth noting that competently modelled Colima clay figures, whether of people, including officials, warriors or religious dignitaries, or of dogs and other animals, are frequently in caricature, reflecting the humour of the potters who found amusement in thus portraying the life of their world.

Figures of unusual character were also produced in the state of Guanajuato. These pottery figures, belonging to a class known as 'pretty-lady', are somewhat flattened in shape, the features indicated by clay fillets. Early Guanajuato figurines are not generally found painted or slip decorated, but later examples survive that are lavishly painted in polychrome, chiefly in black, white and red geometrical designs.

In AD 980 the Toltecs founded Tula, their principal city, where the arts subsequently flourished with the development of the peculiar flamboyant style associated with Toltec culture. The Toltecs invented two outstanding, vital types of pottery now classified as 'plumbate' ware and 'fine orange' ware. The wares were contemporaneous. Judging from specimens excavated in far apart areas of Mexico, it is thought that both plumbate and fine orange wares were either distributed in trade or actually made in all regions where the Toltecs held sway.

Plumbate ware is among the most singular pottery produced in pre-Columbian America. It is fundamentally different from other soft contemporary wares made in Mexico in that the paste fired into a hard body. Bulbous jars and some other types of vessels are found in varying shape. Plumbate pottery has a distinctive lustrous appearance, and this, combined with incised decoration, gives the ware its extraordinary character. Ornate incised designs typical of Toltec art were cut

72 TWO FIGURINES:
(*left*) From Chupicuara
(Guanajuato) 300 BC to
AD 200. *H 9in*; (*right*)
from Querendaro,
Michoacan. 300 BC to
AD 200. *H 5½in*. Both
Mexican

before the application of slip to wares. Plumbate ware varies in colour from olive to black. Gods and animals, frequently depicted in Toltec art, appear constantly in decoration of plumbate ware. Vases exist with figures moulded to the sides. Sometimes a vessel evidently intended for ceremonial use is found fashioned in the form of an animal or bird. As in earlier cultures, vases were made in all shapes and sizes for a multiplicity of purposes, almost invariably either supported on tripods or on pedestal bases. Incised decoration executed on plumbate wares is occasionally fine, but generally wares display careless workmanship and poor finish.

Where or how plumbate ware originated can only be guessed at. It is fairly certain that the ware was being made by about AD 1000. The fact that early examples have been excavated on far apart ancient sites has given rise to uncertainty concerning the source of origin. Almost certainly, the ware was distributed over a wide area through trade. It appears most probable that the ware originated on the Pacific coast of Mexico. The appellation plumbate ware is somewhat misleading as it leads to an erroneous assumption that the paste had lead mixed in to produce a glazed effect. Lustrous finish was achieved by a different technique which vitally depended upon high firing in a reducing furnace, to a degree of around 950°C. The clay, of a special type probably originally discovered by natives acquainted with the nature and craft of pottery, most likely changed colour, assuming a variety of tones, in firing, due to the presence of oxygen not easily controlled. Whether or not the lustrous surface of the ware was obtained by applying two coats of slip, as is surmised, is not known for certain.

Fine orange ware appears to have been made with greater concern for finish and quality than indicated in plumbate ware. A vital difference between fine orange ware and other pottery produced in Mexico over a long period is that any kind of tempering medium is absent from the former. Two varieties were made, although the paste is fundamentally the same, smooth and fine in texture and evenly coloured. The essential difference between the two types of fine orange ware is that the surface of one is smooth and matt while that of the other is hard with a slightly lustrous appearance.

Shape and manner of decoration of fine orange ware greatly varies, largely depending upon the locality in which it is found. It has been suggested that the existence of so many diversely shaped and decorated specimens of fine orange ware proves that the ware was not made exclusively in one locality from where it was distributed, but that only the raw clay was traded and that potters in widely separated regions made their own fine orange ware.

As the centuries passed, prior to the arrival of Europeans in Mexico and Central America, potters gradually forsook their high artistic standards. Toltec influence initiated an artistic decline which became markedly visible with increasing preference for harsh colour contrasts, flamboyant decoration and eccentric form. Over-elaboration and poor craftsmanship mar a large proportion of late wares. It is as curious as it was unfortunate that as the potters learned more about materials and developed their ability to produce more durable wares by improved firing techniques their artistic sensibility declined.

Far to the south of the Isthmus of Panama, in the central Andean region, the highly advanced ancient civilisations of South America produced superb pottery in immeasurable variety. Between the rise of the Mochica and Nazca cultures and the destruction of the Inca empire potters working in a vast region throughout successive centuries developed their productions along individualistic lines.

The Mochica people were well established and in an advanced state of civilisation by about the beginning of the Christian era, or perhaps a few centuries earlier, living principally in the valley of the Chicama river adjacent to the north coast of Peru. At about the same time, in the Nazca valley coastal region far to the south, the Nazca culture entered upon a period of remarkable artistic development.

Mochica pottery attained its peak of technical and artistic excellence in splendid ceremonial wares. The potters were among the first in South America to master the technique of ceramic modelling in the round. As moulds were extensively used, reproduction was a common practice, but with interesting variations occurring in examples, carried out during decoration and finishing. Decoration chiefly consisted of low-relief ornament painted red and white, with touches of black added at a later period. Vessels of many shapes were produced, a large proportion in rep-

73 VASE. Maya. Classic period, c fifth to sixth century AD. Mexican. H 5½in

resentation of human and animal forms, the entire body or alternatively the head only.

Whatever the mode of decoration, low relief or painted design, it was generally stylised. Scenes from everyday life and religious ceremonial were depicted. Decoration on jars was richly varied, often depicting people at work, scenery, buildings and a variety of animals, birds, flora and fruits. Whistling jars were popular and were commonly made in representation of birds.

Nazca pottery was technically superior to that of the Mochicas, but artistically the wares of both cultures reached about the same level and exhibited a degree of affinity in style and decoration. The two cultures were roughly contemporaneous. However, due to the separation of the Mochica and Nazca peoples by about a thousand miles of wild mountainous terrain it is improbable that more than slight contact, even if that, was maintained between the two.

The finest Nazca pottery is thin and obviously made by craftsmen who cared about their work. Most objects were finished with polishing. Low or pressed relief decoration, as commonly found on Mochica pottery, is absent from Nazca wares, while modelling in the round, a technique practised with great accomplishment by Mochica potters, was rarely attempted by Nazca craftsmen. Vessels in representation of stylised human and animal heads were favourite Nazca pottery forms. The most commonly produced wares were jars of utilitarian or ceremonial character made in an extraordinary variety of shapes and sizes. Globular jars with two connected short tubular spouts are usually striking objects, often lavishly decorated with finely painted designs in numerous colours. Brilliant polychrome painting on a slip ground was a favourite Nazca mode of decoration on jars, bowls and beakers. As many as eight colours appear on a single vessel. Varying colour tones were popular, the palette usually comprising yellow, grey, red, brown, violet, black and white. Designs are usually outlined in black. At first, a dark red background was used almost exclusively, but this was later superseded by a white slip ground. Decoration on numerous extant examples depicts stylised life forms. Vessels intended exclusively for use in ceremony are decorated with religious motifs and scenes.

In the highland region south of Lake Titicaca, around the ancient site of Tiahuanaco, just inside the western border of Bolivia, pottery has been excavated comparable in quality with the finest Mochica and Nazca wares with which it is probably contemporaneous. Tiahuanaco pottery is usually painted in polychrome. The finest examples yet discovered have a red slip ground with decoration applied in a colour range of grey, yellow or brown, the design outlined in black or white. Geometrical designs are common. Examples have been found decorated with stylised condors and pumas. It was apparently conventional in the decoration of Tiahuanaco pottery to depict animals and birds in profile, often with the eyes half black and half white.

Mochica, Nazca and Tiahuanaco pottery belongs to the most fruitful period in their respective cultures. With the lapse of centuries skill declined although ancient traditions endured. Later potters worked in the old traditions but the quality of their wares became much inferior. Pottery made during times of strife and cultural decline exhibits coarseness made all the more repellent by comparison with the delicately ornamented, refined productions of earlier centuries.

With the rise of the Incas ancient South American ceramic art reached its final flowering. The finest wares were produced during the expansion of the empire in the fifteenth century. Comparatively few shapes were made, chiefly jars, bowls and plates, not overlooking the curious drinking vessel known to the Incas as a *paccha*, a red-bodied object usually painted in polychrome and polished. Geometrical and stylised plant designs were characteristic Inca decoration, occasionally with the addition of conventionalised insects and llamas.

Inca ceramic art, which itself was derivative, influenced potters throughout the vast area of the empire. Developments in techniques and styles emanated from Cuzco and were ultimately adopted by potters in territories under Inca rule, with the result that in the last decades before the arrival of the Spanish conquerors much of the pottery made in the region of the central Andes and adjoining areas was more or less uniform in style, conforming to the shapes and modes of decoration favoured and perhaps decreed by Inca rulers.

COLONIAL NORTH AMERICA

Folk pottery, principally comprising earthenware vessels of simple character, was the earliest ceramic ware produced in the American colonies by immigrant potters from England and Europe. Naturally, potters followed the traditional techniques of their native lands; in consequence for generations American pottery closely resembled that of Western Europe. Differences of character that subsequently developed were not necessarily the outcome of any conscious desire on the part of colonial potters to invent new techniques or introduce new styles, but were more often promoted by necessity owing to differences in materials available or the special needs of the settlers who purchased the wares. In early colonial times communities in the sparsely populated colonies lived austerely, requiring only serviceable utilitarian pots. No potter would have considered it worthwhile to make other than plain wares that his customers needed and could afford to buy. Until the eighteenth century little attempt was made by colonial potters, however enterprising and inventive, to employ their skill in production of 'fancy' wares. At first, whenever styles changed, they usually did so because newly-imported wares from Europe were copied and in this respect immigrant potters endeavoured to keep abreast of fashion.

Surviving records mention Dutch and English potters at work in various places during the seventeenth century, but little early documentary evidence concerning American colonial potters has come to light. We know of Philip Drinker working at Charlestown, Massachusetts, in 1635, and others, including John Pride who settled in Salem as a potter at about the same time, but information is sketchy. The first colonial pottery of importance was established in 1688 by Dr Daniel Coxe, an English physician who owned land in west New Jersey. The new works arose on a site at Burlington, New Jersey. Coxe subsequently became physician to Queen Anne. Little is known concerning the venture and the man behind it other than the somewhat surprising fact that Dr Coxe never set foot in America. He apparently employed an Englishman to manage his factory.

Potters trained in Europe who arrived in the colonies with intention of practising their skills were not invariably successful in making use of available materials to meet their needs. Potter's clay was plentiful throughout most of the colonies, but quality varied and clays in some localities proved unsuitable for specific purposes. Owing to a scarcity of lead and tin, vital in the production of glaze, new techniques and some measure of innovation became imperative. Although many immigrant potters were capable of making and decorating excellent earthenware, particularly potters from England who had trained in Staffordshire, and Frenchmen experienced in the production of faience, until prosperity and more peaceful times arrived high

74 SWEETMEAT DISH.
Bonnin and Morris,
Philadelphia. Porcelain.
Colonial American.
H 5½in

standards in pottery were not demanded. For a long period pottery continued to be imported from Europe, chiefly from England and Holland. Thus European influence on styles was maintained while the colonial potter was only expected to supply comparatively coarse wares.

Changes gradually came about, however, and the lot of the colonial potter improved. Materials were abundant, with unlimited supplies of wood for heating kilns. As potters became more prosperous they undertook to train apprentices in traditional methods, although as time passed these were generally discontinued in favour of new technical and artistic developments. In this way, wares were designed to meet the changing needs of progressive communities. The European tradition was eliminated in time and later American folk pottery assumed its peculiar characteristics.

As he usually operated a humble kiln, lacked financial resources and found his trade restricted, the less fortunate, unaspiring potter made only wares he experienced no difficulty in selling. Earthenware domestic pots were produced by immigrant folk potters from the early decades of the seventeenth century through to the Revolution. Stoneware was first made in the colonies at the beginning of the eighteenth century and after the Revolution largely superseded earthenware for use in the home. Salt-glazed stoneware became the principal product in the new century. Both the earthenware and stoneware traditions have endured and are now practised with success by eminent modern American potters.

The earliest examples of American colonial earthenware – redware – excavated at Jamestown, Virginia, date from the period 1630–50. Early redware is extremely fragile and, when unglazed, is porous. Presumably, only utilitarian wares were made at Jamestown. Other wares were probably shipped to the colony from England. It was not long, however, before Jamestown potters were producing lead-glazed wares.

Potters living in early colonial America often engaged in other work besides making pottery. Many worked small farms. While they grew and tended crops they gathered and prepared pottery materials. Preparation of the clay was usually well under way by the early autumn when the harvest had been gathered in. Clay was dug up and made ready for use in the spring. Preparing the clay for winter storage was a process that varied among potters. Most followed the method used by the ancient Greeks – which has survived through the centuries – of preparation in pits. The clay was thoroughly mixed and left covered with water in a shallow pit. This allowed the right consistency to be obtained while stones and grit were eliminated by sinking to the bottom. In the next stage of operations the clay was removed from the pit and strained through a horsehair sieve. The moist clay was then placed in a second adjacent pit known as a 'sun-kiln' where it was evenly spread out in successive layers, each layer left to dry out to a practical working consistency before being covered by the next layer. Finally, the clay was cut into convenient-sized blocks and stored away for the winter.

As noted, early American folk pottery was essentially utilitarian in character, extremely simple in shape and with a minimum of decoration. Ornament usually consisted of lines executed with a stick or impressions made with the finger upon the moist clay. As a rule, potters produced vessels by throwing on the wheel, applying decoration when the pot was shaped.

The use of glaze by colonial potters began with the introduction of pure lead glaze produced by a method which became common practice, that of dusting powdered galena over the surface of wares before firing. Only thin glazing was achieved by this technique. Owing to difficulty in obtaining materials, at first only the insides of wares were glazed. By this means vessels were rendered watertight and were less troublesome to clean. When supplies of lead became easier to obtain and less costly, colonial potters considerably improved their methods of glazing. Use of liquid glaze, produced by mixing galena, red lead or litharge with white sand and water, enabled potters to dip wares and thereby achieve evenly distributed glazing inside and out. At a later stage of technical development it became the practice to mix a proportion of loam or clay with sand and lead in order to obtain a thicker, more colourful glaze.

Like the ancient Chinese potters, American colonial potters fired their earthenware once only. Wares, which were previously shaped on the wheel and decorated, were left to dry out before glaze was applied, followed by firing. A once-fired technique saved time and labour, and no problems were created in glazing while dusting on galena remained the general method. Later, when coloured glazes became popular, the single-firing technique proved less satisfactory.

Although wares made by immigrant potters continued to improve in quality with the increasing prosperity and development of the colonies it was a long time before they were regarded as being anything but inferior to wares imported from Europe. It was probably due to this widely held opinion, generally based more on fancy than fact, that colonial potters refrained from the production of anything but utilitarian wares. They were not encouraged to compete with European pottery concerns that supplied ever-increasing quantities of wares to the colonies both before and after the Revolution. Colonial potters were in consequence slow to attempt making ornamental wares and their productions showed little change in style for decades. A certain characteristic lightness and charm in the manner of decoration of American folk pottery evolved towards the end of the eighteenth century, but the post-Revolution era was reached before potters began seeking to improve the style and quality of their wares in an effort to rival imported wares and capture a share of the market.

Labour did not present the same problems to the modest colonial potter in the seventeenth century, who often worked single-handed, as in the following century when increasing numbers of skilled potters arrived in the colonies. By the middle of the eighteenth century the location of raw materials was generally known. Wherever extensive deposits of suitable clays were found potters newly arrived from Europe tended to settle in groups. Skilled labour and trade became centred in certain areas where apprentices could receive adequate training and feel confident of finding work when they had served their time. Owing to the abundance of materials throughout the colonies pottery-making centres sprang up in widely separated localities.

Proximity to one another in a particular area and the use of materials obtained from the same sources inevitably resulted in groups of potters producing similar wares. Exchange of technical information and ideas, and unrestrained emulation of each other's techniques and styles, resulted in close similarity between wares made in various centres so that it eventually became easy to distinguish the productions of respective groups by individual characteristics.

A potter's entire family was often involved in making pottery. A pottery founded by an immigrant potter was sometimes operated by his descendants through successive generations. A master potter might, for example, instruct his sons in the techniques of his craft and, by their adherence to certain traditions from one generation to another, the wares of a particular family became identifiable. Apprentices sometimes married their master's daughters and thus, through sons and daughters, family tradition was perpetuated.

Earthenware was chiefly produced in the New England colonies, particularly in Massachusetts and Connecticut, also in East Pennsylvania. Stoneware, for which Vermont subsequently became noted, was a later product. German-speaking immigrant potters, commonly referred to as Pennsylvania Dutch, who settled around Philadelphia and in Germantown, were mainly responsible for the growth of a flourishing pottery industry in Pennsylvania. The German earthenware tradition was kept alive in numerous small potteries established by Germans in a wide area

75 POT. Stoneware. Decorated with bird holding grapes. Boston, Massachusetts, c1795. American. *H 12½in*

extending as far south as Maryland and Virginia. Red clay and pipe clay were plentiful in Pennsylvania, also lead for use in glazing. German potters thus immediately and easily procured most of the essential materials for continuing to work as formerly in their native land. All types of earthenware were produced, colour and quality varying according to the type of clay obtainable locally. Redware was made in large quantities. White, brown and yellow earthenwares were less commonly produced. 'Tulip' motifs were commonly used in decoration of Pennsylvania Dutch wares.

Colonial potters working from the mid-eighteenth century onwards found hitherto scarce materials much easier to obtain and in many instances less costly. Materials still only obtainable from Europe reached colonial ports regularly and were more quickly distributed. Colouring oxides, used in glazing, were readily obtainable in America by the mid-eighteenth century, but remained costly. Potters tended to rely upon iron oxides found locally for yellows and browns – yellow was also obtained from antimony – and upon manganese oxide for brown and black. Copper oxide, which was expensive, yielded green used chiefly in decoration.

76 PLATE. By Johannes Neesz. Red earthenware. Pennsylvania German, c1810.
American. D 12½in

For readers unacquainted with American folk pottery it may be of interest and
indeed advisable to state here that far from being dull and drab in appearance,
as may mistakenly be concluded, much American folk pottery is attractively
coloured. Only a limited number of colouring oxides were available but potters
displayed ingenuity when using them in decoration. The body of wares was generally
coloured brown, varying from light to dark in tone, sometimes appearing almost
black.

As glazing materials were costly and even at a relatively late date techniques
followed in applying glaze decoratively were known or practised by only a comparatively few potters, for a long period decoration on earthenware remained
simple. New England potters for the most part scarcely deviated from their characteristic use of straight and wavy lines, a decorative style which continued in favour
until well into the eighteenth century. As colouring oxides became more readily
available potters desiring to impart brightness to their wares applied splashes of

colour with a brush. The colours often ran into the glaze and down the sides of wares, with a resultant pleasing effect. When later New England potters ventured to improve on traditional methods of decoration they devised a technique of applying clear glaze over coloured slip, with charming results.

Potters in Pennsylvania and New England frequently made use of the cogglewheel in decoration of wares. The wheel consisted of clay or wooden rollers engraved with a continuous pattern which were rolled across the surface of wares before they hardened.

Early colonial potters used two types of wheel in throwing. A 'kick and paw' wheel, as it was called, more generally used by European potters, was driven by operating a foot-lever. Potters from England usually preferred to use the foot-powered 'kick' or treadle wheel. Both English and Continental immigrant potters were in the majority trained in uses of the wheel, consequently their wares were much better shaped and finished than most pottery produced in America before the advent of European colonists.

Newly arrived potters from Europe naturally introduced the latest techniques developed in their homelands. Itinerant potters, who gained knowledge of improved methods as they travelled the colonies, were much less frequently encountered before the Revolution than after. As the eighteenth century progressed numbers of itinerant craftsmen earned a comfortable living working for short periods for different masters as they travelled from one locality to another. Skilled labour remained scarce for decades. Some craftsmen found it more profitable and less hazardous to work for a master for as long as they felt inclined before moving on than to set up their own workshops even when they possessed the capital to do so. Many potters who led a wandering life in the colonies continued to acquire technical knowledge which they passed on to the masters for whom they worked. Thus new ideas were transmitted from one craftsman to another.

In the last decade of the eighteenth century colonial housewives began to appreciate the superiority of stoneware over earthenware for domestic pots. At about the same time an increasing awareness of the danger to health from the use of lead glaze on household wares gave rise to uneasiness.

It is not known for certain which potter or potters first produced stoneware in the American colonies. William Crolius, an immigrant potter from Germany, made stoneware in the vicinity of New York at about the beginning of the 1730s. According to records, Anthony Duché and his sons were making stoneware in Philadelphia late in the 1720s.

Crolius, who was born near Coblenz in Germany in 1700, became an important and successful potter after emigrating to America in 1718. He was evidently trained in the techniques of pottery manufacture at a comparatively early age, in all probability before he left Europe. Almost certainly, the first kiln erected in the New York area for the production of stoneware was owned by William Crolius. The

Crolius Pottery became one of the most successful and longest surviving concerns of its kind in the locality, continued in operation by the founder's descendants until its closure in 1887. A stoneware pottery set up in about 1740 by John Remmey, an emigrant from the Rhineland who married Crolius's sister-in-law, flourished until 1820.

In about 1740, at Charlestown, Massachusetts, a prosperous earthenware manufacturer, Isaac Parker, became the first New England potter to experiment in stoneware production. Parker exhausted his financial reserves in endeavouring to invent or obtain a formula. A grant awarded him by the General Court to aid him in continuing experiments was received too late, only shortly before his death. Parker's widow, Grace, assisted by James Duché, a son of Anthony Duché, continued her husband's experiments. Costly transportation of clays after local materials were found unsuitable led Mrs Parker and her partners – she had meantime enlisted the support of her brother-in-law Thomas Symmes – to the verge of bankruptcy. When Mrs Parker and Symmes both died in 1754 experiments came to an end. Stoneware was not produced in Massachusetts until the late 1770s when William Seaver of Taunton set up a kiln and succeeded in manufacturing stoneware that could be sold at a competitive price by blending local clay with stoneware clay transported from New Jersey.

Clay vital in production of stoneware was at first obtained principally from New Jersey. The clay was used by a number of potters who later specialised in making

77 CROCK. Red earthenware. Incised decoration. Colonial American. H 10in

stoneware, including the well-known States family of potters who established kilns in various parts of Connecticut. Adam States, believed to be an immigrant potter from Holland, who established a pottery at Greenwich, Connecticut, in 1750, was probably the first potter to manufacture stoneware in Connecticut. German immigrant potters who settled in East Pennsylvania, where German-speaking communities became established, at first produced only earthenware in their native tradition. As stoneware superseded earthenware in general usage the Germans found it expedient to concentrate on its production while continuing to make quantities of earthenware. In addition to rich deposits in New Jersey and Delaware, stoneware clay was plentiful in East Pennsylvania, an advantage the German potters exploited to the full. Stoneware produced by German-speaking potters was primarily functional, conventional in design and generally plain, but this did not altogether exclude decoration mainly embodying *sgraffiato* and use of coloured slip.

Inevitably, as happened in Europe following the discovery of the porcelain secret at Meissen and the establishment of Augustus the Strong's royal factory, a number of enterprising colonial potters endeavoured to penetrate the mysteries surrounding porcelain production and become the first to manufacture it in America. White clay deposits discovered in the vicinity of Philadelphia gave hope of successful experiments but attempts to make porcelain proved abortive.

At this juncture, in a curious and somewhat obscure commercial connection between potters in the American colonies and England, Andrew Duché, a son of Anthony Duché the French Huguenot potter, takes his place in a chain of events. If his dubious claims may be believed, Andrew Duché was the first American potter to produce porcelain in his workshop in Savannah, Georgia.

Andrew Duché was born in Philadelphia. Four years after his marriage in 1731 he settled in New Windsor, South Carolina. According to records, in the summer of 1737, at Savannah, Sir Roger Lacey, Crown Agent for the Colony of Georgia to the Cherokee Indians, brought Duché's aims and circumstances to the notice of General Oglethorpe. As a result, Duché was granted financial aid in establishing an earthenware factory at Savannah in 1738.

In or about 1739 Duché claimed that he had discovered how to make porcelain and sought further financial aid from the trustees in order to purchase equipment and extend his workshop. A grant was applied for on the ground that porcelain manufacture would prove of great economic benefit to the colony. Duché made sweeping claims. Ignoring the fact that porcelain was already being produced in Europe at Meissen and Vienna he announced that he was the first man outside Asia to discover the porcelain secret. Moreover, Duché claimed to have located the essential materials within a convenient distance from Savannah.

By the late summer of 1741 Duché was planning a voyage to England, intending, as he informed his friends, to take specimens of his porcelain wares to London. After successive delays he arrived in London at the end of May 1743 and is believed to have remained in England at least until the end of 1744.

It appears highly probable that sometime during 1744 Duché made the acquaintance of Edward Heylin and Thomas Frye, founders of the Bow porcelain factory, and approached them with a business proposition. This may be deduced from the fact that when Heylin and Frye took out a patent in December 1744 they proposed to make porcelain using *kaolin*, known as *unaker* to the Cherokee Indians in America, from whose territory it was to be obtained. It may be presumed that, having interested Heylin and Frye in the clay, whether or not they were shown actual samples of porcelain made from it, Duché offered to keep them supplied with regular shipments. There is some uncertainty as to whether the Cherokees took the clay from the 'back of Carolina' or the 'back of Virginia' as is variously stated in contemporary accounts. Cookworthy believed the clay was obtained from Virginia.

Writing in May 1745, William Cookworthy, founder of the short-lived Plymouth Pottery in England, reported to a friend that he had met a visitor from the American colonies who had shown him specimens of porcelain as fine as the Chinese ware and that the unnamed man had acquired tracts of land from the Indians where clay deposits were located. Cookworthy was apparently offered unlimited supplies to be shipped from America. It may reasonably be concluded that the man Cookworthy referred to was Andrew Duché.

Although Duché must have taken examples of porcelain to England, which he presumably showed to the Bow partners and to Cookworthy, there remains considerable doubt as to whether the wares were his authentic productions and, if so, whether or not the specimens were crude and of experimental character. It appears that in all circumstances, however, the three men were sufficiently impressed by Duché's story and proposition, and by what he had to show them, to listen with complete credulity. The present general consensus of opinion is that Duché never actually made porcelain, or if he did so only a few experimental pieces were made that he took to England. No porcelain made by Duché is known to survive and no documentary evidence has yet come to light to prove that porcelain was produced on a commercial scale in the Duché factory at Savannah.

Bonnin and Morris of Southwark, Philadelphia, were undoubtedly the first Americans to manufacture porcelain on a commercial scale. Theirs is the earliest American porcelain known, of which only a few examples remain extant. The factory was established in 1769 and closed in 1772. Despite the quality and attractiveness of Bonnin and Morris's wares their venture was doomed to failure from the start, largely due to overwhelming competition from English manufacturers supported by the Philadelphia dealers who imported their wares.

Bonnin took the initiative in the manufacture of porcelain, using a white clay procured from White Clay Creek in Delaware. A frame building was erected to serve as a factory in Prime Street, Philadelphia. The majority of the workmen engaged were Englishmen, either previously settled in the locality or specially brought over from England to work in the new factory. When news reached England that a porcelain factory had been set up in Philadelphia to supply the colonists with fine wares the ultimate ruination of the venture was swiftly contrived and achieved.

Bonnin and Morris claimed that their porcelain was as good as any imported wares, particularly that of Bow, a factory specifically mentioned in their first advertisement soliciting orders. In July 1771 the Southwark factory stated in an advertisement that, having obtained adequate supplies of zaffre, it was able to supply blue-and-white wares of the finest quality.

That some unspecified connection existed between the Bonnin and Morris factory and that of Bow can hardly be doubted. That the Bow factory was mentioned in the American factory's initial advertisement and that workmen were procured from London – probably former Bow employees – and, most significantly, the unquestionable similarity between Bow porcelain and authenticated Bonnin and Morris wares, appears more than coincidental. Analysis in England and America has left no doubt of the similarity of pastes used, particularly as both are notable for their bone-ash content, indicating the use of bones in composition. Bonnin and Morris's soft porcelain is sometimes erroneously and misleadingly referred to as creamware.

English manufacturers proceeded to dump large consignments of pottery and porcelain in the colony, undercutting Bonnin and Morris with low prices and presenting a dazzling variety of wares offered through dealers. As the result of this intensive competitive campaign, the American firm failed to hold out financially. An appeal to the trustees for aid was refused. Morris withdrew from the partnership in 1771 and removed to North Carolina. Bonnin continued to struggle on alone in the face of mounting difficulties. In 1772 he was compelled to close the factory, which inflicted great hardship, especially on the workmen who had been lured from England by the prospect of rich reward.

After the unfortunate Bonnin and Morris venture, which deserved a kinder fate, the subsequent development of porcelain production in America belongs to the nineteenth century.

THE UNITED STATES

Compared with the history and development of ceramic art in the Old World and pre-Columbian America, that of the United States since the end of the Revolution may appear dull and even inconsequential. While no ceramic discoveries of such major importance as, for example, the discovery of the porcelain secret at Meissen or the development of parian ware by English potters, have yet been made in the United States, to dismiss the work of American potters, especially that of modern experimentalists, as of little consequence or interest would be both unwise and unjustified.

American research in ceramics, introduction of new materials and development of new techniques during the past fifty years have greatly extended technical knowledge in the field. Vital new concepts in ceramic art will undoubtedly in course of time strongly influence the potter.

Neither should it too readily be concluded that because for generations the art of the potter in America reflected European traditions and styles it completely lacked originality. It has been noted in preceding pages that by the middle of the eighteenth century, and possibly earlier, colonial potters began to evolve techniques and styles that were peculiarly their own. From the beginning of the nineteenth century, when the new nation was gathering strength, except where the European tradition persisted until a comparatively late date, the wares of American potters became increasingly more distinctive and within a few decades were easily distinguishable from contemporary European pottery.

After the Revolution earthenware and stoneware continued to be produced in the old folk pottery tradition. Earthenware gradually lost its popularity while, despite its comparatively high cost, the demand for stoneware increased. During the first three decades of the nineteenth century the number of potteries operating in the United States grew rapidly. As stoneware ousted earthenware in popular demand more enterprising potters became interested in profiting from production on a wider commercial scale. In 1808 Samuel Sullivan established his stoneware factory at Zanesville, Muskingham County, Ohio. Sullivan's factory was the first of a large number of concerns producing similar wares established in the vicinity during the ensuing thirty years. Joseph Brier became a successful stoneware manufacturer at Jonathan Creek near Zanesville. Before mid-century Zanesville was a leading pottery centre noted for its stoneware. Abundance of materials, available labour and cheap river transportation encouraged many skilled potters trained in the east to set up kilns in the Ohio river valley.

As had begun to happen in the preceding century, immigrant potters from

78 PITCHER. Hound
handle. Rockingham
brown glaze. Nineteenth
century, American.
H 12in

Europe congregated in areas where materials were plentiful. Many found employment in the first factories established in the United States for the mass-production of pottery. The principal factories sprang up in Bennington, Vermont, East Liverpool, Ohio, and Trenton, New Jersey.

A factory destined to become important in the annals of American ceramics was founded at Bennington in 1793 by Captain John Norton. Only earthenware was produced at first, but by about 1814 Norton had acquired sufficient technical knowledge to commence manufacture of salt-glazed stonewares. In 1831, by which time creamware and 'Rockingham' brownware were being produced, the son of the founder, Judge Lyman Norton, transferred the works to Bennington Village. In 1837, when the factory was under the direction of Julius Norton, grandson of Captain John, an outstanding personality concerned in the development of American ceramics, Christopher Webber Fenton, joined the firm. Fenton is not sometimes referred to as 'the American Josiah Wedgwood' without good reason. He was energetic, clever and ambitious. Three years after his arrival at Bennington he entered into partnership with Julius Norton. Although the association lasted only three years, for Fenton they proved to be vital years of experiment in new techniques. He was spurred on by his over-riding ambition to become a leading figure in what he hoped would develop into the most important pottery manufacturing centre in the United States.

It was probably at Fenton's instigation that John Harrison, an English potter formerly employed at Copeland and Garrett's factory in England, was invited to take up employment at Bennington. Harrison was soon interesting his employers in new production techniques, including the commercial potential of parian ware, originally developed at the Copeland factory and of which some account has already been given.

Fenton learned many techniques from Harrison, in particular the skilful blending of clays and advanced glazing processes. Experimentation occupied Fenton during most of his working day. After the dissolution of his partnership with Norton, when they continued on good terms, Fenton installed equipment in a corner of the factory building and carried on with his experiments in ceramic processes. While endeavouring to effect further improvement in some of Harrison's complex glazing techniques, Fenton succeeded in devising a simple process for colouring transparent glaze which he patented in 1849. Fenton's process entailed a first firing of the ware to the biscuit followed by dipping in clear glaze. In the second and final stage the ware was sprinkled with coloured oxides which produced a pleasing mottled glaze in varying tones of green, blue, yellow and orange.

Brown and grey stonewares, lead-glazed redware and slip-decorated earthenware of various kinds continued to be made in the United States by potters in small concerns throughout the nineteenth century. Country craftsmen skilled in traditional pottery techniques did not, as a rule, venture beyond routine production according to long usage. Experiments were left to large concerns always seeking to introduce novel wares. It was principally in the factories that the dream of manufacturing porcelain in America was revived.

Despite the disastrous failure of the Bonnin and Morris factory, the prospect of successfully manufacturing porcelain wares continued to hold out promise of rich reward to ambitious potters. At least two Americans claimed to have made porcelain before William E. Tucker achieved the distinction of being the first American successfully to manufacture porcelain commercially and hold his own against foreign competition. Dr Henry Mead of New York announced his successful porcelain experiments in 1816. From the only known surviving example, it is evident that Mead produced soft porcelain. In 1824 Abraham Miller of Philadelphia claimed to have made porcelain and is believed to have exhibited a specimen. The Jersey City Porcelain and Earthenware Company, subsequently known as the American Pottery Manufacturing Company, is reputed to have made porcelain in 1826.

William Tucker began his career as a decorator of whiteware. After setting up as a master potter in 1826 he engaged in manufacturing creamware before becoming interested in the production of porcelain. After Tucker was joined in partnership by Judge Joseph Hemphill in 1832 the factory was considerably extended and a number of skilled workmen and artists trained in Europe in porcelain production and decoration joined the concern. Tucker and his partner produced a range of excellent porcelain wares until 1838. The porcelain body was notable for its whiteness. Finely executed painted decoration admirably enhanced the beauty of Tucker porcelain. Empire-style wares, undoubtedly Tucker's finest productions, made in

79 PITCHER. From the
Tucker factory,
Philadelphia. Porcelain.
Nineteenth century,
American. *H 8½in*

earlier years, were sometimes left undecorated or, as is found on later examples, simply decorated in a restrained manner in sepia tones touched with gilt. In his late period Tucker altered the form and decoration of his wares when more elaborate shapes were lavishly embellished with polychrome floral designs.

Notwithstanding Tucker's moderate success in manufacturing porcelain, other American pottery concerns in existence at the period did not rush to follow his example. Stoneware appeared safer and more profitable than risking vast amounts of capital in setting up porcelain kilns. The desire to manufacture porcelain was outweighed by fears of financial difficulties, especially as wealthy Americans of the time were more inclined to adorn their homes with porcelain imported from Europe and the Orient. Tucker's only serious competitor was the firm of Smith, Fife and Company whose attractive ornamental wares in Grecian design ran Tucker's porcelain close in popularity.

Charles Cartledge established a porcelain works at Greenpoint, Brooklyn. The factory became noted for the quality and variety of its wares. During nine productive years, from 1847 to 1856, the most outstanding craftsman in the factory was Josiah Jones who served Cartledge as chief modeller. White soft-paste porcelain domestic wares were the principal products of the factory, also door furniture and buttons. Jones is reputed to have modelled a series of porcelain busts. The identities of decorators employed by Cartledge are not known but the standard of decoration executed on fine tablewares was remarkably high, indicating that Cartledge was fortunate enough to employ a team of accomplished ceramic artists. Probably some, if not all, received their training in European porcelain factories.

During the 1860s the Union Porcelain Works attracted a good deal of attention with fine wares produced under the direction of Thomas C. Smith. Americans were at last beginning to realise that porcelain as fine as any made in Europe at the period could be produced in their own country where materials were abundant and skilled labour waited to be employed. Thomas Smith succeeded in arousing greater interest and admiration for his wares than Tucker achieved. Sometime after 1870 a gifted modeller, Karl Müller, joined the firm. He worked chiefly in rococo style, inspired by eighteenth-century German porcelain. Müller's work ranked among the finest in the United States at the period. He did not allow his intense admiration for rococo to conflict with realism in modelling. Müller's models were generally realistic and vigorously executed, and for the most part remarkable for close attention to detail.

In a different form of ceramic art John Rogers of New York became celebrated for his charming terracotta 'Rogers groups', in great demand in the 1860s and 1870s. Rogers's terracottas were admired for their delightful portrayal of contemporary American life and character. Although it was a little-known fact at the time, other well-known American sculptors had a hand in modelling some of the finest terracotta figures accepted as Rogers's exclusive work.

American ceramic sculpture was slow to develop through the nineteenth century and in fact only came to the fore in American ceramic art after the end of World War I when the numbers of studio potters in the United States began steadily increasing. During the last decades of the nineteenth century, when the Ohio river valley had long been a pottery producing area, a number of leading potters became interested in the promotion of special training in ceramic sculpture. The idea took root but the volume of response was discouragingly small. Not until the early twentieth century was ceramics to any appreciable extent regarded as art by Americans; and the second decade of the century had almost passed before the work of eminent studio potters made real impact. A few pioneers in the field were responsible for the slow advancement made in interesting the American public in ceramic sculpture. R. Guy Cowan of the Cowan Pottery at Rocky River, Ohio, gave an energetic and inspiring lead during the years 1913–31, which culminated in the foundation of the American school of ceramic sculpture.

The standard of decoration on wares made in American pottery manufacturing concerns remained at a low ebb almost until the end of the nineteenth century. Towards the close of the century leading pottery manufacturers became cognisant of the truth, that if American wares were ever to compete successfully with European imported wares their artistic standard needed to be improved effectively. It was realised that it was not enough to employ modellers, decorators and workmen trained in European factories. A need for technical training centres and schools of design where American artists could be properly trained in techniques was felt to be urgent. Largely due to the tireless efforts of Edward Orton Jr, a department of ceramics was set up in Ohio State University in 1894.

Charles Fergus Binns, born in England in 1857, became one of the foremost

80 BENJAMIN FRANKLIN. Parian bust by Ott and Brewer, Trenton, New Jersey,
c1875. American. *H 7½in*

individuals to influence the development of American ceramics. It is hardly an exaggeration to state that but for the enthusiasm and creative energy of Binns the artistic trend of early twentieth-century American ceramics would have been different, also fundamental techniques practised by studio potters in the United States today. Dr Binns came of a family long associated with ceramics. He trained in English factories at Derby and Worcester and before emigrating to the United States held a supervisory post in the Royal Worcester factory. Binns began his long career as an educator and technologist in ceramics in New Jersey where he directed a ceramics trade school. In 1900 he became the first director of New York State College of Ceramics at Alfred, where he pursued a distinguished career through the ensuing thirty-five years.

As a potter of remarkable originality and technical skill, allied to superb artistic accomplishment, Binns has had few equals in the United States. He passionately admired Chinese pottery, especially of the Ch'ing dynasty, and his enthusiasm led him to imitate Chinese wares in his early period. His emulation of Chinese pottery considerably influenced other potters with whom he associated. Binns was brilliantly successful with stoneware glazes, always subdued in colour and tone, yet somehow extraordinarily luminous. Perhaps the most commendable feature of his work during a period when over-elaboration was rife in all forms of decoration is that his pots were free of fussiness, their great charm emanating from their simple form and restrained ornamentation. Binns occasionally made his bowls and vases in two parts, using a template pattern, which enabled him to obtain precisely the shape required. In all aspects of his work Binns aimed at perfection. Always an idealist, he strove hard to convince others, as he himself was convinced, that the potter's art had no limitations and that ultimately potters would achieve refinement of form and texture far superior to anything then known. Among Binns's pupils, who carried on in his tradition, were Arthur Baggs, John F. McMahon, Marion L. Fordick and, for a brief period, Adelaide A. Robineau.

Without doubt, Adelaide Alsop Robineau was one of the most remarkable women of her era, a gifted ceramist whose work won her international esteem over a long period lasting until her death in 1929. She was keenly interested in high-fired porcelain and devoted much time to studying ancient Chinese techniques in firing at high temperatures. Mrs Robineau also studied painting. Her enthusiasm for pottery was aroused during a two-week course of instruction under Charles F. Binns.

When Mrs Robineau began production of her porcelain masterpieces in her hill-top studio at Syracuse she had high hopes and ideals, but little dreamed how far her art would take her to success in her own country and subsequent international fame. She achieved recognition as a leading ceramist, a brilliant designer and artist in ceramic sculpture and most other branches of ceramic art. Although high-firing techniques remained her special field of study, prompting her continuous experiments, Mrs Robineau did not confine her interest to one method and style. She acquired her skill initially by closely studying the techniques of others, but was

81 PITCHER. Dark brown glaze, decorated with flowers in red, brown, green and yellow. Rookwood Pottery, Cincinnati, Ohio. Nineteenth century, American. *H 10in*

rarely imitative, preferring to rely upon her own taste and judgement of what constituted good or bad design.

Before Mrs Robineau launched into her brilliant career as a potter numerous American women became interested in what is known as art pottery. It is believed that the Philadelphia Centennial Exhibition of 1876, with a display of art pottery, attracted women into taking up pottery decoration as a pastime. Members of the Cincinnati Pottery Club founded in 1879 were mainly concerned with decorative design on pottery. A much more ambitious organisation came into existence in

82   TUREEN. Stoneware. By Peter Voulkos. American. *H 12in*

1880 when Maria Longworth Storer founded the Rookwood Pottery of Cincinnati, Ohio. From merely painting pottery as a hobby the accomplished, enterprising ladies of the Rookwood Pottery launched into production of wares. Pottery made by Rookwood craftswomen was tasteful and colourful, according to contemporary taste, exhibiting marked Japanese influence, with a preference for honey-coloured and red decorative glazes. Rookwood wares undoubtedly had shortcomings but the venture achieved commercial success.

Nearer to the present day, since the end of World War II the productions of a number of brilliant American potters have attracted international interest. In 1943, Gisela Richter, then curator of Roman and Greek art at the Metropolitan Museum, New York, stated that in her opinion American pottery and ceramic sculpture were 'abreast of, if not superior' to anything in production in pre-war Europe. Such an opinion was naturally not widely shared by Europeans. Nevertheless, American achievements in ceramics have continued to surprise and captivate an increasingly appreciative and perceptive public during post-war decades.

The end of World War II released an unprecedented spurt of creative energy in ceramic art and invention in the United States. For example, among varying types of figures produced by modern American studio potters perhaps their most significant common characteristic is a refreshing originality, not expressed in form and ornament alone but also in unusual ways that the clay medium itself is exploited. It may well be that ceramic art in the United States has suffered from over-experimentation in materials, design and techniques, but where innovation has been tempered with sound artistic judgement in the application of new ideas the outcome has often proved successful and occasionally sensational.

In the 1950s Edward Marshall Boehm became celebrated for his fine animal and bird figures in hard-paste porcelain produced in his studio at Trenton. Boehm, a native of Maryland, born near Baltimore, spent much of his earlier working life among animals, which stood him in good stead when, nearing the age of forty, he was attracted to ceramic sculpture. He established his studio at Trenton in 1949 and rapidly gained high repute for fascinating animal and bird figures executed in a style reminiscent of Meissen. A team of repairers assembled the separate parts of figures produced from moulds, working closely to a plaster model of the original clay figure. The quality of modelling and exquisite colouring imparts a unique grace and beauty to Boehm's figures and they are now highly prized as collectors' items.

Since the beginning of the present century American artist potters have been closely associated with the development of modern ceramics within and outside the United States, in both the introduction and use of new materials and *avant-garde* styles and techniques. In early decades studio potters continued to be influenced by primitive Japanese pottery, but by the 1930s, as appreciation of the simple beauty and interest of American folk pottery deepened, much American studio pottery assumed a more than merely superficial resemblance to traditional colonial wares. A steady movement away from the production of wares of functional form occurred, gathering momentum through the war years. With the coming of peace a new spirit of experiment and enterprise became manifest in the work of American artist potters. Sculptural form took precedence over the purely functional, while the decorative appeal of wares became increasingly important. A taste for asymmetrical abstract forms developed, with linear decoration and splashes of colour applied over coarse-textured surfaces. When innovation became fashionable potters evolved new technical processes in the creation of wares with textured surfaces. Among potters who gave the lead in the introduction of new forms and textures were Gertrude and Otto Natzler, Carlton Ball, David Weinrib, Henry Varnum Poor, Peter Voulkos, Antonio Prieto and Franz Wildenhain.

Since the end of World War II a number of eminent American artist potters have increasingly made use of the wheel, supporting a conviction which has gained ground in many studios that thrown wares possess quality and character to a greater extent than moulded or cast wares. By making the fullest use of the wheel and adopting advanced glazing and firing techniques certain contemporary potters in the United States believe, and in many instances have proved, that production of variegated and unusual surface textures is facilitated. Primitive art, be it Asiatic, European, pre-Columbian American or early colonial American, continues to be a major source of inspiration for American potters. Without slavish adherence to ancient forms and traditions, many studio potters working in the United States today still obviously derive their art and techniques from ancient sources, notwithstanding that their productions frequently reveal differences in materials and methods which renders them essentially modern.

Among leading American potters whose work, largely of experimental and therefore unusual character, has made vital impact within and beyond the borders of the United States is Daniel Rhodes. His experiments with new materials and original approach to form and ornament have widely influenced Rhodes's contemporaries in their own work and attitudes. Rhodes, already a successful potter of repute, working mainly in traditional styles, began moving away from conventional ceramic techniques during the mid-1950s. He was among the first artist potters of repute working in the United States virtually to abandon use of the wheel to work almost entirely with his hands. Moreover, in deserting tradition in order to introduce new processes, Rhodes initiated a new concept of ceramic art in America that subsequently had far-reaching and unexpectedly powerful influence on ceramics elsewhere, particularly in Europe.

At the outset, following his decision to break with tradition, Rhodes concentrated on making unglazed pots left in the biscuit, often with rough-textured surfaces over which he applied clay slip. His most remarkable innovations included the insertion of layers of fibreglass into wares which fused with the clay during firing and produced a material with exceptional plastic and tensile qualities. Rhodes's work with this material is extraordinarily spirited and original. Other potters, principally those specialising in ceramic sculpture, adopted Rhodes's fibreglass and clay fusing process by which they obtained a material that permitted the creation of ceramic forms hitherto unknown. A new class of ceramic sculpture consequently appeared, created by potters who excelled in Rhodes's technique. As was to be expected, not everyone admired these novel creations, but even critics who found little aesthetic appeal in works that lacked the smooth refinement generally looked for in ceramic sculpture were in the majority impressed and intrigued by the greater scope in composition offered to potters who mastered the technique.

After the appearance of Rhodes's wares in his new style, many ceramic artists followed his lead in producing ceramic objects designed solely to please the eye and grace their surroundings. Utility became unimportant. Wares in conventional form and materials continued to be made by studio potters who preferred to follow a safe course that promised more commissions and easier disposal of wares on the market. Others, however, though for the most part in less extreme form than Rhodes and potters who closely emulated his style, concentrated on producing works designed to give purely visual delight.

Peter Voulkos progressed from making pots of conventional utilitarian character to dramatic ceramic sculpture. Voulkos works with characteristic verve and boldness, investing the majority of his creations with a robust quality that distinguishes

83 BOTTLE. Stoneware.
By Gertrud and Otto
Natzler. *H 10¼in*

them from the works of the majority of his contemporaries. As a dexterous manipulator of clays in his ceramic sculpture Voulkos displays superior skill and imagination, expressing his individuality in his work in whatever mood it may be conceived and executed. The somewhat ponderous character of Voulkos's more important compositions, with surfaces hammered and scraped to obtain the desired
texture, does not lessen their attraction, but rather lends dignity to objects rendered
striking by their solidity.

In certain respects, mainly pertaining to form, Voulkos's work shows affinity
with that of Rhodes. During the 1950s, coinciding with Rhodes's experimental
period in ceramic sculpture, Voulkos also moved from making bowls and pots into
the sphere of ceramic sculpture. Two men, without question potters supreme,
initiated a change in the scope and tempo of the potter's art in America. In their
respective ways, by practical demonstration and inspiration derived from their
works by other craftsmen, the two master potters enormously influenced the trend
of ceramic art in the United States. Future development of ceramics in America,
in the studio – and to some extent in the pottery industry in the paramount matter

of design – will owe much to the initiative and accomplishment of Rhodes and Voulkos.

Techniques and styles either originated or largely developed by American potters over the past fifty years have been widely imitated and have strongly influenced the work of potters in most Western countries. A number of successful American potters developed unmistakable, distinctive styles and techniques by which their work can be instantly recognised.

Paul Soldner demonstrated how massive forms with glazed surfaces varying in texture can be impressively rendered without dull heaviness. In different forms and treatment Soldner made excellent use of the slab process, originated by potters in ancient China, in which a vessel is built up or ornamented with clay slabs. These may be previously rolled out upon textured surfaces to obtain a pattern, or beaten or rolled with tools to acquire surface texture before assembling. Decoration applied to Soldner's stoneware bottles is sometimes striking, for example his use of granules of shale embedded in the clay, or patterns in cascading effect produced by covering white slip with a thin coat of iron-oxide-coloured glaze.

Arthur Handy achieved remarkable dexterity in throwing on the wheel. Among his finest works is a quickly thrown stoneware jar retaining heavily impressed finger marks, the vessel evidently drawn into a squarish shape while the clay remained moist. Decorative opaque magnesia glaze, apparently applied with deliberate carelessness over black and grey slip, was left to run down over the body of the jar. Handy is seen at his best in what may at first glance appear to be forms created by chance or on impulse during the throwing process. Glaze seldom appears to be other than casually applied. Handy's style is easy and direct, investing his wares with the same fluid grace observable in ancient Chinese pottery.

Eunice Prieto also made pleasant, effective use of flowing glazes generously applied over the inside and outside of vessels, particularly attractive bowls.

James Secrest achieved excellent results in the creation of unusual forms by combining throwing with the slab technique. His attractive stoneware footed bowls attest to his mastery of technique. The foot and base of the bowl may be formed by throwing. Slabs, previously pressed to give them a raised surface texture, are held in position by joining at the ends and firmly fixing to the base. The textured surface of the slabbed bowl upon its plain cylindrical foot and the balanced proportions of the piece combine to create a sculptural effect, illustrating the close relationship of pottery to sculpture.

Philip Secrest specialised in the production of stonewares with interesting glazed and unglazed surfaces. An unusual and pleasing textured band often seen encircling pots by Secrest is achieved by scraping glaze away from a roughened surface. Some of Secrest's most attractive wares have a burnt-orange-coloured body decorated with a contrasting soft grey glaze.

Theodore Randall, an experimentalist, made excellent use of pressing as a creative technique. He sometimes used slabs pressed on an incised surface in building up his stoneware pots usually finished with a top formed of coiled clay.

Randall also made pots from joined-up sections pressed in moulds and fired to the biscuit.

Vivika and Otto Heino's wares are outstanding for unusual and attractive decoration. The Heinos' simple process of applying thick glaze and scratching through it with a pointed tool before firing produces striking results. During firing the lines scratched through the glaze become well-defined patterns penetrating to the body of the ware.

Stanley Rosen, on the other hand, has often preferred to leave his wares unglazed inside and outside. Decoration may consist of applied white, black and brown slip. Rosen does not despise use of colour, but has always regarded form as of paramount importance, with modelling and surface treatment only of slightly less vital consideration. Nearly all Rosen's boldly conceived works exhibit complex surface modelling with little reliance placed on coloured glaze for decorative effect. The wares are solid, occasionally monumental in conception, and invariably display an admirable mastery of techniques.

Many other potters have pioneered and experimented, contributing to the continuing development of American ceramic art. As Daniel Rhodes has observed, the creation of pottery is something of an adventure wherein, at the end, the potter may perhaps find himself. No art or craft is closer to nature. The American artist potter, possibly to a greater extent than his fellows in the Old World, who are perhaps still more consciously influenced by ancient traditions, is forward-looking and responsive to innovation. Therefore, it may be anticipated that future progress in ceramics will largely be initiated in the United States. Much depends upon to what extent and for how long, creative art and individual expression of art, in whatever form, can resist ever-increasing pressures that threaten the ultimate elimination of independent artists and craftsmen, and the extinction of true art.

BIBLIOGRAPHY

Works are listed in order of publication

CHINA

Chinese Symbolism. W. F. Mayers. London, 1874

A History and Description of Chinese Porcelain. W. Cosmo Monkhouse. With notes by S. W. Bushell. London, 1901

A Description of Chinese Pottery and Porcelain. (A translation of the T'ao Shuo.) S. W. Bushell. Oxford, 1910

Chinese Pottery and Porcelain. R. L. Hobson, London, 1915

The Beginnings of Porcelain in China. B. Laufer. Chicago, 1917

The Wares of the Ming Dynasty. R. L. Hobson. London, 1922

The Art of the Chinese Potter. R. L. Hobson and A. C. Hetherington. London, 1923

Ming and Ch'ing Porcelains. E. Bluett. London, 1933

The Ceramic Art of China and Other Countries of the Far East. W. B. Honey. London, 1944

Chinese Ceramic Glazes. A. C. Hetherington. London, 1948

Later Chinese Porcelain. S. Jenyns. London, 1951

Ming Pottery and Porcelain. S. Jenyns. London, 1953

Oriental Blue and White. Sir Harry Garner. London, 1954

Pottery Refinements or 'Tao Ya'. Edited Sayer. London, 1959

Illustrated Catalogue of Porcelains Decorated in Underglaze Blue and Copper Red in the Percival David Foundation of Chinese Art. Margaret Medley. London, 1963

Chinese Porcelain. Anthony Du Boulay. London, 1963

Chinese Blue and White. Ann Franks. London, 1969

KOREA

Corean Pottery. W. B. Honey. London, 1947

The Koreans and their Culture. C. Osgood. New York, 1951

The Ceramic Art of Korea. G. M. Compertz. London, 1961

Korean Celadon. G. M. Compertz and C. Kim. London, 1963

JAPAN

Kakiemon and Nabishema Wares. Saiko-Kwai. Tokyo, 1929

A Selection of Famous Japanese Ceramic Wares. Meito-Sen Nishon. Tokyo, 1932–8

Masterpieces of Pottery and Porcelain in Japan. Seitchi Okada. Kyoto, 1934
Ceramic Art of Japan. T. Mitsouka. Tokyo, 1949
Japanese Ceramics from Ancient to Modern Times. Fujio Koyama. Oakland Art
    Museum, USA, 1961
Ceramic Art of Japan. Hugo Munsterberg. Tokyo, 1964
Japanese Porcelain. S. Jenyns. London, 1965
Potter in Japan. Bernard Leach. London, 1967
Japanese Pottery. S. Jenyns. London, 1971

WESTERN ASIA AND ISLAM

Egyptian Ceramic Art. H. Wallis. London, 1900
La Céramique dans l'Art Musulman. H. Rivière. Paris, 1913
A Guide to the Islamic Pottery of the Near East. R. L. Hobson. British Museum,
    London, 1932
A Survey of Persian Art. Edited A. Pope. London, 1938
A Handbook of Muhammadan Art. M. S. Dimond. Metropolitan Museum, New
    York, 1944
Early Islamic Pottery: Mesopotamia, Egypt and Persia. Arthur Lane. London, 1947
The Early Sgraffito Ware of the Near East. Arthur Lane. London, 1948
Later Islamic Pottery. Arthur Lane. London, 1957
Ancient Iran. Edith Porada. London, 1965
Medieval Middle Eastern Pottery. J. W. Allan. London, 1971

GREECE

The Craft of Athenian Pottery. G. A. M. Richter. New York, 1923
A Handbook of Greek Black-figured Vases. J. C. Hoppin. Paris, 1924
Attic Vase Painting. C. Seltman. New York, 1933
Potter and Painter in Ancient Athens. J. O. Beazley. London, 1946
Greek Pottery. Arthur Lane. London, 1948
Greek Terracottas. T. Webster. London, 1950
Greek Painted Pottery. R. M. Cook. London, 1960
History of Greek Vase Painting. P. Arias, M. Hirmer, B. B. Shefton. New York,
    1962
Hellenistic Art. T. Webster. London, 1967
Greek Geometric Pottery. J. N. Coldstream. London, 1968

ITALY

La Manifattura della Porcellane di Doccia. C. Lorenzini. Florence, 1861
Notes on Venetian Ceramics. W. R. Drake. London, 1868
A History and Description of Italian Maiolica. M. Solon. London, 1907
Vinovo e le Sue Porcellane. L. De-Mauri. Milan, 1923
Catalogo delle Porcellane dei Medici. G. Liverani. Faenza, 1936
Italian Maiolica. Bernard Rackham. London, 1952

Italian Porcelain. Arthur Lane. London, 1954
Capodimonte and Buen Retiro Porcelain. A. W. Frothingham. New York, 1955
Five Centuries of Italian Maiolica. G. Liverani. New York, 1960
Italian Porcelain. F. Stozzi. London, 1967
Maiolica, Delft and Faience. G. Scavizzi. London, 1970

GERMANY AND AUSTRIA

Geschichte der Bayerischen Porzellan Manufaktur Nymphenburg. Friedrich H. Hofman. Leipzig, 1921–3
Wiener Keramik. W. Rochowansky. Vienna, 1923
Meissner Porzellan. Ernst Zimmerman. Leipzig, 1924
German Porcelain. W. B. Honey. London, 1947
Dresden China. W. B. Honey. London, 1947
Old Viennese Porcelain. Strohmar-Novak, trans A. von Zeppelin. Vienna, 1950
Vienna Porcelain of the Du Paquier Period. J. F. Hayward. London, 1952
18th Century German Porcelain. George Savage. London, 1958
Book of Porcelain. Straehelin. Trans from German by M. Bullock. London, 1966

FRANCE

A History and Description of French Porcelain. E. S. Ayscher. London, 1905
Histoire de Manufactures Français de Porcellaine. Comte X. de Chavagnac and Marquis A. de Grollier. Paris, 1906
Le Biscuit de Sèvres. E. Bourgeois. Paris, 1909
La Céramique Française. R. Peyre. Paris, 1910
French Faience. Arthur Lane. London, 1948
Les Poteries Française. H. Haug. Paris, 1948
La Porcelaine de Sèvres. P. Verlet, S. Grandjean, M. Bruner. Paris, 1953
French Porcelain. W. B. Honey. London, 1954
Les Poteries et les Faiences Française. A. Lisur-Tardy. Paris, 1957
French Porcelain of the 18th Century. George Savage. London, 1960
French Porcelain. H. Laudais. London, 1961

ENGLAND

History of the Staffordshire Potteries. Simeon Shaw. London, 1829
Life of Josiah Wedgwood. E. Meteyard. London, 1865–6
The Art of the Old English Potter. M. Solon. London, 1883
Potters: Their Arts and Crafts. Sparkes and Gandy. London, 1897
A History and Description of English Earthenware and Stoneware. William A. Burton. London, 1904
English Porcelain Figures of the 18th Century. W. King. London, 1925
English Pottery and Porcelain. W. B. Honey. London, 1933
British Potters and Pottery Today. C. E. Bunt. London, 1950
English Country Pottery. R. G. Haggar. London, 1950

Nineteenth Century English Pottery and Porcelain. G. Bemrose. London, 1952
English Porcelain of the Eighteenth Century. J. L. Dixon. London, 1952
Wedgwood. W. Mankowitz. London, 1953
Artist Potters in England. Muriel Rose. London, 1955
English Porcelain and Bone China. G. B. and T. Hughes. London, 1955
Longton Hall Porcelain. B. Watney. London, 1957
English Porcelain Figures of the Eighteenth Century. Arthur Lane. London, 1957
Victorian Pottery and Porcelain. G. B. Hughes. London, 1959
English Pottery and Porcelain. George Savage. New York, 1961
Victorian Pottery. H. Wakefield. London, 1962
English Pottery and Porcelain Figures. G. B. Hughes. London, 1964
English Porcelain 1745–1850. Edited Charleston. London, 1965
Master Potters of the Industrial Revolution. Bevis Hiller. London, 1965
English Country Pottery. P. Brears. Newton Abbot, 1971
Derby Porcelain. Barrett and Thorpe. London, 1971

AMERICA (ANCIENT)
The Ancient Maya. S. G. Morley. Stanford, 1944
Mexico South. Miguel Covarrubias. London, 1948
Plumbate. A Mesoamerican Trade Ware. Anna D. Shepherd. Carnegie Institute of Washington, 1948
Andean Culture History. American Museum of Natural History. Washington, 1949
Prehistoric Indians of the Southwest. H. M. Wormington. Denver Museum of Natural History. 2nd edn, Denver, 1951
The Art of Ancient Peru. Heinrich Ubbelohde-Doering. London, 1952
Ancient American Pottery. G. H. S. Bushell and A. Digby. London, 1955

AMERICA (COLONIAL AND UNITED STATES)
The Pottery and Porcelain of the United States. E. A. Barber. New York, 1901
Lead Glazed Pottery. E. A. Barber. Pennsylvania Museum. Philadelphia, 1907
Early American Folk Pottery. Alber Hastings Pitkin. Hartford, Conn, 1918
The Potters and Potteries of Bennington. John Spargo. Boston, 1926
Notes on American Ceramics 1607–1943. A. W. Clement. Brooklyn Museum, New York, 1944
Our Pioneer Potters. A. W. Clement. New York, 1947
American Potters and Pottery. John Ramsay. New York, 1947
Early New England Potters and their Wares. Lura Woodside Watkins. Harvard, 1950
Early American Designs: Ceramics. E. O. Christensen. New York, 1952
Early Potters and Potteries of New York State. William F. Ketcham Jnr. New York, 1970
Early American Folk Pottery. Harold F. Guilland. Philadelphia, 1971

BIBLIOGRAPHY

GENERAL

The Manual of Practical Potting. Charles F. Binns. New York, 1901

Salt Glazed Stoneware: Germany, Flanders, England and the United States. E. A. Barber. Pennsylvania Museum, Philadelphia, 1903

Porcelain, A Sketch of its Nature, Art and Manufacture. William Burton. London, 1906

Three Books of the Potter's Art. Cipiano Piccolpassi, trans by Bernard Rackham. Victoria and Albert Museum, London, 1934

The Art of the Potter. W. B. Honey. London, 1935

Pottery and Ceramics. Ernst Rosenthal. London, 1949

European Ceramic Art from the End of the Middle Ages to about 1815. W. B. Honey. London, 1952

Stoneware and Porcelain: The Art of High-fired Pottery. Daniel Rhodes. Philadelphia, 1959; England, 1960

The Book of Pottery and Porcelain. Warren E. Cox. New York, 1960

2,000 Years of Oriental Ceramics. F. Koyama and J. Figgess. New York, 1961

Understanding Pottery Glazes. David Green. London, 1963

Potter's Work. Bernard Leach. London, 1967

ACKNOWLEDGEMENTS

I am indebted to a number of people on both sides of the Atlantic who allowed me to benefit from their expert knowledge in resolving various research problems. My thanks are expressed to all.

Among friends and associates in England I am grateful to John Howard for suggesting a practical arrangement of the work. Thanks are due to directors, curators, etc, of British museums and galleries for their willing assistance and advice, not least in becoming actively concerned in the matter of providing photographs: these include Michael R. Parkinson, Keeper of Decorative Arts, the City Art Gallery, Manchester; A. R. Mountford, FMA, Director of the City Museum and Art Gallery, Stoke-on-Trent; John Thompson, MA, AMA, Director of Bradford City Art Gallery and Museums; staff members at Hertford House (Wallace Collection), London, staff members at the British Museum, London, and staff members at the Victoria and Albert Museum, London.

I also wish to thank Messrs Christie, Manson and Woods for photographs and to express my appreciation of the way in which the firm's press office staff rendered valuable assistance and expended considerable time in meeting my requirements.

I am indebted to Robert Williams, of Messrs Winifred Williams, London and Eastbourne, for his practical interest in the work and providing photographs.

In America, Carl Hannen allowed me to draw on his extensive expert knowledge of Oriental ceramics concerning points relating to various ancient techniques. Thanks are due to Dr Thomas Lawton, Assistant Director of the Freer Gallery of Art, Washington, for advice and assistance. Kind interest and practical assistance received from J. Jefferson Miller II, Curator of the Division of Ceramics and Glass, the Smithsonian Institution, Washington, is much appreciated.

Thanks are expressed to Vera Bawden for producing the typescript.

The photographs in this volume are reproduced by courtesy of the following:
12, Bradford City Art Gallery and Museum; 26, 30, the City of Manchester Art Gallery; 24, 25, 28, 44, 55, 56, 57, 58, 59, 60, 61, 62, 64, 65, 68, 69, 70, 71, 72, 73, the City Museum and Art Gallery, Stoke-on-Trent; 6, 11, 14, 15, 16, 17, 18, 22, 23, the Freer Gallery of Art, Smithsonian Institution, Washington DC; 1, 2, 3, 4, 5, 7, 8, 9, 10, 13, 19, 20, 32, 34, 35, 36, 37, 38, 39, 40, 41, 42, 43, 47, 49, 50, 51, Messrs Christie, Manson and Woods; 45, 48, 66, 67, Messrs Winifred Williams, London and Eastbourne; 74, 75, 76, 77, 78, 79, 80, 81, 82, 83, the National Museum of History and Technology, Smithsonian Institution, Washington DC; 27, 54, the Trustees of the British Museum; 52, 53, the Trustees of the Wallace Collection, London.

INDEX